# FAR & AWAY

## TRUE TALES from an INTERNATIONAL LIFE

## RUSSELL SUNSHINE

Park Place Publications
Pacific Grove, California

First Edition March 2016
Designed by Patricia Hamilton

Photos from the author's personal archives.
Photo processing and digitalization by Bay Photo Lab of Monterey.
Cover photo: the author visiting the Benedictine Monastery at
Norcia, Italy, 2000. Photographer: Nancy Swing


Published by
Park Place Publications
Pacific Grove, California
www.parkplacepublications.com

ISBN: 978-1-943887-19-4
Printed in U.S.A.

~ FOR NANCY ~

*Beloved life partner, intrepid humsafar,*
*and unflagging editorial advisor*

# THE PAST AS PROLOGUE

Since my earliest days, I've been magnetically attracted to travel. As a child, I'd sit on the floor in my parents' Los Angeles home and tug back issues of *National Geographic* out of snug bookshelf rows. Explorers' black-and-white snapshots would lead my imagination to remote and exotic lands.

When reading a book or an article, if an unfamiliar place-name blocked my progress, I'd detour to a dictionary or atlas to solve the puzzle. There I'd struggle with phonetic symbols and accent marks, hesitantly imitating alien sounds. If I could spot the new name on a map, I'd sweep outward circles until I could locate some recognizable reference point. Tracing my index finger along jigsaw boundaries, I'd try to memorize the discovery's neighborhood.

Into early adolescence, my travelling consisted of excursions organized and chaperoned by parents or schools. By college, I was relishing the pleasure of researching my own international expeditions. Never-been-there-before was a threshold criterion for selecting destinations. Trip-planning became recreation in its own right. Where and when to go, how to get there and how much to budget? What to take, where to stay, what to see? It hardly mattered that many plotted itineraries never made it beyond my desktop.

Then and later, for the trips that did materialize, departures were the payoff for all that preparation. While fellow travelers often fretted and complained, for me the boarding of a plane or a train gave visceral pleasure. When a plane lifted off, I'd take care not to jostle tight-jawed seatmates. Away at last!

I savored the process of moving from A to B. Except when rushing to meet a professional deadline, I was in no hurry for a voyage to end. I loved watching streaming landscapes unspool outside train windows. On marathon transoceanic flights, I contentedly lapsed into suspended animation. A family mantra paraphrased Robert Louis Stevenson: "It's better to journey hopefully than to arrive."

In the developing countries where I did most of my professional travelling, delays and diversions would routinely disrupt the best-laid plans. But even busted schedules could offer the gift of unanticipated encounters and adventures. I soon aspired to a Zen attitude of not clinging too tightly to expectations.

My career as an international-development consultant created opportunities for not merely visiting foreign countries but staying on. I worked in over 40 of them, living long-term in eight. These extended sojourns permitted much deeper immersions than quick in-and-out tourism. In this working context, paying attention to local values and customs was not merely good manners; it was essential for cross-cultural effectiveness. On all these assignments, the baseline challenges were the same. How could I enter a country as an outside advisor, often communicating through interpreters, and earn the trust of the host-government leaders who were my chief clients? And how could I help those leaders to consider international best practices that they could successfully adopt or adapt to suit national needs and conditions?

Periodically returning to America, I'd contribute tales from the trail to friends' holiday tables. Now happily retired, I'd like to share a selection with a broader circle—serving up a taste of my passion for the far and away.

Most of these tales are about travelling. The rest describe living and working abroad. Some are humorous, others serious. A few are scary. I hope you'll find several eye-opening and moving.

These are true first-person accounts recording dates, places and even conversations to the best of my recollection. Fortunately, I haven't had to rely on fading memories for details. For decades, Nancy and I sent regular "fam-letts" from overseas to loved ones in the States. We also exchanged correspondence with each other when working in separate countries. Retained copies of those letters have now given me an invaluable trove of contemporary source materials. With this archival fact-checker, I've been able to plug narrative gaps and prune creeping embellishments.

Maps have been included for geographical orientation, and photos to put faces on the cast of characters. A few names have been changed to protect the privacy of persons still in sensitive positions. The tales are grouped in a chronological sequence of chapters. Most chapters deal with a single long-term destination. Brief introductions provide background. What led me to that destination? What was I working on while I was there?

Please feel free to dip in at any spot. Or proceed straight through to trace the lifetime arc. My wish is that one or more of these sketches may stimulate you to reach for your own passport.

Since most of these stories emerged from my international career, I would like to acknowledge with deep respect and gratitude key individuals who inspired and sustained that professional journey. Nurturing mentors Alice Ilchman in New Delhi, Tony Beilenson in Sacramento and Dick Buxbaum in Berkeley. Exemplary clients Nick Kassum in Tanzania, Liu Peilong in China and Ameerah Haq in Laos.

Sincere thanks also to Patricia Hamilton for her deft and creative design services in guiding this long-delayed project to final publication.

*Russell Sunshine*
*February 2016*

# CONTENTS

*Contents continued*

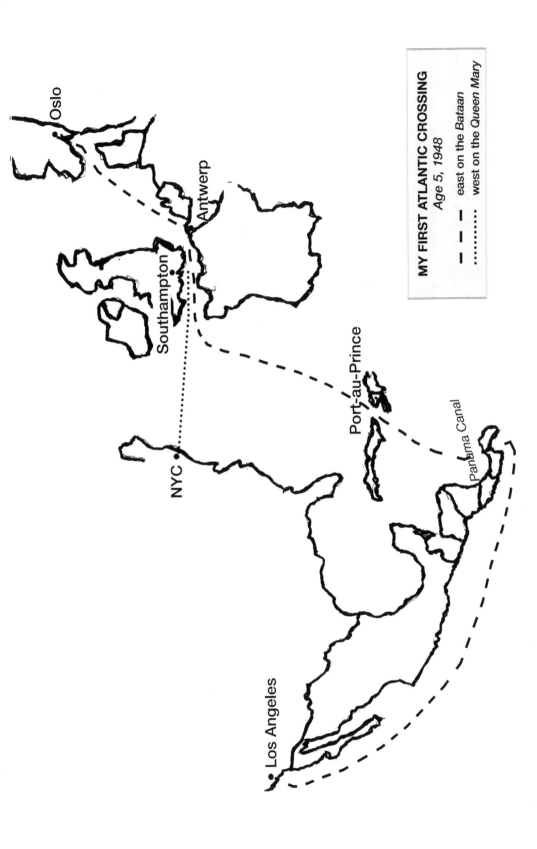

MY FIRST ATLANTIC CROSSING
*Age 5, 1948*

– – – east on the *Bataan*
· · · · · · · west on the *Queen Mary*

Oslo

Antwerp

Southampton

Port-au-Prince

NYC

Panama Canal

Los Angeles

# CHAPTER ONE

# CHILDHOOD INSPIRATIONS

Ours was a traveling family. Both sets of my grandparents were immigrants. Dad's father came from Budapest in Austria-Hungary; his mother, from Strasbourg in Alsace-Lorraine. As they stepped ashore at Ellis Island in the 1890s, family lore has it that a helpful immigration officer tried to do them a favor. Judging that he wouldn't be the only American to have difficulty pronouncing and spelling "Sonnenschein," he wrote down an on-the-spot translation. It's been "Sunshine" ever since.

The Rough-Rider President was at the peak of popularity on Dad's birthdate in 1906. So in another symbol of New World, turn-of-the-century, optimism, Dad was named Theodore Roosevelt Sunshine ("Ted" for short).

His father was reputed, although only in whispers, to have enjoyed infrequent success as a Mississippi riverboat gambler. To help support seven siblings, Dad left his native St. Louis while still in his teens. Venturing first to Arkansas and then California, he sought his fortune in the new agribusiness industry.

Mother's parents were British, from Durham and Newcastle in northern England. Her father, a civil engineer, specialized in the design and construction of railroad bridges. His first overseas posting was to Southern Africa while still in his early twenties. By the time he and his wife were starting a family, Grandad was helping the Canadian Pacific Railway race across the North American continent.

Mom was born half-way along that construction route on the Alberta prairie, also in 1906. Her parents lingered in Vancouver before leading their two daughters southward to join the sizeable British expatriate community in Los Angeles.

*Headin' West. Grandfather with my mother on the Alberta frontier. Calgary 1909.*

I will always be charmed that Mom and Dad—Miss Grieve and Mr. Sunshine—first met while ice-dancing to a live orchestra in L.A.'s Glacier Palace. After marrying in 1931, my parents had three sons, born five years apart starting in 1938—Bob, Russell and Doug. My earliest memories include ambitious car treks to fabled Wild West jamborees: the Pendleton Roundup in Oregon and the Calgary Stampede near my mother's birthplace.

My forebears were also story-tellers, with travel tales featured in the repertoire. Mom and Dad were animated raconteurs, his style tending to the softly dramatic, hers to droll humor. Her older sister Nora and her cousin Ethel could be relied on to offer excerpts from their own immigrant sagas, narrated in resilient Geordie accents. Some of my parents' stories were about my grandparents. Others, about Mom and Dad's early days of marriage before kids came along. I didn't understand all the details or punch lines. But the recitations were stored in my memory bank.

The setting for the telling was as important as the content. The family circle always gravitated to my parents' den, a cozy nook more inviting than the formal living room. I've a vivid sensation of paneled bookshelves topped with antique pewter tankards, the welcoming warmth of the coal-burning hearth, deep cushions on the red leather couch. And a purring cat, always a cat.

# Grandfather's Campfire

### Southern Rhodesia 1898

The runner wouldn't take no for an answer. Boots off, stocking feet propped over his crude cabin's front-porch railing, my grandfather was weary from fatigue and dehydration. Definitely not in a mood to make even the short trek back to the African workers' compound. His reflex reaction was to defer the shaman's summons until first thing the next morning.

But the messenger held his ground, just below the porch steps. He looked down at his feet, shifting his weight from one leg to the other, without retreating. Apparently he preferred to risk a dressing-down from the *bwana* than to face the consequences of returning unaccompanied to his dispatcher.

Although still in his early twenties, Grandfather wore two hats in this remote location: site manager and civil engineer. Hundreds of miles upcountry, he fully grasped the necessity of maintaining smooth relations with his local workforce. Progress on this railway bridge was already weeks behind schedule. Showing respect for the shaman—part healer, part magistrate, part parish priest—only made common sense. On reflection, the tribal elder wouldn't have disturbed him with a late-night call if it didn't demand immediate action.

*Grandfather Robert Grieve (seated, center) up-country in Southern Africa. 1898.*

With boots back on, my grandfather followed his anxious escort through the bush. At the compound, nothing was normal. The cordial hubbub of community evenings was eerily doused. No swirls of dust raised by squealing kids, no banging of pots and pans, no aromas of frying onions, no huddles of gossiping workers smoking after-dinner pipes.

The central space was deserted. Hut entries were closed. In the silence, the campfire crackled like gunshots.

The withered shaman sat alone on a fireside log. His arthritic back, draped in a plain cloth, was curved in a permanent C. He raised a parchment hand to gesture his visitor to sit beside him. Grandfather did as beckoned and awaited an explanation.

"Look into the fire." The shaman's resonant voice was imperative but not unkind.

My grandfather stared into the bright orange core. Still fatigued and uncertain what was being asked, for some moments he noticed nothing unusual. Then, within the flames, an image coalesced. At first it merely shimmered, hinting blurred shapes. But steadily, the focus sharpened to present a crisp picture.

In the center of a square room stood a sturdy bed. A man's figure lay under the covers, head propped on a pillow. His hands were crossed over a book. A woman in black knelt by the bed, leaning across it, hands touching the man's.

Other figures, male and female, filled the edge of the frame. Two windows were dark and curtained. Oil lamps gave soft light.

My grandfather gasped with recognition. He was looking at his parent's bedroom in Durham, England. The two central figures were his parents. Eyes closed, face slack, his father was obviously dead. But his mother was moving. No still photograph this, her torso rose and fell with sobs.

The background row was equally identifiable—all my grandfather's brothers and sisters. Except James, studying on the Continent. Some pairs clasped hands. Watching and waiting. Now their vigil was over.

The shaman placed gentle fingers on my Grandfather's forearm. "*Bwana*, so sorry for this big sadness."

With the words, the image was gone. Only flickering flames and collapsing kindling as before.

My grandfather staggered to his feet and stumbled back to his cabin. His head swirled with a storm of emotions—confusion and disbelief, skepticism and grief.

Two weeks later, a wrinkled telegram made its way up from Pretoria.

"MAY 15. ROBERT: DAD PASSED IN HIS SLEEP LAST NIGHT WITHOUT SUFFERING. MOTHER AND ALL BEARING UP. IAN."

"Last night." May 14.

The night of the campfire.

# SPIFFY

*Bakersfield, California 1935*

Dad thought it would be nice to combine business with pleasure. Tom Peppers, his boss at the produce brokerage, had asked him to drive north from Los Angeles into the San Joaquin Valley to meet with key clients. The firm needed to tally the big melon growers' yield expectations and harvest schedules in order to plot rail-shipment requirements for the selling season. Phone calls could collect the basic numbers. But there was no substitute for face-to-face contact when brokering competition was heating up.

Dad asked Mom if she'd like to come along. *The L.A. Times* had just published an enticing write-up on the upgraded Bakersfield Inn. The review touted "the most attractive accommodations within 100 miles." She could sample the amenities while he drove out to the fields. In the evenings, they'd enjoy the good food and the Inn's dance band imported from San Francisco.

Mom was delighted. In those early days of their marriage, my parents liked to travel together whenever they could afford it. This time Dad's expenses would be covered by his firm, so they'd just need a bit extra for her.

Dad was loading their bags into the car when he realized her acceptance came with strings attached. Mom was crossing the front lawn with Spiffy in her arms.

*My parents, newlyweds Sally and Ted Sunshine. Olvera Street,*
*Los Angeles 1931.*

"My sister's out of town through the weekend," she explained. "She can't sit the cat."

"Sally, don't even think of it," Dad protested. "You know the Inn won't accept pets. They won't risk their new carpets."

"Ted, leave it to me. Spiffy will be good as gold."

As if taking in every parry in this exchange, the normally demanding white Persian was meekly purring. He never budged or bolted when Mom arranged his favorite towel on the car's back seat and laid him on it.

Dad looked at his wristwatch. They had to get started if he was going to arrive in time for his afternoon appointments. He saw no way out. When the cat dozed contentedly through North Hollywood and Encino, up and over the Ridge Route, and then down the Grapevine into Bakersfield, he wondered what his wife had slipped into Spiffy's milk.

In the 1930s, even automobile travel was a dressy affair. My parents walked into the Bakersfield Inn wearing suits and hats. High heels and gloves completed Mom's tailored ensemble. Winter temperatures in the Valley seldom dropped to near-freezing. So the white fox fur draped over her forearm was a borderline affectation. But eccentric attire was already becoming a California signature and the Inn management welcomed panache.

Dad was nervous during check-in. But Mom's accessory thankfully didn't twitch. Were they going to get away with it?

The couple followed the bellhop's loaded luggage cart across the foyer to the gleaming bank of elevators. Double doors slid silently open and they all piled in. The uniformed operator asked for their floor.

"Five, please," Dad answered distractedly, determined to concentrate on the pleasure he knew Mom would take in the panoramic view.

"All the way it is." The operator rotated the lever with a flick of the wrist and the cabin lurched into sudden ascent.

"YEEEEEEEEOOOOOOOOWWWWWWWWWW!"

Spiffy had had enough. Slumping comatose over Mom's arm was well within his dramatic range. Flying in a motorized box had never been part of the bargain.

His massive bulk exploded straight up past startled faces and jostled hats. Rotating like an Olympic gymnast as he levitated, Spiffy slammed into the smart elevator's ceiling screen upside down, grasping the burnished brass with 20 desperate claws.

The oscillating howl filled the claustrophobic cube. Dad slumped against the back wall. The shocked operator and bellhop looked to Mom for their crisis cue. No perspiration on *her* lip, she communicated non-verbal volumes. She had heard nothing untoward. She had no connection with the wild animal whose pulsing tail was dangling three inches in front of her nose. If the employees would merely remain calm, she and her husband would see no need to report this unfortunate incident to the pair's superiors.

Like many emergencies, this one lasted an eternity and an instant. The elevator operator regained enough consciousness to stop at the fifth floor. When he opened the doors, Spiffy relaxed his death grip.

Mom reached up with a nonchalant glove and retrieved the errant fox fur. Dad let go of the hand rail and unlocked his knees.

With the room key and cart, the bellhop led the way out. "Follow me, please. Five seventeen is to your left."

My parents agreed that the hotel floor show never matched the opening act.

*Spiffy in repose. Los Angeles 1935.*

# High Flyer

### Mid-Atlantic 1948

One week out from Los Angeles, my brother Bob and I were already bored. We'd exhausted the ship's confined spaces that were not off-limits. Hearts and Monopoly couldn't hold our attention. Erupting with excess energy, we were a constant nuisance.

Transatlantic crossings were rapidly resuming three years after VE day. But demand for passenger berths far outstripped supply. The *Bataan* was the only ship Dad had been able to book from L.A.'s Long Beach Harbor. The Norwegian freighter could accommodate only 14 passengers. He'd reserved a three-bunk cabin for his wife and two sons. Dad had recently launched his own brokerage firm, so he'd have to stay home and mind the store.

After 20 years of residence in California, Mom remained a loyal subject of the British Crown. She was expecting her third child in August, so she knew she'd find it difficult to do any more international traveling for several years. Before that birth, she was determined to visit her English cousins, escorting two steamer-trunks crammed with canned goods, staples and other treats they'd been deprived of throughout the War, and since then by continued rationing.

Bob was ten. I'd just turned five. At first we loved the compact freighter. Everything was new and inviting—decks and passageways to

*The* Bataan, *ready to get to work. Los Angeles Harbor 1948.*

explore, fresh paint and diesel fumes to backtrack to their sources, the ship's rolling pitch to balance against. From our perch on the bow high above Panama Canal locks, we spied tiny mechanical donkeys hauling massive bow lines like determined Dinky Toys.

Port-Au-Prince quayside was exciting but scary from my three-foot height. While the crew re-provisioned, our shore party made slow progress through the raucous street markets. Holding on to Mother with one hand and Bob with the other, I felt overwhelmed but fascinated by Creole banter, ebony elbows, slippery fish guts and sparring pups. A battering rain squall made the footing even more treacherous.

After Haiti, as the ship's novelty began to wear off, my brother and I felt increasingly cramped. Our cabin was a closet, all drawers and doors. The captain's bridge, packed with navigation wheels, radar and blinking lights, was fascinating but out-of-bounds. So were the cavernous fore and aft holds, deafening with the screech of cranes and signals bellowed between decks and depths. A careless deckhand had lost a forearm in a winch loading coffee beans off Santo Domingo. We hadn't seen the accident but had heard the frantic screams. Now Bob and I had been ordered to stay clear of those treacherous pits.

Sparky, the radio operator, did more than his fair share to keep us entertained. His second finger danced on the keypad, Morse code clicking an express train over tracks. During transmission lulls, he let us tap out our own make-believe messages.

The ship's Scandinavian menus were tasty, if unfamiliar. Bob and I were soon wolfing down pickled herring, rye flatbread and hard white cheeses, not to mention sweet red-dwarf bananas and juice-dripping papayas.

But even these treats left interminable hours to occupy ourselves. The working vessel could spare no space for play areas or sports facilities, much less a pool. The passenger manifest included no other kids. And, as Mom sternly relayed, the adults had made clear to the Captain that they had not paid high fares to be disturbed by "rampaging boys."

From Hispaniola, it was open sailing. The freighter was now heavily laden, so our Atlantic crossing would take a fortnight. Bob and I fidgeted and skirmished. The ship's metal surfaces bounced back heat from the sun above and engines below. They burned to the touch. Mom was seven months' pregnant and must have suffered from the humidity and unrelieved chaperoning. She grew cross with our tussles. We did our best to keep out of her sight and away from the sacrosanct adult reading room.

One glaring morning we raced up the metal stairway that was bolted to the back of the freighter's superstructure. Its three flights zigzagged from the rear deck up to a narrow platform encircling the bridge. Built strictly for the crew's use, the steps were narrow and utilitarian, open except for a narrow-pipe handrail.

We played tag at top speed. Bob's legs were much longer. He always won, but this time I thought I could just make it to the top before he caught up. I looked back to gauge my shrinking lead. He was taking two stairs at a time. Head twisted over my left shoulder, I reached for the railing with my right hand.

I missed it and followed the hand into space.

When I opened my eyes, Mom was standing on one side of me, the Captain on the other. I was lying flat on my back under a loose sheet. It was cold. I moved my hands and found I was wearing only underpants. What had happened to my clothes?

There was some sort of thin mattress under me, and a hard metal surface under that.

Beyond my bare feet, I could see a paneled wall covered by framed photographs, triangular pennants and nautical charts. I recognized the Captain's cabin. I'd been inside it only once, during his pre-departure reception. But Bob and I had also peered in on furtive hide-and-seek romps. Now sunlight poured through twin portholes.

Mom's eyes were shimmering. Something was wrong. She never cried.

"He's come back," the Captain murmured. "It wasn't his time to go."

I felt awkward being talked about by adults as if I wasn't there. And shivery without my clothes. I rolled over on my left side to get up. The Captain restrained me with a gentle hand.

My head hurt all over, front and back. I reached up to my forehead and touched a soft gauze bandage. The skin under it felt stiff, burning and raw, like a knee skinned on playground asphalt. My whole right side was tender from shoulder to knee. I peeked under the sheet and spotted rainbow bruises. The colors were darkest where the bones hurt the worst, at my elbow and hip.

When Bob was allowed to visit my makeshift infirmary, he was unnaturally subdued. I pressed him to fill in the blanks.

"You must have lost your balance," he began. "You just angled out and kept on going, between the handrail and the stairs. I thought you might sail right into the pit. But you dropped real fast. Bounced on the other flight of stairs below us. Then flopped onto the deck."

My brother paused for a breath. "You didn't make a sound. I was the only one screaming."

I'd taken most of that first impact on my forehead. The metal stair scraped the skin off from temple to temple. By the time I'd hit the hardwood deck, I'd rotated in the air and landed on my right side and the back of my head. That last smack was hard enough to embed a long splinter under my scalp. But the adults had more serious problems to worry about. I was concussed and unconscious. I stayed out for 48 hours.

In mid-Atlantic, we were days from landfall or another vessel. Since the *Bataan* was a freighter, it was not required to carry a doctor on board. By good fortune, one of the other passengers had a sizable medical kit in his trunk. They sprinkled powdered sulfa across my forehead to ward off infection.

Then they waited. And prayed.

Once I woke up, my recovery was swift and uncomplicated. In England, a thorough examination revealed no residual damage to bones or nerves. My flexible child's frame and light weight had probably saved my life.

Over time, that wooden sliver became a curiously comforting companion. A secret talisman from my first trip abroad. I carried it with me everywhere. When I ran my fingers over the welt, everything came back. The glare of the sky. The steep stairs. The clang of Bob's feet catching up. Just never the handrail.

*With my older brother Bob and chaperone.*
*Tower of London 1948.*

# Pear Soup

*Los Angeles, Mid–Atlantic 1954*

Dad's face was ashen. No after-work cocktails and caviar cheese tonight by the cozy den fire. He collapsed, slumped-shouldered, into the wooden kitchen chair.

"Tell me about it," Mom gently urged.

"A phone call from New York. The pears are on deck."

"I don't know what that means."

"What it means is pear mush in the mid-Atlantic. Pear soup by the Southampton docks."

The bitter outburst animated my father as Mom pulled out a second chair. In a halting monotone, he laid out the sorry tale.

Dad normally worked as a produce broker, a middleman negotiating contracts between California growers and wholesale buyers scattered across North America or even in Europe. Safeway, A&P, Kroger's, and other giant supermarket chains were his core customers. Navel and Valencia oranges, honeydew and cantaloupe melons were his main commodities. Dad took over responsibility for the crops at the packing-house loading dock, hired rail cars or trucks, and monitored hourly prices to get his farmer-clients the best return.

The entire high-speed produce industry rode on trust. Normally, a grower released his shipment before Dad had found a buyer, leaving the broker to make a sale while the wheels rolled. From bare-bones offices above Seventh & Central in the L.A. Produce Market, Dad and his staff worked the telephones and teletypes from 6 a.m. to 5 p.m., coaxing customers in multiple time zones.

Hundreds or thousands of miles away, buyers honored the prices Dad quoted over the phone, relying on his word and reputation for the unseen goods' quality, condition and timely delivery. As he relied on them to have sufficient funds in the bank to make prompt payment.

Dad had founded Pacific Coast Fruit Distributors in the boom years just after World War II. Buying out his two partners, he expanded steadily and was prospering in the early 1950s. He worked on high volume and low commission. But periodically, the inveterate risk-taker would seize opportunities for higher rewards. When the odds seemed right, he purchased crops for his own account.

The Bartlett pears had been too tempting to pass up. The prerequisites for windfall profits were all in place. A bumper crop of exceptional fruit from the Ukiah Valley. A farmer with a surplus, offering a bargain farm-gate price. And an English importer volunteering to pay a premium, in order to place a precious holiday treat on the tables of London consumers. Dad borrowed from his local branch bank, bought a huge shipment of the pears and rushed it by rail across the United States to the New York docks. Loaded into a chartered freighter's refrigerated hold, the shipment was timed to arrive in England in peak condition.

Except the pears were on deck. Exposed, un-refrigerated, to sun and wind. Dad's New York agent blamed the harbor freight-forwarder. The forwarder blamed the ship's crew. It made little difference. In 1954, international transport of highly perishable commodities was uninsurable, and years-long lawsuits were unlikely to recover even legal expenses.

*PCFD: Dad's brokerage logo. Los Angeles Produce Market 1955.*

"How bad is it?" Mom cut to the chase. "Will we lose the house?"

"The house and my car. Yours is paid for."

"Will we have to take the boys out of private school?"

"They can probably stay till the end of the fall semester. After that, it'll be public school for all three."

"Who will you have to lay off?"

"George, Paul and Joe have agreed to take a salary cut. The rest I'll have to let go."

"Can you see any way out?"

"The ship's beyond recall."

Mom stood up. "Then let's go down in style."

Normally, I'd help out at my parents' parties by passing around hors d'oeuvres and collecting empty glasses. This one was catered. The kitchen was crowded with strangers in white jackets and aprons. The back porch was stacked with full boxes and platters. A piano trio was in full swing at the far end of the veranda. Couples were dancing on the patio. Mom and Dad had given their three sons an abbreviated version of our family crisis. But they'd sworn us to secrecy. No guest was aware of our pending ruin. Fall parties required no special occasion in '50s L.A. Everyone seemed to be having a grand old time.

I answered the front doorbell. The capped Western Union man needed a signature on his receipt for a wire. I found Dad, who signed the form. He opened the distinctive yellow envelope without enthusiasm. But then he ran off to pull Mom into the comparative quiet of the den.

I tried to decode the clipped text that fluttered to the floor.

"WORSTEVER NOR ATLAN BLIZZARD STOP TWO INCH POWDER BLANKETING PEAR CRATES STOP YOURE ONE LUCKY ESSO BEE STOP."

My parents hugged for the longest time.

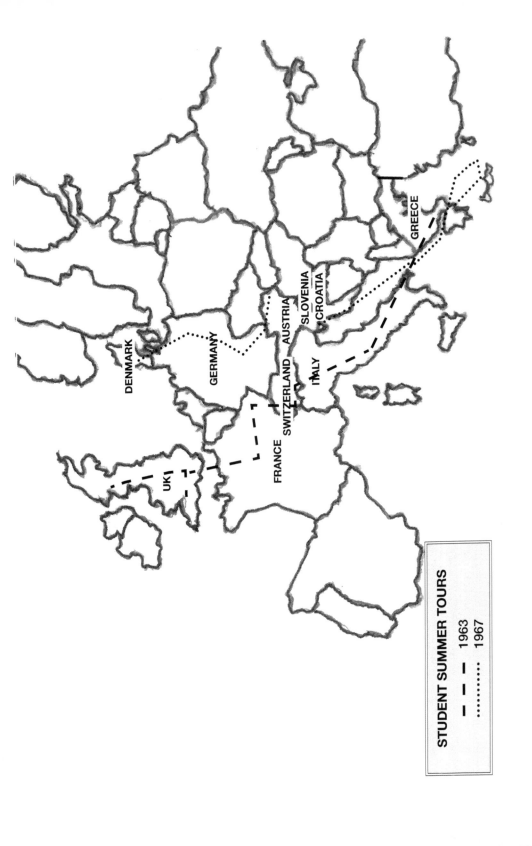

STUDENT SUMMER TOURS

1963

1967

## Chapter Two

# FIRST STEPS ON MY OWN

In my early teens, I ventured forth for the first time without adult supervision, joining a kids-only camping trip into California's High Sierras.

After junior year of college, a summer job at a youth conference in Strasbourg, France financed my first solo trip abroad. With conference duties completed, I made good use of a student Euro-rail pass to sightsee as far south as Athens.

Europe lured me again between law-school terms. Shouldering a backpack and sleeping in youth hostels, I became an expert at international travel on five dollars a day.

# CITY SLICKERS

*Los Angeles and Kings Canyon National Park 1958*

"Guys, listen up. I've got a great idea."

"Another one? God save us."

John was pumped up. Ed's sarcasm tipped him off he'd have to do some selling.

We were sitting together in what had become our regular spot in the Hollywood High schoolyard at recess. The vantage point let us check out the parade of girls without appearing to stare. Ed and Mike, the Bates twins, were John's faithful posse. They always fell into line, but first he had to get them up to speed.

"Summer school's over at the end of next week. Fall term doesn't start till September." Then remembering the odd man out, "For you too, Russ?"

The three of them went to Notre Dame High in Sherman Oaks. I was at Harvard School in North Hollywood. "Same for me. Second week of September."

"So what are we all going to do in the meantime?"

"You tell us, Uncle John." Wise-guy Mike winked at us. "Here it comes."

"Kings Canyon."

Ed smirked. "What's that, a new theme park?"

"A National Park. Which means it's free."

Now the twins started double-teaming him. "Free for what? What's there to do?"

"Where is it and how do you get there?"

John kept his eye on the prize. "There's great hiking and camping. The Park's up in the High Sierras. East of Fresno. My dad can drive us up and back, as long as we travel on weekends when he'll be off work." And after a pause, "I already asked him."

I'd never known anyone like John Lynch. My Harvard School classmates were almost all Protestants, from privileged families living in Beverly Hills or L.A.'s Wilshire District. Their fathers were corporate executives, high-powered lawyers or movie-studio heads. John was an Irish Catholic. His dad was a blue-collar worker. In a labor union. Our high schools were only two miles apart but we lived in different worlds. The only reason we'd been thrown together was summer-school typing class at Hollywood High.

John had answers for everything. With self-confidence and humor, he could make those answers convincing. There were leaders at my school too, especially football and basketball captains. But John had street smarts. I was a year ahead of myself in school and had just turned 15. John and the twins were 16 and seemed much more mature.

Once he'd made his initial pitch without turning us off, John consolidated his gains. Kings Canyon was right next door to Sequoia National Park, which we'd all heard about. But it was much less crowded. Sleeping outdoors wouldn't cost us a thing, apart from some basic gear and rations. The twins climbed quickly on board.

John got me to introduce him to my parents. I noticed how polite and well-prepared he was when answering their questions. He'd even brought a map. To my surprise, my folks quickly gave their approval for my joining the unchaperoned expedition. Maybe they saw this as an opportunity for me to do some growing up.

Trip-planning moved quickly forward. The four of us descended on the Army Surplus store near our summer school to load up on low-budget backpacks, sleeping bags, boots and freeze-dried food. We gave little or no thought to the hike itself. It all seemed so simple. We were physically fit from playing school sports. I ran Cross-Country, for God's sake. This would just be a walk. What could go wrong in a National Park, with rangers all around wearing those funny hats?

The drive up from L.A. took longer than planned. So John's father continued on, without stopping, past the Park Visitors' Center and Ranger Station at Cedar Creek, straight to the trailheads at the end of Kings Canyon. As our self-appointed Team Leader, John had pre-selected the more remote Paradise Valley Trail, instead of the shorter one along Copper Creek.

Our excitement built as Mr. Lynch drove away. We laced up our new hiking boots and hoisted unfamiliar packs. A large printed sign was unavoidable at the edge of the parking lot.

"ATTENTION, CAMPERS! Mountain lions have been spotted in the vicinity. Black bears are also common." The fine print advised on what to do and not do if one of these threats were encountered.

We joined in mocking the key instruction: "Don't run. Stay calm." Mike danced around the sign, shouting "Here, Kitty-kitty!"

Filled with adrenalin, we started off at a fast pace. But we soon figured out this was a harder slog than running up and down a basketball court or around a track. A lot of the trail was steep and slow-going, almost a dirt stairway with thick tree roots as steps. Our overstuffed backpacks grew steadily heavier. We hadn't factored in the trail's 1,500-foot gain, or the thinning air as we approached its 7,000-foot summit. Both made it harder to get our wind.

We were all unprepared for the five-plus hours it took us to reach Paradise Valley. By the time we'd selected a campsite, we were too bushed to do more than gulp down some cold food and climb into our thin sleeping bags. I privately took inventory of hot spots and blisters on my toes and heels. Soon I dropped into unconsciousness, lulled by the burble of the Kings River's South Fork.

In the morning we rebounded, preparing a hot breakfast over a campfire and taking stock of our surroundings. "Paradise Valley" was a geographer's exaggeration. A more accurate description was a narrow gorge. Maybe lower down, the terrain opened out into a true meadow. But where we were the converging valley sides were sheer cliffs only a couple of hundred yards apart. I was content to recuperate from the ascent, just lounging around our campsite. But the twins seemed to twitch with surplus energy. They kept daring each other to scale the dominating cliff wall directly across the watercourse.

Uninterested in helping with kitchen cleanup, they set off upstream. "To go exploring," as they described their impulsive agenda to John. He had to remind them to fill their canteens. And to argue with them to tie windbreakers around their waists, in case they were still out when temperatures dropped.

He and I expected the normally ravenous pair to turn up for lunch, but John joked that the Bates boys had more brawn than brains. By mid-afternoon, he thought he heard them across the valley and insisted on searching in case they needed a hand. I watched him walk upstream and then ford the Fork to enter a wooded gash in the opposite cliff where a gradual slope promised possible footing.

I tried to follow his progress but quickly lost sight of him. After that, I heard and saw nothing for what seemed like hours. The cliff face was still golden in full sunlight. But I noticed the shadows advancing with surprising speed across the narrow valley floor.

Then John shouted my name from out of the sky. He sounded far off, so I scanned the cliff face up and down, then side to side. I almost puked when I spotted three small figures half-way up the vertical wall. For the first time I realized they all could die.

"We need help…help…help" came the echo, rebounding off the cliff behind me.

"Is anyone hurt?" I shouted back from the streambed.

"Ed's ankle."

"What?"

"Ed's hurt his ankle."

"Can you slide down?

"Too steep. Dropped onto a ledge."

"How can I help?"

"GO...GET...THE...RANGERS!" Smoky-the-Bear hats were no longer a joke.

I recalled the Ranger Station next to the Visitors' Center that we'd driven past on the way in. If I could hike back down to the parking lot, I could catch a lift to the Station. I loaded a small plastic bag with granola, filled my canteen and carried my flashlight in my hand. Before starting out, I applied Band-Aids to my tender feet and pulled on an extra pair of hiking socks. I yelled up to my stranded companions that I'd bring help soon. The pledge sounded hollow even before it echoed.

They didn't answer. I felt discouraged but tried to comfort myself that they were saving their strength. I set off full of purpose. But as day turned to night and my own energy drained, I sank into a zombie plod, one foot in front of the other.

A twig snapped like a whip crack, yanking me out of my fog. I jolted to a halt, peering ahead towards the source of the sound. Without my noticing, the full moon had completed its arc, reducing the walkable overhead glare to a diffuse, depth-distorting glow. Now all my senses were on full-alert.

The trail sloped downward in front of me, snaking between giant boulders. No breath of wind. Even the pine-bough tips were motionless. Maybe I'd imagined the sound. For sure, no other hiker would be tromping about at three a.m. No one normal, at least.

Another noise, from the same direction. Not my imagination twice in a row. Softer this time, like a foot in the dust. My mind flashed back to the trailhead warning sign. Lion or bear?

I tried to stay still, palm on canteen to keep it from clanging against my belt. Moving only my eyeballs, I scanned my surroundings for a safe perch if it was a predator. No chance. They could out-climb and out-run me in this terrain. Cold sweat ran down my chest. I couldn't see a damned thing around the bend. And no way was I going to reveal my own location by switching on my flashlight.

Five minutes? 15? I had to keep going, get down and out of the woods. Frightened almost to paralysis, I forced myself to inch forward, each step sounding amplified. Peering over the rocks, I made out two pale reflecting eyes and almost peed in my jeans. Four feet off the ground. Holy shit! A big one.

Jangling bells as the creature shifted weight. Christ Almighty! Mountain lions don't telegraph their whereabouts with bell collars! Flashlight on. A pack mule had slipped its tether. Welcome to the Wild West, Kit Carson. I laughed out loud but blushed with shame.

Negotiating a truce and squeezing past the fearsome mule, I was eager to make up for lost time. But the moon had set, so I was walking by starlight, feeling for footing over rocks and roots. My narrow flashlight beam seemed to hinder as much as it helped. I switched it off again.

It was past dawn when I reached the trailhead. Somehow I'd expected there'd be early hikers with vehicles in the parking lot. Not a soul. Nothing for it but to keep on slogging, five more miles to the Ranger Station. I straggled in by eight a.m. The station was tight as a drum. Soon the first Ranger drove up and opened the office. He barked at me to hold my horses until he could get the lights turned on and coffee on the stove.

I blurted out my emergency.

"I know it seems like the end of the world to you, Sonny. But's it's no big deal to us. City slickers stub their toes and demand to be medevacked every day of the week. By now I'm sure your panicked buddies have wiggled their way off the ledge. They're probably chowing down on bacon and pancakes. Including your share."

I rattled off my arguments to convince him to take the situation seriously. I'd seen for myself where the boys were trapped. If they'd slid onto the ledge as John had called out, the only way off of it was hundreds of feet straight down. And Ed already had an injured ankle.

A second Ranger arrived to join the conversation. He seemed less dismissive than his colleague and invited me to pinpoint our camp's location on their large-scale topo map. I was embarrassed by my inability to do that with certainty. But a distinctive bend in the South Fork gave me the marker I needed to hone in on the area with confidence.

The more positive Ranger reacted. "We need to call in a chopper to check this out."

"Money and fuel wasted," the first man snorted. "But it sure as hell beats sending in a climbing team on a spooked teenybopper's say-so."

After a series of phone calls, a Cessna was summoned, in place of the helicopter out-of-commission for maintenance. I felt dismay but also vindication when a radioed call from the aircraft confirmed there were still three figures on the cliff.

Now everything shifted into high gear. Before noon, a team of six trained Search & Rescue volunteers assembled at the Station, complete with horse trailers and climbing gear. Another supplier delivered pack mules to the trailhead to carry that gear while the climbers rode their own horses. Six team members, six horses.

The bad-tempered Ranger seemed to remember me as an afterthought. "You can hitch a ride in a truck as far as the trailhead. After that, if you want to return to the scene, you're on your own."

Just before we left the station, I was allowed to phone my parents to alert them to the situation. I assured my mom I was safe but asked her to contact Mrs. Lynch, without giving too many details, since we didn't yet know how this was all going to turn out.

By the time I struggled up to our campsite in late afternoon, the drama was mostly over. The team had scoped out the cliff face and determined that going up from the valley floor was more practical than trying to rappel down from above. The three best climbers had roped up and ascended hand over hand to the ledge, driving pins along their vertical route.

The ground crew explained to me what we were watching through binoculars. First the climbers gave my friends energy drinks to replace their electrolytes. Next they wrapped Ed's ankle in a soft boot and belayed him down while their colleagues below guided the ropes. Mike came next, John second, and then the three rescuers.

There was no round of back-slapping for a job safely completed. But also no tongue-lashing. On closer examination, Ed's ankle was only strained. With a new wrapping, it could bear weight. The laconic crew drank some water, chewed some trail snacks, re-loaded the pack mules and rode off down the mountain. Their chief told us to rest overnight at our campsite, walk out the next morning and report to the Ranger Station. They'd phone our parents to assure them everyone was okay. And they'd ask John's father to meet us at the trailhead with his car.

After dinner, I expected the twins to collapse with exhaustion. But they started egging each other on around the campfire.

"Admit it, Ed. You were scared shitless."

"Not likely, brother. Chilled maybe, but never spooked. Unlike you. You couldn't stop yammerin'."

"Just didn't want to fall asleep and roll off the ledge. Not in a hurry to find out if I can really fly in my dreams."

I couldn't believe the brothers were so egotistical. "What about the men?"

"What men?" Ed looked annoyed at my interruption of the fraternal duet.

"The three who risked their necks rescuing you."

He threw up his arms. "Don't be a chump, Russ. Those guys are paid an arm and a leg. And the clock starts ticking the moment they get the call."

"Time and a half on weekends." Mike had his brother's back.

Leader John wasn't saying a word. I wanted to draw him in. "What do you think about what happened up there?"

"I'm just glad we got down in one piece."

The next day at the station, the bad-tempered Ranger read us the riot act. He ticked off our shortcomings, from rank inexperience and lack of supervision, to ignorance of the terrain, to scaling cliff faces without know-how or equipment. John's father fidgeted in his chair as the Ranger itemized the high costs of the rescue, including the spotter aircraft, and complained that only Federal regulations prohibited the National Park Service from sending the bill to our parents. The twins grinned. But for once they kept their mouths shut.

While our drama had been playing out, the press must have had an inside source within the Park Service. *The Los Angeles Times* had given us a banner headline.

*L.A. Times August 22, 1958.*

We'd even bumped Elizabeth Taylor's latest divorce.

Tallying the 40-plus miles I'd logged up and down, my Cross-Country teammates at Harvard School were impressed by my endurance. My own self-assessment was less charitable. Even without a points-deduction for ambush by pack mule, I rated myself merely the least of four fools.

# EMERALDS ON THE SEINE

*Paris 1963*

"Wake up, boys! Help! Thief! Thief!"

The screams pierced my dream like high-voltage probes. I struggled to the surface, groping for my bearings. Where was I? Who was shouting?

Paris. Just arrived from New York. My new boss's apartment. He'd given Bill and me a place to stay before we moved on to our Strasbourg summer jobs.

"He's getting away! Stop him!"

A gaunt figure leaned into our dark bedroom, silhouetted against a back-lit hallway. Eugene Metz. The boss's polio-stiffened frame was unmistakable.

Still disoriented but with an accelerating heartbeat, I vaulted out of bed in my jockey shorts, no thought for eyeglasses on the nightstand.

Mr. Metz pivoted back into the light, jabbing the air with a skeletal finger: "There! There he goes!"

I could make out a blurred figure retreating down the bowling alley of a hallway. I sprinted after him, bare feet on cool hardwood floors. Bill pounded behind me.

I caught up with the man at the apartment's front door. He was turning the brass handle and pulling the door inwards. I slammed into his upper body, driving him past the angled door and pinning him against the corridor wall.

Panting into his face and still grasping his arms, I got my first clear look at my quarry. A tanned, handsome Caucasian in his late thirties. The man was well-groomed and clean-shaven, giving off some subtle cologne.

Despite my assault on his tuxedo, he put up zero resistance. No swearing, no struggle. He confronted my grimace with mild amusement, his muscles totally relaxed.

It didn't compute.

My brain caught up with my body. Mr. Metz hadn't been able to take us to dinner because his British superior was flying in unexpectedly from London. This dapper guy was no crook. He had to be the cross-Channel CEO. And I'd just strong-armed him. In my new boss's home. In my undershorts.

I dropped chagrined arms and shuffled back a step.

"Look, Mister, I'm terribly sorry. I thought—"

And with a dancer's glide, the cool cavalier was through the front door.

"Noooooo!" Mr. Metz wailed, closing the distance. "You had him! You let him go!"

Bill rushed past me out the opening and I flew after them both. The apartment-house vestibule wrapped around a wrought-iron staircase that looped to ground level in oblong spirals. We were four levels up.

Our hare had a sizable lead. We could hear the rhythmic tap of his dress shoes on the marble stairs. He ran in darkness. Bill salvaged some light by slapping the time switches next to each level's elevator doors. The pulsing bursts lit the staid space like a Grade-B thriller as we descended two steps at a time.

Outside the apartment building, the pavement in this fashionable *arrondissement* was still cobble-stoned. Domed and slippery from mist, the stones made a treacherous surface for a sprint and hammered our bare soles. One hundred yards ahead, the thief looked like he was having similar problems, advancing in short stutter steps.

He headed down the slight slope to the graveled path above the Seine, gaining ground until we reached the flat surface. Then he wove in and out of a phalanx of parked vehicles beneath irregular streetlights.

And was gone. Into this black alley. Or that one. Not a trace.

We hobbled back like humbled hounds. In the apartment, a trio of gendarmes was taking a statement from our despondent host. This being the high-rent district, an officer in beribboned tunic and pristine kepi was overseeing two patrolmen.

The one in charge scoffed at our bedraggled near-nudity. "No futbol trophy, American boys? Perhaps you missed your padded uniforms?"

I hated his mockery. His razor creases and mirrored shoe-tops suggested they'd never been soiled by a vulgar puddle. I wished we'd dragged our prey back to dump on his gleaming feet. But we hadn't. So we slumped in two chairs and recovered our wind, while Mr. Metz explained for the police notebook how the tuxedoed thief had gained entry to his home.

Like Bill and me, the arriving London executive had opted to retire early. With Mr. Metz's wife away visiting South American relatives and his apartment's guest bedroom already occupied by the two of us, he found accommodations for his supervisor at a posh Paris hotel. Then our host strolled to a riverside cafe to enjoy a solitary liqueur.

At the next table, a young man in evening dress struck up a conversation in English, commenting on the headline in Mr. Metz's copy of the *International Herald Tribune*. After a casual but cordial exchange, Mr. Metz invited the stranger to join him at his table. Over drinks, the gentleman introduced himself as Charles Langley and sketched his particulars. A historian specializing in the French Revolution at a respected English university, Langley was in Paris researching original sources and had just splurged on an evening at the Opera.

Without wanting to be presumptuous, Mr. Metz glimpsed an opportunity. He knew that British academics were poorly paid. He had two American student employees on his hands, a wife out of town, and a visiting superior to whom he owed priority attention. Risking a rebuff, he asked the historian if he'd be willing to give his two houseguests an orientation to Paris, in consideration for a stipend, of course. At first, the man bristled, huffing that tour-guiding was hardly his métier. But after Mr. Metz's apology, he promptly relaxed. Acknowledging that he knew Paris like the back of his hand, he also conceded, with evident embarrassment, that he could make good use of the honorarium.

Mr. Metz suggested they return together to his apartment. He'd introduce Langley to his student guests. If the Americans had made no prior plans, the trio could arrange an informal sightseeing itinerary for the next couple of days.

Back at the flat, Mr. Metz discovered that Bill and I were dead to the world. He proposed postponing introductions until the next morning and offered the scholar a nightcap. Langley accepted, continued to chat with aplomb and then asked if he could use the bathroom. Mr. Metz pointed out the appropriate hallway door, just beyond the dining room. After some time, he became concerned when the man did not return. Thinking that Langley might have taken ill, he walked along to the guest bathroom, only to find its light out and door open.

Mr. Metz wondered if the professor had misunderstood his directions and gone too far down the hallway in search of the toilet. Our host spotted a light in the master bedroom at the back of the apartment. He walked the length of the corridor and stepped into the suite.

Langley was leaning over Mrs. Metz's dressing table, coolly slipping her jewels into trim tuxedo pockets like after-dinner mints.

In an instant, Mr. Metz fitted the pieces together. The household staff had sent the carpets out for cleaning. So Langley must have heard him approaching on the hallway floor. Yet despite imminent detection, the thief had calmly completed his plucking until the glass tabletop was swept clean. This disdainful composure rammed home to Mr. Metz, beyond any doubt, that he was confronting no amateur opportunist.

Looking up in the mirror, Langley turned and silently crossed the room. He reached up gracefully with his right hand as if to straighten Mr. Metz's necktie, and grasped him tightly by the throat. "Not. One. Word."

He stepped past his pinioned victim and released his grip. Mr. Metz gasped and began to collapse on frail, quaking legs. Langley strolled down the long corridor, unrushed and unruffled.

Struggling for balance, Mr. Metz grabbed at the door frame. He pulled himself around the corner and lurched into his guests' darkened room.

"Wake up, boys! Help! Thief! Thief!" My entrance cue.

The commander preened his mustache. "We know it is no consolation, Monsieur Metz, but you are not this serpent's first victim. This was the fourth robbery of the summer with the same modus operandi."

In broad strokes, the police profiled the predator's pattern. The thief cruised Seine-side cafes to stalk elderly English-speakers. Always presentable, well-spoken and diffident, he let his lonely interlocutors drive the conversational pace. Then he deftly seized openings for closer contact. He had consistently eluded capture, despite loud complaints by rattled café proprietors and stake-outs by plain-clothed teams.

The commander concluded. "Monsieur Metz, when you are able, we will need an itemized inventory of the stolen items. In candor, however, you're unlikely to recover the goods, even if we catch him. They'll be fenced before we submit our report."

Changing tone, he broke out in a supportive grin. "Naturally, Monsieur, you are covered by insurance. And as we all know from our sky-rocketing premiums, the insurance companies can well afford to pay the occasional claim."

Mr. Metz seemed near tears as he haltingly replied. His Latin American wife had brought to her marriage a dowry of Colombian emeralds. Always kept in a bank vault, the jewelry was due for reappraisal upon expiration of the current term of its insurance coverage. Mr. Metz had taken the emeralds out of the bank for this valuation. But he'd been forced by his superior's unscheduled arrival from London to postpone the appointment with the appraiser until the following morning. So for this night alone—12 short hours out of 18 married years—the jewels had been doubly exposed—out of their vault and uninsured.

Mr. Metz was too genteel, and too distraught, to enumerate sums. But we could count the zeroes from his pallor. "Professor Langley" would never have to teach again.

## Laura's Villa

*Florence/Firenze 1963*

Laura's parting invitation at the Strasbourg conference looped and beckoned like a musical refrain. "*Caro* Russell, don't you dare pass through Firenze without giving me a call."

Now here I was in the city of Dante and Michelangelo, checked into a no-star *pensione* and unpacking clothes crushed like cornflakes by an overwhelmed backpack. Even my toothbrush looked permanently pleated.

I'd unfolded the wrinkled note so many times that I had the number memorized. I lifted the receiver on the hallway telephone. The landlady took up a comfortable eavesdropping position behind the kitchen door.

Then I got cold feet. What if Laura hadn't been serious and I put her on the spot? What if there was a local boyfriend unamused by parachuting foreigners? What the hell, nothing ventured. I dialed and took a breath.

"Bravo! You are here!" Laura's warmth thawed my toes. "I was afraid you might be too busy to call. When did you arrive? How long can you stay?"

I rushed to retrieve my carefully rehearsed script. "Just got in. For three days, then on to Rome. Can you join me for coffee somewhere in town? My treat, of course. Your only obligation is to find your way here. My guidebook map requires a magnifying glass and I'm disoriented after nine hours on three trains."

I'd checked and rechecked my lira cache. If she didn't order pastry with her cappuccino, I could cover both cups and get back on budget by skipping only dinner.

"Don't be silly, Russell. You're a guest in my town. Tuscan tradition demands that I bring you home. Besides, Sandro's just back from the States. My older brother, I told you about him. He'll welcome the chance to practice his American slang. My parents just shudder."

"Then your family will want to be alone with him."

"Nonsense; we're Italians. Besides, he'll be here for six weeks. You'll be gone in three days. Come this afternoon if you're free. My parents are having a small reception to honor *il figlio prodigo.*"

Laura's impulsive energy was contagious. But "reception" jangled alarm bells.

"I'm just traveling with a backpack. Your folks wouldn't find me presentable."

"You underestimate them. You'll do fine. It's outdoors and informal."

"What time is the party? Can you dictate some phonetic directions that I can mimic for a bus driver?"

"Any time after four. But local buses are hopeless. Where's your hotel? I'll send a car."

More jangles. Did my fellow student command a motor pool? I recited the *pensione* address.

Despite Laura's breeziness, I was confident that jeans and a T-shirt fell outside "informal's" permissible boundaries. For a gratuity, my landlady begrudgingly quick-pressed my one dress shirt and rumpled suit. I spent the balance of my snack fund on an inadequate bouquet from a street vendor.

My uneasiness spiked again when I spotted the slowing car. Black and gleaming, tinted windows, understated but classy. The chauffeur only made it worse. His suit was better than mine, his cap from Central

Casting. He sized me up as he stepped around the car. A left-shoulder shrug fluently conveyed disapproval and resignation.

I hesitated, then opted for the back seat. No need to give this jerk satisfaction by riding shotgun. The leather upholstery was firm but supple. We pulled away from the curb in silence. I'd mastered only survival Italian and didn't know one soccer star from another. Besides, family guests probably didn't chat with the help.

He crossed the Arno. Another bad sign. I recalled the shaded-blue area on my tourist map—a posh enclave. We climbed gentle switchbacks past protective ivied walls.

I slunk lower into the plush seat. This reunion had been a mistake. Any lingering hope evaporated when we turned in at 15-foot wrought-iron gates. Two bright uniforms checked my name against a clipboard guest-list before waving us through.

The ascending driveway was a glorious *allée* of laden orange trees and umbrella pines. We emerged onto a graveled quadrangle before a three-story villa. The driver barely paused to let me out. He wheeled away as if embarrassed to be seen delivering this tacky cargo.

I stood and gawked until rescued by a welcoming wave from a young man whose features marked him as Laura's brother. Unlike his compact sister, Alessandro was tall and thin. But his ebony eyes and eyebrows were a giveaway. He wore trousers and a shirt but also a necktie. So I hadn't guessed entirely wrong about attire.

Alessandro kindly volunteered that he'd enjoy having a few moments to chat in English. He had just completed marathon medical exams at New York University and was looking forward to his summer break. He apologized that his sister was still getting ready but assured me she'd be down shortly.

My host led me around the corner of the house onto a lawn as expansive as a fairway. We stood on a terrace above the river, with an unobstructed view of Brunelleschi's signature dome. A marble balustrade lined the perimeter, leading the eye to an elegant swimming pool and canopied gazebos.

A covey of neglected young women beckoned Alessandro to return. I thanked him for taking time away from his guests when he was the honoree. With a relaxed smile, he handed me off to his mother. *Signora* Paroli set her glass on a waiter's tray and approached on long legs.

Her silk dress shimmered in jade and aquamarine. Her short hair surprised me, more *a la moda* than matronly. She gleamed in the sunlight with bright gold accessories. By American standards, she was overloaded. But somehow she carried it off without clamor or ostentation.

Laura's mother radiated warmth. Both hands came up to clasp mine in greeting.

"Mr. Sunshine, welcome to our home. May I call you 'Russell'? Laura has told us so much about you. But, please, you must excuse my English. I almost never have an opportunity to practice and my lessons were more years ago than I'd prefer you to speculate."

Not a blink at my weary costume. Not a missed syllable despite her linguistic apology. The lady's gentle courtesy calmed what must have been my evident self-consciousness.

"Laura will be here in a moment. Her father was unfortunately called away for an emergency. He's a surgeon, as my daughter may have told you."

On cue, Laura descended the villa's rear staircase and added her welcome with a warm kiss on each cheek. A chic party dress had replaced student jeans. The daughter evidently resembled her father more than her mother but the two women shared a magnetic sparkle. Accepting my wimpy bouquet with appreciation before passing it off to a servant, she steered our conversation to familiar topics—my post-conference itinerary and mutual Strasbourg friends.

As we strolled and chatted, I had a chance to observe the assembled guests. Some were more casually dressed than my awkward suit, but all were stylish, and confident. I was surprised by the wide range of ages, from toddlers to octogenarians. The hugs and kisses, within and across genders, were unfamiliar to me but seemed totally natural. Steady laughter drifted across the pool, refined but in no way brittle or false.

I sensed this was an inner circle, more than casual acquaintances.

The afternoon went quickly, lubricated by flutes of *prosecco* topped up by attentive waiters. I relaxed just enough to admire the gracious sophistication of the Paroli entourage.

As things wound down, Laura was called away by her mother to say goodbye to departing guests. Alessandro seized the moment to take me aside.

"Russell, I need to speak with you about a diplomatically delicate matter. This would be ridiculous in New York, or even Milano, but Firenze is still surprisingly provincial. Laura could not accept your kind invitation to coffee."

"Not to worry. She explained to me about your welcome-home party."

"Yes, I'm glad you could join us on such short notice. But, no, my sister would have had to turn you down in any case. Single young women of our class—if I can use that word to an American—are not permitted to be seen alone with a man outside their family circle."

"Alessandro, you're kidding, right? Laura's 23 and just returned from four weeks alone in Strasbourg."

"Ah, but that's the power of appearances. It's what we're *seen* to do that must be constrained."

"I hope you don't think I'd ravish your sister in the town square?" Beneath my banter, I felt incredulous, even a smidge insulted.

Alessandro's good humor lowered the temperature. With hands up, "Everything's cool. Even this close to the Cathedral, two sugars in a *cappuccino* is no mortal sin. Please do not misunderstand. I'm not the Latin heavy. And my sister is not chasing you away. To the contrary, she's determined to see you again before you leave Florence. But for that to happen, when we are back in our parents' nest her older brother must act as chaperone."

Alessandro could probably read disappointment as well as amusement on my American face. He showed tact by playing to the latter response. "*Signor* Russell Sunshine, Alessandro and Laura Paroli would be pleased if you would join them for rustic fare on Thursday evening at 8 o'clock. Transport, without surly driver, will be provided."

We met towards the end of my stay, after I'd done the obligatory Uffizi and David. The playful Alessandro was all business behind the wheel. He drove his Alfa Romeo, in gloves, like a Formula One veteran.

In no time, we reached an ancient inn in the Tuscan countryside. A quiet alcove had been reserved. Thanks to a solicitous proprietor and with no menus in sight, we dined on home-made pasta and grilled veal chops garnished with red peppers and eggplant, all accompanied by a robust Barolo.

The sole awkward moment arose when the innkeeper presented a regional specialty with a flourish. I could not cope with the platter of tiny birds, freshly trapped in a net and crisped in their skins, eyes and all. Alessandro eased me past discomfort, sweeping my share onto his plate. His Brooklyn growl would win no awards, but was nonetheless deeply appreciated. "It's your loss, Buddy."

Tiramisu, espressos and grappa rounded out the memorable meal.

Our last evening together was cordial and confiding. Three was never a crowd. We candidly shared plans and prospects. Laura was going to follow her male relatives into medicine. Brother and sister had deep affection for Florence, family and friends. But they were realistic enough to accept that foreign study might lure them permanently abroad.

*Europe on $5/day. 1967.*

# GREEN BEANS AND BEATLES

*Croatia 1967*

The glib travel agents in Rijeka had made it sound irresistible. Betina was a Dalmatian jewel, a pristine islet lapped by turquoise waters, a bustling fishing village. In a poster phrase, "the real Croatia, unspoiled and undiscovered."

When the rackety bus dropped me in the main plaza at a moonless 10 p.m., no one had told the local inhabitants about their hamlet's rave reviews. Betina by night was barely breathing. Talk about rolling up the sidewalks when the sun goes down. I knew that fishermen had to make an early start, but no teenagers, no tourists, no insomniac retirees?

I took it as inauspicious that the bus driver asked me twice whether I was sure this was my correct destination. I offloaded my backpack, and he wasted no time re-crossing the one-lane causeway that connected the island to the coastal road.

As my eyes adjusted to the dispiriting gloom, I made out one faintly lit bar in the far corner of the town square. I set my pack down by an outside table. No one emerged so I stepped inside to order a beer. The inert barman nodded that he'd send it out, presumably via the oblivious waitress smoking in the corner. The only customers were two drunks hunched over their glasses at the end of the counter.

My lodging requirements were unassuming. But from my sidewalk vantage point, I couldn't spot even a *pensione* or youth-hostel placard. So I finished my beer and went back inside to ask for help.

I might as well have been mute. English, French, and my few words of Italian drew no response from the barman or maid. Even my crude mime of sleeping earned only blank stares. I was getting the message that bustling Betina had no beds on offer.

At this point, one of the lolling drinkers regained sufficient consciousness to gesture that I should follow him across the square. Down a side lane, he stopped and hollered in front of a nondescript facade. An interior light came on, an upstairs window opened, words were exchanged, and I was ushered in through the house's front door by a teenage boy speaking primary-school French.

Bruno Balin introduced himself and said I could unroll my sleeping bag on the kitchen floor. It had been a long day. I was glad to end it indoors.

Mama clomped downstairs at six the next morning to organize breakfast. She handed me a metal bowl of cold water to wash my face in the cluttered courtyard. Over bitter coffee and a hard roll, Bruno explained good-naturedly how his family had been elected as my hosts. The drunk had heard my unsuccessful attempt to seek information in French. Bruno was just back from a failed working stint in Lyon. As the village's only foreign-language speaker, he was nominated by default as Director of Hospitality.

The nominee seemed delighted by this diversion. I sensed that his foreign termination and premature homecoming had caused the family to lose face as well as income. Bruno bounced at the chance to get out of the house and show me around.

We stepped outside and into the square. It exhibited little more animation than the previous evening. The bar-front tables were now occupied by garrulous old men in worn jackets and caps. But no vehicles were in evidence, no radios blaring.

We walked around the small island in less than two hours. The touted coastline was undeveloped and uninspiring. The shallows were attractively transparent, but minefields of giant ebony sea urchins ruled out any prospect of wading.

Bruno rattled on about how cramped he was feeling in his backwater birthplace. He railed against his bullying French boss who had obviously had it in for him. He pumped me for information about America and England. Pop music seemed his obsessive escape.

When we made it back to his house for lunch, the prevailing poverty and the imposition my visit was causing came into cruel focus. For the day's principal meal, Bruno's mother served green beans and green beans. Steamed with garlic for the main course. Cold with lemon juice for the salad. Home-made wine that could have powered a trawler washed it down.

After a communal nap that seemed to retard the already sluggish pace, Bruno slyly revealed his proposed itinerary for the guest who fell to earth. That evening, the neighboring village was hosting a touring band. A rock band, no less. Direct from Zagreb. Not London, but for sure the hottest group ever to hit this coastal cul-de-sac. Bruno would be my guide. And I, his leverage for extracting permission to attend from dubious parents.

At dusk, we walked for an hour—first, over the causeway, then inland on a one-lane dirt road and footpaths across rocky fields. En route we passed and greeted a number of Bruno's friends, quietly emerging from their own closed houses. Their stares confirmed that word had spread of the Balins' alien tenant.

Despite the special occasion, dress was strictly informal. Jeans and T-shirts for the guys. Tame skirts and blouses for the girls. Sturdy walking shoes were de rigueur. The balmy Mediterranean evening relieved us of any need for jackets or caps.

Our destination was a stone-walled settlement undulating up a gentle hillside. Like Betina, it too was anchored by a small public square. But at 30 yards on a side, with no relieving harbor vista, this plaza felt much more confining.

The visiting musicians were setting up on a makeshift stage. With studied nonchalance, they plugged in an electronic keyboard and amplifiers, twanged guitars, beat drum riffs, tapped and tested stage-front mikes.

I was reminded of a junior-high school dance in the American hinterland. Girls and boys hugged the walls in gender-segregated clusters, giggling and gossiping, curious but shy. Here, the obligatory chaperones were not school teachers earning overtime but wizened grandmothers uniformly shrouded in widows' black. They tracked their charges like beady-eyed crows.

The music, when it began, was tame and clunky, a C-team repertoire of inadequate rehearsals and erratic chords. Some numbers were evidently regional favorites, but Bruno assured me that unrecognized others topped the Continental charts.

I was surprised to see that the group's leader was the female vocalist, bold and assertive in a red dress and high heels. With elbow-length sleeves and a modest bodice, she was anything but sleazy. But her very presence at the front of an all-male combo was sending a ripple through the locals.

By the band's first break, the crowd still had not come alive. I counted over 100 bodies packing the small plaza, so the concert's appeal was evidently magnetic. And circulating bottles and glasses of beer and wine confirmed that someone was dispensing lubrication. Still, the inhibited throng was hanging back. So far, married, middle-aged couples had been the only, tentative, dancers.

Bruno pulled me aside excitedly. He and his friends had told the vocalist they had an American visitor. She was vexed by the limp audience and had an inspiration for breaking the ice. The band had just learned a half-dozen Beatles tunes. They would turn up the volume for rock and roll. But I had to dance with her to show the villagers how.

I was startled but amused by the benign conspiracy. I'd already sensed that dozens of youngsters were itching to enter in, if only someone would take the first steps. My dancing would win no prizes at the smallest

Stateside party. But on a Dalmatian hillside, I figured I was a medal contender.

Besides, the sweat on Bruno's upper lip made it clear he had put himself on the line. His proxy could help him climb back from discredit. It was the alien's turn to earn those green beans.

Deal struck, the singer apparently decided that total immersion was the best therapy for this comatose crowd. She made no announcement but climbed down from the stage and strutted boldly to the center of the square. The curious throng parted, easing back in concentric waves. With a wink and a firm handshake, my *agente provocateuse* took up her position just in front of me. A fast downbeat with her raised right arm and we were off.

"AH WANNA HOLD YUR HAND! AH WANNA HOLD YUR HA-AA-AND, AH WANNA HOLD YUR HAND!"

The lead singer's defection had left her backups struggling with beat, diction and harmony. But the amplified volume drowned all deficiencies. The sunburst of young smiles showed the tune was familiar.

I took my own cue from my dancing partner, matching her subdued rendition of The Twist. The teens understood she had upped the ante. Their cheer ricocheted off of ancient stone walls.

No fair critic could have judged our gyrations suggestive. Our bland routine would have bored American preschoolers. But the guardian grandmothers had a different take. Black forms rose as one from the perimeter benches and snatched their virgin treasures by the wrists.

Brief bedlam prevailed as the stewards hustled the maidens through gridlocked arches. The last chords skidded to defeated silence.

Bruno beamed the whole way back down to the coast. Liverpool still set the standard. But things were definitely looking up for Dalmatia's hidden jewel.

# A Path Not Taken

*Corfu 1967*

I landed on Corfu after a sleepless overnight ferry ride down the Adriatic from Dubrovnik. A viscous espresso at a dockside kiosk jolted my batteries. But I was still less than alert when I spotted a Tourism Office just beyond the harbor parking lot. I'd expected to have to walk into town to find orientation information, so this was a break.

I set down my pack on the office's front porch and tapped on the cracked-open door.

"Come in, come in. I just stopped by to drop off some brochures. But God knows where Dimitri is, so you're in luck. You get the Regional Director."

My host seemed at once gruff and ironic. His English was thickly accented but comprehensible. Since he didn't stand up, offer further introduction or shake my hand, I followed his lead and took the chair directly facing the massive desk.

The Director was in his fifties, portly with gray-violet bags under his eyes, sporting an aroused porcupine's coiffure. His three-piece suit had seen better days, though a neat bow tie and trimmed mustache showed he still took some pains with his appearance. Peter Lorre with a taste for *retsina*.

He was fidgeting and obviously impatient, so I got straight to the point.

"Mr. Director, I've read about Corfu from a distance, but I want to see the real thing for myself. What remains of the Greeks and Venetians, but also Durrell's villa and village folk festivals, if any are on?"

"And how long have you budgeted, young man, for this comprehensive exploration?"

"Three days. I'm booked onward to Ios and then Santorini on Tuesday. But I've got long legs and can cover a lot of ground in a few hours. Besides, your distances here are so short."

"While our island may be just a speck to American eyes," he countered with an aggrieved eyebrow, "its history is rich and layered. What is more, you are not yet too late—almost but not quite—to sample some surviving vestiges of that grandeur. Forget about the Durrells, by the way. They are long gone and were colonial dilettantes when they were here."

He leaned forward. "But three days to savor Corfu is a poor jest. An insult, if I thought it were intentional. Give me, give yourself, three weeks and I will do for you what I haven't done for another foreigner this year. I will grant your wish, show you Corfu as it was, and as it remains, if one only knows where and how to look. Not garish postcards. Columns and amphitheaters, to be sure, but something more precious—fascinating survivors behind the walls."

Now it was my turn to fidget. I was powerfully attracted by this insider's offer of access. Obviously, there were personalities and experiences not even hinted at in my paperback guidebook. But my itinerary was fixed and my momentum compelling. Three weeks for a single destination was unthinkable. Corfu was only the first island on my Aegean loop. What about the other four?

Besides, why had this guy selected me for his VIP package? Clearly, I had no money. Yet this puffed-up bureaucrat didn't strike me as a sexual predator. What was his game?

"Why me?" I blurted out.

"How frank should I be? Because I had to talk to you while Dimitri slept off Friday night. Because I am bored in this backwater post while awaiting my overdue promotion to Athens. Because I am sick of ignorant Americans ticking us off checklists like some third-tier rest-stop. Because you are obviously naive but seem genuinely curious."

I tensed my shoulders in hesitation.

Like a jaded bazaar vendor, the Director labored to close the deal. "Young man, don't make this complicated. Few choices in life are so unambiguous. Think of yourself as a swimmer in one of our fabled coves. You can thrash across, disturbing the surface. Or you can take a deep breath and plunge into the depths. But to plunge takes more time, more commitment. And you can't find submerged treasures without a guide. It's entirely up to you. Sprint or dive. But make up your mind. I'm already late for an appointment in town."

I stared at my feet. "I just can't stay." It came out as a reflex, with no pro-and-con balancing. Somehow I felt threatened by the prospect of surrendering my plan. My itinerary's fully allocated calendar squares represented security far from home.

The Director waved me out the door with a dismissive shrug. My last glimpse of him was stuffing disordered papers into a battered briefcase.

Now I was on my own. But *my* Corfu was a waste of time. Although I had relished *Prospero's Cell*, Lawrence Durrell's magical cliff-face home was sealed off behind locked gates. No folk dances were scheduled during my stay. The *souvlaki* was gristly, more mutton than lamb. "Local crafts" bore imported labels.

I shuttled on to my next island destination, already regretting forfeited treasures in the depths.

◧ ▨ ◧

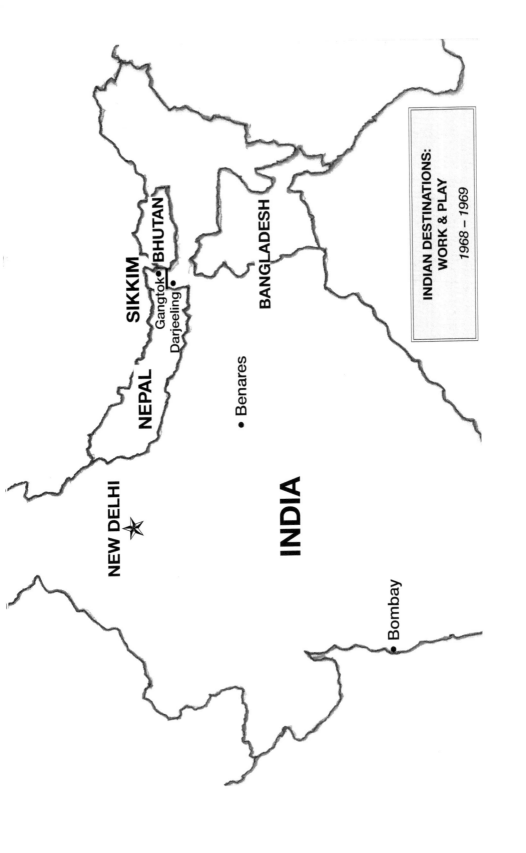

## Chapter Three

# INDIA:
# THIRD-WORLD INITIATION

The Berkeley Professional Schools Program in India was both innovative and practical. The University of California selected 12 new graduates from the professional schools on its Berkeley campus—Architecture, Business, City Planning, Criminology, Education, Industrial Relations, Law, Optometry, Public Health and Social Welfare—and transported us to India's national capital. In 1968, I was one of two Program Fellows chosen from the Law School. Craig Scott, my good friend and classmate, was the other.

In New Delhi, the Fellows dispersed for four days every week to host agencies where we conducted individual research in our respective disciplines. On Fridays, the full dozen reassembled for a rolling seminar on Indian culture and politics, featuring candid conversations with respected national leaders and thinkers. Group excursions to historical sites and invitations to arts performances enriched our layered immersion. Despite our disparate personalities and priorities, we all found India fascinating and impressive, enervating and exasperating.

*Berkeley Professional Schools Fellows in India. New Delhi 1968.*
*(I'm third from the left in the back row.)*

My research on the link between Indian legal education and law practice carried me far afield, from my main working base at Delhi University to law faculties in Bombay (now Mumbai) and Ernakulum. Taking advantage of generous breaks scheduled by the Berkeley Program to encourage individual exploration, I crisscrossed the vast Subcontinent in rattling Third-Class trains. In the south, I visited Madras (now Tamil Nadu) and Kerala, hopping across the straits to Ceylon (Sri Lanka). In western Rajasthan, I circled through the princely fortress towns of Bikaner, Jaipur, Jodhpur and Udaipur. In the north, I schlepped a backpack over Rohtang Pass from Hindu Kulu and Manali to Buddhist Lahaul and Spiti. In the east, I got as far as Darjeeling and Sikkim.

This was my first long-term residence in a foreign country, and in a non-Western developing country as a bonus. If this debut hadn't worked out, you wouldn't be reading this book. But after an initial period of destabilizing adjustment, I grew to relish the unpredictable magic of cross-cultural encounters.

By the end of my 16-month Indian sojourn, the die was cast. I had found my niche and my passion abroad.

*Crossing Rohtang Pass.*
*Himachal Pradesh 1969.*

# Stepping Out

## *New Delhi 1968*

Now that we'd arrived in India after an exhausting series of hops across the Pacific and East Asia, most of our colleagues were recuperating from jet lag. But four of us were restless and jumped at our first invitation to a public function. The American Embassy had obtained for our Berkeley Program complimentary passes to the Indian Independence Day festivities on the Maidan, the sprawling public park separating Old Delhi from New. With two lawyers, a nurse and a social worker in our quartet, we joked that we were qualified to deal with almost any contingency.

Our taxi driver threaded his way through near-gridlock and pointed us in the direction of some uniformed police at our destination. We climbed out of the cab and did a collective double-take. It was easily the largest crowd any of us had ever seen. A packed mass of humanity stretched to the horizon. The next day's newspapers would estimate the throng at one million. To us, it felt as if the celebration had drawn the capital's entire population.

We made our way to the officers and flashed our passes. They waved us into a chute they'd laid out across the grass, its metal partitions like heavy bicycle racks wrapped in red and white tape. This impromptu corridor was mainly for notables' chauffeur-driven cars, but it was doubling as a right-of-way for privileged pedestrians. We were thankful we'd dressed up for the occasion. Craig and I had on suits and ties, despite the humid heat. Kay and Marybeth were in dresses. The reserved passageway eased our progress through the crowd like an express lane.

An elevated stage had been set up for the speeches. Shiny bunting in the national colors of green, orange and white draped across its front. An alphabet of radio call letters topped the bundle of center-stage microphones. Trim rows of folding chairs for invited guests had been arranged on the grass immediately in front of the stage, the first few rows roped off for designated VIPs. We found four seats among the also-rans.

Almost as soon as we were seated, we were up again for the Indian national anthem. Then back down, taking our cues from the surrounding guests. Three religious representatives—a Hindu, a Sikh and a Muslim—blessed the commemoration. Next, a seemingly endless parade of speakers took turns at the microphones. The mimeographed handout on our seats listed them as national and local politicians. Several aging veterans from India's Independence Movement were also introduced and acknowledged with applause. Twenty years on, these respected freedom-fighters were still sporting homespun cotton outfits championed by Mahatma Gandhi, as well as Nehru's signature campaign caps. Top brass from the military services rounded out the queue of what turned out to be preliminary presenters.

It was far too early in our stay for us to identify most of these celebrities. None of us was a specialist in Indian politics. Thanks to our weekly roundtables, we'd soon become familiar with major players' names and faces. But now, even the few leaders we already knew were difficult to recognize on this dais. The glaring spotlights flattened their faces into unnatural masks. Dusk accentuated these theatrical distortions.

Prime Minister Indira Gandhi was the headliner. Rising from her seat, she received an instantaneous greeting from what looked like a Congress Party claque bunched off to one side of the stage. By the time she approached the rostrum, this prompting had the desired effect of inspiring a rousing cheer from the crowd. Like the other orators, she spoke in Hindi. Our pre-departure language-cramming in California hadn't been adequate for us to keep up with her rapid pace. But we could infer from the national holiday and the expectant pauses for applause that this was standard patriotic fare.

At last the marathon agenda had been covered. The crowd turned away from the stage and we followed their gaze. Two huge papier-mâché effigies of Rama and Ravana, the potent adversaries from India's beloved folk epic, the Ramayana, loomed over a cleared space just beyond the dais. Their colors dazzled in the crossing spotlights, red and gold for the hero, black and silver for the villain. Their elaborate headgear towered 50 feet above kindling banked around their bases.

The band filled the air with a brass fanfare. Attendants stepped forward to touch flaring torches to the giants' hems. Flames whooshed into the darkening sky. The multitude roared its approval, overpowering the trumpets. Sheets of shiny paper flaked off the disintegrating figures, wafting up in flimsy patches. We could feel the heat 100 yards away. The bonfires crackled, the exposed bamboo frames collapsed, snapping and popping. Twin pyres bathed the satisfied, supercharged crowd in pulsing brilliance.

As the fires subsided, the VIPs were directed to their idling cortege. The four of us had talked in advance about retracing our entry route along the taped corridor. But now security guards with orange-tipped flashlights reserved that channel for vehicles only. No provision had apparently been made for the exit of invited pedestrians. We tried to caucus above the happy din but couldn't make ourselves heard. We fell back on sign language, agreed on a plausible direction and started off, confident we could find a taxi at any edge of the park.

The crowd was so dense that we walked in pairs. Four abreast was out of the question. Kay and Craig were in front, Marybeth and I just behind. At six-feet-one, I was above average height back in California. On the Subcontinent, I was basketball material. I could see over almost all of the heads from here to infinity. With few exceptions, they were adult males, uniformly black-haired and mostly young. Several female politicians had shared the rostrum but the surging spectators included few women or kids.

The crowd's slow progress was halting and borderline claustrophobic. We drew stares, some whistles, and several pigeon-English taunts.

"Hey, Sahibs, where you come from? Where you going? Take me with you!"

The bold ones played to their pals for laughs. But the mood struck me as harmless and joshing, like contented fans dispersing after a stadium win.

Marybeth's sudden halt pulled me up short.

"Take my hand," she shouted in my right ear. "Walk closer." Her jaw was rigid, cheeks flushed. We barely knew each other but it was obvious she was livid.

"What's wrong, Marybeth? What's the matter?"

"They're grabbing me!" she snapped. "Front and back!"

"Who? Who's grabbing you?"

"Them!" she screamed.

I finally realized she meant the young bucks walking right by our sides. These joking kids were groping an escorted foreign woman. Maybe the bonfires had sparked their hormones and the massed anonymity was fanning their bravado?

Before I could warn Craig and Kay, they also jerked to a halt. Kay spun towards the young Indian next to her and slapped him with full force across the face.

His hands flew up in pain and shame. "What you do?" he yelped. "Why you strike me, *Fereng*?"

Craig jumped into the breach. "You know damned well why she hit you, Buster! Back off and keep your hands to yourself!"

Marybeth and I rushed forward to join them. The four of us were crammed together. I began to experience everything in slow-motion. In a heartbeat, the giddy revelers transformed into a howling mob. It was like a sci-fi shape-shift. I watched it happen. I heard it. I felt it. But it couldn't be real.

Almost palpable rage swelled up from the bodies pressing against us, radiating outwards in an invisible wave. A much larger block of the festival crowd caught the rolling frenzy. The previously random buzz became focused. It syncopated into manic jeers. No one had yet struck us but more than a few raised fists were silhouetted against the glare. I was sure that in seconds we'd be bashed and trampled.

By reflex, our four backs wheeled inwards. Bumping up against each other, we flinched, facing the mob. I flashed on a movie image of covered wagons circled against a different kind of Indians. Across the carpet of heads, I spotted metal helmets, wide in the brim, flat in the crown, like World War I doughboys. Another cinema cliché pinged my hyper-aroused consciousness—"Here comes the cavalry!"

Somehow they sliced swiftly through the crush. I could make them out clearly now, a squad of ten soldiers or military police, uniformly tall and thin. All in short-sleeved khaki shirts, baggy shorts, taut knee socks, high boots, and those helmets, secured with chinstraps. It was a flying wedge, a triangle formation for penetrating crowds.

"Squad, Halt!"

The wedge stopped with a high-stepping, two-beat boot slam like the Guard changing at Buckingham Palace. Even the barked command was in English. A three-striped sergeant stepped forward. I couldn't make out where he'd come from in the wedge. He was just there, inches from my face, under rigid self-control. At close range, I stared at a left eye blinking in a tic just above a prominent mole.

He vibrated with a British palm-turned-outward salute. "On my signal, get inside and stay inside!"

Inside? I almost erupted in hysterical laughter. He sounded like my mother issuing a childhood ultimatum to come in from the backyard and go up to my room. Inside where? Gulping air, I realized he meant the wedge.

"Squad, About!"

In unison, the soldiers pivoted 180 degrees. The point man stepped through the center, pulling the two sides after him as the arrowhead reversed and reformed.

And to us, "Now move!"

We staggered trembling into the small pocket, pushing forward, instinctively distancing ourselves from the triangle's open rear, which the sergeant now sealed.

"*Lathis*, Up!"

Only now did I spot the slender staves, bamboo rods three feet long, shafts girded in metal bands. Stock still, each soldier raised his staff in a two-handed grasp, like an American baseball bat.

The mob was a monster sensing it was about to lose its prey. It flexed inwards, howls intensifying.

"Point, Attack!"

Bending his knees and throwing his weight forward in a sudden fluid lunge, the point man swung his *lathi* with disciplined brutality. No other soldier moved a muscle.

"*Thwonk!*"

The club caught a jeering boy above his left ear and across his face, knocking him senseless. Blood sprayed from his shattered nose, splattering shirts and faces. The point returned to attention as if taking batting practice.

I was sure we'd be devoured by the assaulted beast.

"Squad, Forward Slow!" With a synchronized, measured tread, the wedge eased into gear.

The unconscious boy's friends ducked down to drag his limp body aside. The vacated space was barely sufficient to absorb our creeping advance. There were no further blows but also no separation. Almost imperceptibly, the rows of resisting bodies bowed and yielded to our penetration. Immediately behind, the crush continuously resealed.

Soldiers and mob touched each other on both flanks of the arrowhead. Spiced sweat mixed with the acrid bite of smoke from the pyres. Spit flew from screaming mouths. But those screams seemed more hysterical than hostile—primordial arousal, out-of-control. Inside the frail rolling fence, I felt mentally mesmerized and physically terrified. Scrunching my shoulders down to reduce my exposure, all I earned was a cramp across my upper back.

Our cowed quartet shuffled forward, snug against the protective phalanx. Still the mob let us through. My analytical lawyer's brain protested that this capitulation wasn't logical. Hundreds of packed, shouting bodies should not give way to a dozen silent ones. The sergeant wore a holstered sidearm but never drew or fired it. The batons had demonstrated their crude power, but there were less than ten of them. If the front of the pack would just stop retreating, if two or three more *lathi* smacks drove the youths over the edge, the mob could trample us into a pulp without any conscious decision.

Our slog seemed interminable. I felt nauseous and heavy-limbed. Finally, I spotted car tops and parking-lot signs. I stumbled over a curb. We had reached the Maidan perimeter.

My wristwatch said 9.15. We had left the grandstand at 9 p.m. Fifteen short minutes. Unbelievable.

The pressing mob magically dissolved into a mundane dispersing crowd. Our juvenile assailants slipped away without a parting taunt.

The irony was stone-heavy. In Berkeley, cops had been hated "pigs," violently blocking our right to demonstrate. Tonight they had violently rescued us from a pack not much younger than ourselves.

The sergeant flagged down a cruising taxi and ordered it to take us. I had the longest legs so I climbed in beside the driver. Only then did I feel the painful indentations punched across my right palm. Marybeth's nails.

The sergeant relaxed his rigid discipline. "Go back where you came from," he hissed, slamming my door. "Never come here again."

Thirty-six hours since we'd touched down at Delhi Airport. Welcome to India.

## CROSS PURPOSES

### *New Delhi 1968*

I had a love/hate relationship with Delhi's scooter-taxis. Mostly love. The three-wheelers were the transport of choice for all members of our Berkeley Program. Public buses were undependable and packed like sardines. Driving ourselves would have been suicidal in Delhi traffic, even if we could have run the bureaucratic gauntlet to procure a license and a car.

The roving rickshaws could be hailed on every street corner. And their fares were dirt-cheap. The exasperating exceptions were when our foreign faces inspired unscrupulous inflation. But with humor and patience, even this extortion could often be reduced.

These vehicles were strictly no-frills. Powered by rebuilt motorcycle engines or souped-up lawnmower motors, they belched particulate clouds that we knew must be taking years off our lives. The passenger seats bruised our bums. Rain curtains were useless in drenching monsoons.

But the taxi-wallahs were irresistible desperadoes. They'd slalom through traffic jams at break-neck speed, keeping up a banter combining bravado with obscenities. These pilots' unflappable panache converted grim street-survival to competitive Keep Away.

This morning, while my muttering chauffeur was briefly stymied at a clogged roundabout, I stole another glance at the note Professor Aggarwal had left on my desk the previous evening. The two brief sentences were curiously unsettling: "Mr. Sunshine, could you stop by my office at 9 tomorrow morning. I have the item you are hotly pursuing."

Aggarwal was Chair of the Acquisitions Committee at the Indian Law Institute where I was a Visiting Fellow. No surprise, then, that the Institute's Librarian had relayed to him my complaint about another researcher poaching my reserved periodical.

But how about "please"? And why "hotly pursuing"? Collegial wit or a cross-cultural jab? And why the period after "morning" instead of a question mark? Was he subtly issuing a summons instead of an invitation? Enough parsing paranoia, Sunshine. The guy probably just wants to hand over the magazine. And maybe ask you to lighten up on his librarian.

Screeching tires, a jerk to the left, and exchanged volleys of Punjabi curses yanked me out of my funk. Shaken but braced in the taxi's back seat, I caught a pirate's reassuring grin in the rear-view mirror.

"Not to worry, *Sahib-ji*. Lorry bugger not even close."

"No problem, Ace. Just get me to my meeting in one piece."

Fare paid and limbs counted, I crossed the Institute's sere lawn to its anonymous entrance. The self-effacing structure diverted no attention from the neoclassical grandeur of the Supreme Court, the Institute's imposing patron directly across the road.

Inside I was struck, as every morning, by the demoralizing vacuum. There were more swallows trespassing in foyer niches than scholars working in the expansive facilities. It wasn't getting to this building that sapped my energy. It was arriving here.

Professor Aggarwal answered my knock on his office door. Probably in his early forties, his dark eyes were deep-set in a somber face.

He ignored my outstretched hand, waved me in and closed the door firmly behind us. Then he retreated behind his desk, so I took the chair in front. No collegial side-by-side proximity on the window-sofa for this tête-à-tête. When he leaned forward to place sharp elbows on the cleared desktop, worn suit sleeves were stretched taut. A prominent vein pulsed across his forehead.

"Mr. Sunshine, I've been meaning to have this conversation for some time. I kept hoping it wouldn't be necessary."

"Professor, I'm sure my contretemps with the Institute Librarian doesn't warrant a Committee Chairman's intervention. I just want to borrow the periodical long enough to photocopy one article. Ten minutes max."

"As usual, the American jumps to conclusions, focused on his precious source materials. I suspect you don't even see us most of the time, much less consider the impression you're making."

I was stung by his barb and confused by his vagueness. "Professor Aggarwal, this American needs you to be more explicit. Who is 'us' and what impression?"

"'We', Mr. Sunshine, are your Indian colleagues, the Institute's permanent staff. In two months, you may not have begun to sort us all out. But we've paid more attention to you and your compatriot."

He meant Craig, my flat-mate, the Berkeley Program's other lawyer. "Professor, we can't be that interesting—two foreign Fellows who will only be with you for less than a year. Have we done something to offend?"

"It's what you haven't done that offends. You treat us as if we are unworthy of your personal or professional acquaintance."

"Look, we don't seem to be on the same page this morning. I thought you just wanted to chat about the contested periodical. I'm sorry if I've struck you as anti-social. I'm confident Craig would apologize as well. We're only here part-time each week and we've both been concentrating on organizing field trips around the country to collect our data. So there haven't been many opportunities to get acquainted."

"Mr. Sunshine, I doubt that scholarly dedication is the sole explanation for your indifference. You have never taken time to ask about *our* research, much less to ask our advice on shaping yours."

By now, I was sufficiently provoked to step beyond politeness. "Professor Aggarwal, your criticisms confirm that you favor direct speech. So let me try to be equally frank. You're right. I have found the Institute's inertia disheartening. Thanks to Ford Foundation generosity, you've got a first-rate research facility and a stellar roster of scholars. But I never see more than a half-dozen of you on the job. And most of those are apparently bogged down in a perpetual joint examination of federalism. It's straight out of Dickens. There must be more pressing topics for legal analysis and publication!"

I started to tally impromptu examples on my fingers, but my agitated host cut me off. "Has it never occurred to you that if wish-lists were all that's required, your Indian colleagues could draw them up for themselves?"

"Then why are you all squandering your privileged positions?"

He leaned forward again across the desk. "I wish you had voiced that concern earlier. You might have learned a thing or two. As it is, you have only scratched the surface. Let me give you my perspective. You may trust that each of my colleagues could sketch a parallel profile."

I relaxed a notch for my colleague's narrative. I'd been nonplussed by his pointed attack but was genuinely curious to hear his story. I realized with chagrin that, ten weeks into my Institute tenure, this was my first serious exchange with an Indian counterpart.

"My family is from a village outside Allahabad," he resumed in a less agitated tone. "I was one of the lucky few. I was spotted in primary school as having promise. They shipped me off to a Lucknow boarding school run by missionaries. From there, the doors kept opening. A scholarship to Delhi University. An honors degree in law. A Ford Foundation grant to Columbia University for an LL.M. A teaching appointment back at Delhi, first as instructor, soon as professor. A prized placement at this prestigious Institute. I've been here five years. And here I intend to stay."

Although this résumé was tempered in contrast to his prior combativeness, his complacency was nonetheless irritating. Here was one of the best and the brightest of India's current crop of legal talent. Yet while his country was desperate for technical expertise, he was content to sit on his sinecure.

"Aren't you suffocating?" I challenged. "This place is a tomb."

"Not a tomb, Mr. Sunshine. A monument. These are still early days for the Republic. Our national birthing was traumatic, not to say genocidal. The authorities are taking the long view to restore equilibrium and public confidence. That grace period requires restrained, stable institutions."

The Professor gestured out the window to the Supreme Court. "Like the one that's hosting you. The Justices constitute our Institute Board of Governors. The last thing they wish to hear or read from across the road is any disruptive noise. Our 'perpetual study' of federalism, as you deride it, suits Their Honors to a T."

I felt like jumping on a soapbox. "But that's bald intimidation! The same oppression your Independence Movement struggled against. What about Gandhi, Nehru, and Jinnah? They all used the law to demand and push for economic, political and social change. As independent legal scholars, you've inherited their mantle."

"There is no such thing as 'independent'," he snapped. "At least not applied to a contemporary Indian legal institution. The Supreme Court hires and fires all Institute professionals. Let me deflate your presumptuous pieties with some hard facts. I am the second of seven sons. I had six sisters as well, of whom four survive. My father is a small farmer. My mother teaches primary school. Among 11 siblings, I am the only one to complete secondary school. And not just among my immediate family. The only one in my extended family, including 39 cousins."

The Professor looked inward, as if pained to be confiding. "Everyone in that tribe, and in our surrounding village, looks up to me as the great success. Everyone expects me—needs me—to maintain my elevated position in the national capital. My Institute stipend is modest, even pathetic by your standards. But when supplemented by Delhi Law Faculty lecture fees, this income stream helps keeps rice and *dhal* on the family table, especially during periodic famines."

He had my full attention, for once with no temptation to debate.

"And what do I have to do to keep 50 mouths eating? In a word, nothing. I was selected for this position from among 600 applicants. When my pro forma probation is successfully concluded next spring, I will have earned life tenure. So long as I attract no adverse notice. Keeping my head down, never rocking the boat, a loyal team player. An American should appreciate that—team spirit."

Professor Aggarwal picked up the pace as he concluded his recitation. "Mr. Sunshine, you have a return air ticket to the United States in your pocket and a bright future in some fat-cat law firm. So when you strut through our hallways making facile assumptions about our lack of initiative, you shouldn't be surprised that it gets under our brown skins.

"My colleagues, of course, would never say a word. Some of the older ones still harbor diffidence towards educated Westerners. The rest know you'll be gone soon enough. But I was determined not to let you slip in and out with a closed mind and eyes."

The Professor rose and snatched up a document from a pile on his desk, abruptly terminating our interview. "Take your journal copy. I know you're in a hurry to digest it. I, on the other hand, have nothing but time."

I exited Professor Aggarwal's office with my nose out-of-joint. I wasn't yet receptive, but his tirade had conveyed insights as well as insults. In international relations, how you're feeling matters less than how you're coming across. And for a visiting practitioner, empathy may be more constructive than personal productivity.

# Rainbow Days

*New Delhi 1969*

It depends on what you count. From one perspective, we weren't off to a bad start. Our Berkeley-in-India Program was smoothly launched. Craig, Randy and I had found an affordable flat in a local neighborhood not overrun by other foreigners. Jangpura Extension was only 30 minutes by scooter-taxi from Connaught Circus, New Delhi's central hub, where our host research institutes were located.

Baluram, our houseman, did a reasonable job of keeping up with three bachelors' chronic messiness. And even in a cold-water, one-hotplate kitchen, he could turn out respectable curries. Dr. Sharma, our Hindi tutor, was having uneven success. But already we'd mastered a few pithy phrases to rebuff the most brazen street-vendors.

On the other hand, we still felt so isolated from meaningful contact. Passing pedestrians smiled but seldom spoke. Playing children answered our waves but were kept at a distance by chaperones. In four months we'd been invited into no one's home, not even for tea, although this was one of the world's most hospitable cultures. To be fair, there was no overt hostility, no glares, oaths or vandalism. But our Yankee trio passed in and out of our bustling neighborhood like aliens hermetically sealed in an invisible envelope. We were trying our best to be respectful guests. But resentful loneliness was setting in.

I got up early one Saturday morning to slog through some tedious legal materials. Craig and Randy, my two flat-mates, were still asleep. It was heating up already and the ceiling fan was on the blink. Baluram had opened windows to catch any breeze, but the clamor from the street below seemed unusually raucous. So despite the climbing thermometer, I closed the French windows onto the balcony. I had to get this stuff read over the weekend. I returned to my living-room desk and called out to Baluram to ask that I not be disturbed.

He was always accommodating, even when he thought the *sahibs* were behaving inappropriately. With years of prior experience working for expats, our houseman took foreigners' foibles in stride. So I couldn't believe it a while later when I spotted him out of the corner of my eye. He slipped silently through the front door from the stairwell and was scuttling across the room like a mortified crab.

I barked, trying to hold concentration. "Baluram, I told you I have a deadline."

He halted his lateral creep but didn't respond, bobbing nervously, head bowed, hands clasped in front of him. I was getting annoyed. "Baluram, please tell me what's going on?"

Just then, I sensed we were not alone. I spun my swivel chair. Bold as brass, obviously admitted by my treacherous gatekeeper, Pankaj Butalia had penetrated my sanctum.

I didn't really know Pankaj, but I knew who he was. The Butalias were a large family living on one corner of the hollow square of our apartment block. Devilishly handsome and animated, he was the eldest Butalia child, probably 17 or so. On school days, he'd normally be decked out in the distinctive blazer of St. Stephens, Delhi University's most prestigious college for men.

This morning he was all in white. But it wasn't his outfit that drew my attention. In either hand, he held a softball-sized balloon ominously bulging with colored water—one lime green, one shocking pink.

"Do you want it here," he drawled in his best Spaghetti Western imitation, "or in the street?"

I'd never been fast on my feet. But I could put two and two together. Although the date had snuck up on us, it was *Holi*, the irrepressible Hindu festival of all-bets-off. My foreign friends and I had read about it with unqualified admiration. This highly stratified society had the good sense to set aside one day each year when all rules were suspended. For one day only, no social classes, no castes, no gender discrimination, no reproving elders, no masters and servants. The authorities were prudent enough to keep matters from getting totally out of control. The single sanctioned activity for letting off steam was to douse anyone within range, regardless of status, with volleys of neon liquid.

I knew I was trapped. With as much dignity as I could salvage, I rose from my chair and asked if I might be permitted to change into more suitable attire. My trousers weren't expensive, but I preferred them in beige. My abductor hesitated as if suspecting a ruse. He must have known from his cinema Westerns that Americans were shifty. To tip the scales, I cravenly offered him the prospect of two additional targets sleeping in the next rooms. Pankaj granted me a moment's reprieve, after exacting a solemn pledge that I wouldn't attempt to sound an alarm or leap from a second-floor window.

I had just enough time to wake my still-dozing friends. We jumped into gym shorts, white T-shirts and tennis shoes. Pankaj marched us down to the street. At the top of the stairs, Baluram held open the door, eyes beaming above a crinkled grin.

In our front yard, we confronted Pankaj's co-conspirators: sisters Bela and Urvashi, kid-brother Bunni. They were fidgeting in anticipation, Bela round and confident, Urvashi, slender and intense, youngest Bunni, as always, shy and watchful, taking his cues. The trio's gaudily splattered clothes confirmed they'd rehearsed before stalking big game. Their ambitious arsenal spanned the spectrum from pale yellow to deep purple. Normally quite civilized, now they erupted into tribal ecstasy. Elder Brother had pulled it off.

Their cheers brought home a double irony. All those months that we'd been chafing for contact in the isolation of our second-floor flat, these kids, and probably other neighbors, must have been hovering in parallel frustration a few doors away. And when ultramodern Berkeley graduates couldn't figure out how to break out of their box, a millennia-old Krishna festival provided the key.

Pankaj pulled me back to the present. This was his moment and he was not about to relinquish command. Keeping the gathering throng of eager neighbors at bay, he escorted us to the nearest available wall. He softly inquired if I'd care to take off my spectacles. I resolutely declined.

"Fire!"

The point-blank salvo was disciplined and devastating. We were drenched in a slithering rainbow. The colors ran down our chests like performance art. The crowd's cheers and laughter were deafening, especially since our ears were submerged.

Fair play being gospel for a St. Stephens man, even on *Holi*, Pankaj graciously supplied us with retaliatory ordnance. The spluttering American commandos regrouped with commendable speed. Off we sprinted, ten paces behind our delighted assailants. Soon the entire square was in bedlam. Brilliant showers drenched everyone rash enough to be caught out-of-doors. To my amazement, even stout grandmothers and aunties were entering the fray, sari skirts and petticoats hitched up with one fist, wrist bangles jangling.

In the midst of this chaos, a neighboring barrister was a column of calm, immaculate in pinstripe suit, bowler hat, briefcase and furled umbrella. Daring Bela lofted a vermillion balloon. The black-clad Zorro was unintimidated. "Zaaah!" he shouted, skewering the incoming missile with his umbrella rapier. Then tipping his brim with a wink, he stepped into his waiting car and was whisked away.

Beaming Baluram on the balcony was taking it all in. The entire community was at play. Our community.

That afternoon, Craig, Randy and I were invited to the first of many cordial meals in the Butalia home. We crossed a threshold into their lives, as well as into their dwelling. In the coming months, we joined parents and the kids at a steady stream of films and lectures, recitals and exhibitions. I remember most fondly one outing at the height of New Delhi's garden-wedding season. In our best suits, we three Americans sweated contentedly under a cavernous reception tent, extending the row of six seated Butalias.

"Tell the others, quietly, and follow me out," Mrs. B. whispered in my ear, smoothly lowering her cup and saucer to the grass beneath her folding chair. "We are at the wrong wedding."

With *Holi* as the milestone, more Jangpura neighbors opened their doors. We did our best to reciprocate hospitality, following Baluram's deft, if deferential, guidance.

And those tinted T-shirts? We wore their fading glory for a full season of Sunday-morning touch-football games against the American Embassy's Marine guards.

We liked to think of ourselves as the Indian side.

# River Walks

*Benares[1] 1969*

The lanes were growing narrower and steeper as they sloped down to the river. This was my first walk in Benares, and I was enjoying the random meander. But I had to pay attention to my feet, especially in advancing twilight. The stone paving was uneven and tricky. There was even an occasional stair-step paired with a diagonal gutter. No cars or scooter-taxis could negotiate this warren. That explained the antique wheelbarrows parked at the neighborhood's upper edge, their bantering jockeys ready to shuttle supplies.

Here in the city's oldest quarter, most buildings were three to four stories high. I craned my neck up at rickety balconies and sleeping-porches protruding over the slender passageways. These ad hoc extensions reduced the alleys to canyons, canopied with burdened clotheslines.

I couldn't spot any electric streetlights or wires. The only ground-level illumination gleamed from curbside apartments where kerosene lanterns and oil lamps flickered. Smoke snaked out through open doors and windows, carrying tempting aromas of North Indian cooking: cumin, coriander, garlic, and nutty *ghee*, the all-purpose clarified butter.

As dusk thickened, the slanting streets filled to capacity with pedestrian commuters. Few greetings were exchanged.

---

1 Today, Varanasi.

Benares was an anonymous metropolis, not some intimate village.

An irregular ant-train of small boys surged uphill against the prevailing foot traffic, bobbing and weaving past adult knees and hips. With warning yelps, they squeezed through the crush. Each boy carried a metal brazier suspended from chains like a jeweler's scale. In the center of the 12-inch pan lay a heap of bright embers. The nimble tykes slipped through doorways to deliver hot coals to waiting hearths. Beside the fires, squatting women chopped vegetables on flat stones and stirred simmering pots.

My pinched lane spilled out onto a sprawling embankment overlooking the mighty Ganges. Alley gloom surrendered to a saturated orange glow. To my left and right, tiers of broad steps flanked the riverfront, like a grandstand for giants—Benares's fabled *ghats*. In the distance, the steps seemed to descend straight into the shallows. Directly in front, they stopped at a wide dirt beach.

The entire expanse was illuminated by flaring funeral pyres. Crackling combustion filled the air. Sweating attendants stoked and tended the biers. Beside each pyre, tight clusters of family mourners huddled in white, some wailing, others sobbing or still. Shaven-headed priests chanted Sanskrit prayers, pouring libations of oil over shrouded lifeless forms.

Each pyre had a waiting queue. When a cremation was judged sufficiently advanced, the attendants would unceremoniously tamp down the charred remains. Extinguished bits were swept aside. New logs were added from adjacent piles. At a nod, the next body in line was carried forward, deposited, and a new leave-taking ignited.

Around the base of each bier, small figures darted in and out of what must have been blistering heat. Scooping embers into pans, they scurried away up the hill. I shuddered with recognition. I had traced the ant-caravans to their source.

Since arriving in India, I'd been drawn to Benares as one of the Subcontinent's least Westernized cities. The religious center of the Hindu world, Benares had been continuously occupied for at least 3,000 years.

It was every devout Hindu's fervent wish to make a Benares pilgrimage at least once in a lifetime, like a Muslim's *hajj* to Mecca.

For dying pilgrims, to expire and be cremated on the banks of the Ganges offered redemption and release from reincarnation, the endless cycle of births and deaths. A shortcut to heaven. If one died at home, a second-best, but still valued, blessing could be earned if mourning relatives carried the deceased's ashes to Benares for submersion in the all-absorbing river.

For living pilgrims, the city and its river were hallowed sites of ritual purification. Praying to the patron god Shiva and bathing in the holy stream absolved sins and assuaged suffering. Dawn was the most auspicious moment to perform ablutions.

The morning after I'd witnessed the burning biers, I returned to the *ghats* to watch throngs of devotees greet the new sun with a muted cheer. Some squatted at water's edge, dipping brass pots into the river and sluicing their heads and shoulders. Others waded right in, waist- or even shoulder-high, often ducking under for total immersion. The women were fully clothed in soaked saris. Several kept their heads demurely draped. Most men stripped down to white cotton wraps tucked at the waist. Ascetic *sadhus* bathed without even this simple cloth. The atmosphere was joyful but subdued. There was little chatter, much audible chanting and praying. It was all marvelously incongruous—densely crowded but utterly private, half- or wholly naked yet totally chaste.

The bathers were surrounded by bobbing offerings—marigold garlands, fruits, small votive lamps, as well as less wholesome flotsam. Bustling cremation-attendants were shoveling mounds of ashes, half-burnt logs, even recognizable bones and limbs into the swirling shallows.

I had never felt so alien. But I was impressed by the scene's pious resilience. I felt certain I was observing a rhythm and ritual little varied for millennia.

Yet signs of commercial and technological intrusion were everywhere evident. Vendors' kiosks and billboards were visible in the distance, though still apparently banned from the immediate precincts. Some pilgrims

*Temple ghats from the Ganges. Benares 1969.*

were wearing eyeglasses or wristwatches that they set aside before getting wet. Garish pop music wailed from neighborhood apartments and tea stalls. How much longer, I wondered, could this primordial sanctuary resist total absorption by India's rocketing modernization?

That afternoon, I took one final stroll along the *ghats*. I wandered in some agitation, trying to come to terms with the incongruous tumult of this most sacred site.

An orange caterpillar approaching in the distance interrupted my brooding. As I focused, the undulation transformed into a column of eight Buddhist monks, saffron robes draped over one shoulder, shaven heads gleaming. Their presence in this Hindu center didn't surprise me. Benares was also revered by Buddhists, as the reputed location of Buddha's first sermon.

I guessed these short-statured visitors to be Nepalese. We all raised our hands in the *namaste* greeting, palms together in front of our chests. Most of the monks looked young, in their late teens or early twenties. But the two at the front were older. The leader, at the head of the line, might have been 60. He was compact and plump, standing not much over five feet tall. Thick, wire-rimmed glasses magnified his accepting eyes.

The monk second in line stepped forward to volunteer as interpreter. "Hello, Mister. Where you from?"

"America," I replied, "but I live in New Delhi."

The head monk then silently intervened. With a single raised eyebrow, he seemed to signal to his subordinate that he was literally and figuratively out of line. The tacit reprimand tugged the chagrined acolyte back into place.

The leader now greeted me directly, in halting but understandable Hindi. I mobilized my modest vocabulary to respond in kind. We slipped in and out of English to bridge the gaps. I tried to indicate by posture and tone that I'd meant no discourtesy by speaking first to his eager disciple. The head monk put me at ease with a winning combination of amused animation and spiritual calm.

He explained how he and his charges had come down from Kathmandu to make a circuit of ancient shrines, combining pilgrimage with training. I sketched my own California roots and my professional placement in New Delhi.

"But what of Benares?" the leader inquired. "How do you find this holy place?"

"I'm still taking it in," I cautiously responded. "It's all so strange. Too much to sort out all at once."

"Which part is strange for you?"

"Which isn't? Take the little kids, for example. How can they casually plunder the biers to carry off human remains for kitchen hearths? It seems so disrespectful, even ghoulish."

"The dead no longer need their bones," the monk softly replied. "The boys' families have nothing. This fuel is all they can afford. If the cremation is blessed, perhaps also the supper!"

I was charmed by this older man's serious playfulness. He seemed relaxed and comfortable integrating religious and secular domains. Precisely what I'd been struggling, unsuccessfully, to separate.

At the same time, his nonjudgmental pragmatism struck me as somehow too pat. I swept my arm to encompass the Cecil B. DeMille saga up and down the riverbank. "How can you be so tolerant of these garish rituals? The Buddhism I've read about is disciplined, personal and contemplative. No gods. Some say not even a religion. Hinduism's at the other extreme. A public spectacle with a thousand gods—and still counting. The two paths could hardly be more irreconcilable."

The unruffled monk didn't rise to the bait. "Buddhism, like Hinduism, may take many forms. Some quiet, some louder. Some public, some private. I believe the same may be true of your Western religions. No faith has a monopoly on wisdom. We all walk different paths toward a shared destination."

My sidewalk tutor wrapped it up with a quiet smile. "Try to see past the shrines, the incense, and the garlands."

I longed to extend this provocative dialogue. I found myself surprisingly moved by this chance encounter. Our few moments together had been curiously intimate. But a bustling promenade didn't lend itself to an ecumenical seminar. We all had to move on.

With a nod to his disciples, the head monk took his leave. Another exchange of *namaste*s and we parted company, continuing our pilgrimages in opposite directions.

Short seconds later, an electric jolt zapped the nerve center at the base of my skull. I nearly toppled forward onto the pavement. I began to pivot to confront my apparent assailant. But even as I rotated, I realized I was in no pain. Instead, intense pleasure was coursing through my system. From the point of impact, nerve impulses raced up over my scalp, across tingling cheeks, down my chest, down my spine, along my arms and legs. This was no fantasy. The hairs on my forearms were standing straight up. And my heart was thumping.

I felt supercharged, full of bliss—not merely physical but also mental and emotional. A heightened awareness totally beyond my prior experience. The closest analogy I could summon was a sexual orgasm. But this rush had no erotic dimension.

By this time, I'd spun 180 degrees. I was stunned to discover no one nearby. Not close enough to hurl a stone, much less to strike a body blow. I was completely alone.

Well, not completely. Fifty yards back along the *ghat*, the head monk stood facing me with an ear-to-ear grin. His expression was radiant, kindly, but also impish. His hands were raised in a final prayerful salute. Bowing slightly, he slowly turned and walked away.

# BMW

*Darjeeling and Sikkim 1969*

I climbed down stiffly from my fifth train in three days and hobbled across the station platform. Even at mid-morning, the mountain air was blessedly cool, laced with aromatic whiffs of deodar. Darjeeling wasn't my final destination, merely the gateway to Sikkim. But getting this close after ten months of trying gave me confidence for the first time that things were going to work out.

Craig and I had shared a fascination for Sikkim since childhood. The Himalayan kingdom tucked between Nepal and Bhutan lured us both with schoolboy memories of *Kim* and *Lost Horizon*. We envisioned a forested sanctuary screening monastic retreats, permanent snow ridges and bottomless gorges.

Soon after settling into New Delhi, we'd applied to the Indian Ministry of External Affairs for Sikkimese visas. Our timing could hardly have been worse. Although the kingdom was nominally independent, India was asserting zealous suzerainty over Sikkim's defense and foreign relations. The increasingly belligerent People's Republic of China was flexing its muscles on the kingdom's northern frontier. Indian Cabinet nerves were still raw from border skirmishes in which their troops' lack of preparedness had earned ridicule in the international press.

Our visa request went unacknowledged for nearly a year. We'd given up the expedition as a lost cause when an official response turned up in our mailbox. Without explanation, the curt note denied Craig permission to visit Sikkim at all. My application was granted, but only for 24 hours! We were more annoyed than disappointed. It seemed arbitrary to rule differently on our identical, paired applications. And pointless, even provocative, to give me a single-day's entry when just reaching the border would require a cross-country journey.

We imagined some bored Indian bureaucrat enjoying a small joke at our expense. He must have felt he'd neatly squelched our Yankee wanderlust. We decided to deflate our hypothetical tormentor's balloon. I'd go ahead to Sikkim just for the hell of it. At best, on arrival I could figure out some way to extend my stay. At worst, even a quick glimpse of the kingdom might yield precious memories and snapshots. I felt guilty, but Craig insisted I not cancel the expedition merely because half our party had been turned away.

My rail route took me south-east from Delhi, through Kanpur to Allahabad, due east to Benares and Patna, then north for the slow climb to Darjeeling. The 72-hour slog was a blur of rock-hard compartment benches and inadequate sleeping shelves, snatched station snacks and untended latrines, squalling infants and snoring elders. Third-Class train travel across India was strictly a no-frills proposition. But at a rupee fare equivalent to $12 for 2,500 round-trip miles, I wasn't about to complain.

Even if I hadn't been relieved to get my feet onto solid ground, I'd have been captivated by Darjeeling, a resilient relic of the British Raj. In its heyday a bustling hill station much beloved by the officers and families of the colonial administration, the outpost had blossomed every summer for 100 years as a respite from Calcutta's[2] oppressive heat. Twenty years after Independence, the vertical town's much-faded ambiance was still fetching. I stepped through the gingerbread train station onto a Victorian movie set. My first glance encompassed grand public buildings, stately conifers and timbered cottages edged by English

---

2  Since 2000, Kolkata.

flower gardens. Gaudy pedestrians bustled alongside a quaint parade of horse-drawn carts and carriages.

I asked the local Tourism Office to recommend overnight lodging. They referred me to a nearby bed-and-breakfast run by an Anglo-Indian widow.

The children of mixed marriages between British and Indian parents, Anglo-Indians had provided much of the skilled labor for the colonial government, especially in the national railways. These "half-castes" occupied an economic and social middle ground, never wholly accepted by either community. When the British withdrew in 1947, many Anglo-Indians trailed them back to Europe. Those who stayed on in India tended to assume a low profile in public. In private, they clung tenaciously to their severed British roots.

The Tourism Office had phoned ahead and my hostess greeted me at her garden gate. Mrs. Shaw was a bouncing ball—festive, round and rolling. A pink-and-purple sari sheathed her ample form like a cheery gift-wrap. In a whirl of motion, she patted store-black hair, shook my hand, opened the gate and pulled me through.

Already this generator was up to speed, racing through her short-list of local tourist attractions. When she paused for breath, I injected a word of regret, explaining that I'd be staying in Darjeeling for only one night.

My hostess made no effort to conceal her exasperation. "Dear boy, how can you be so impatient after coming so far? Where could you possibly be going next that competes with Darjeeling's unique appeal?"

"Ma'am, I've no doubt you're right. But I must get on to Sikkim."

Exuberant approval banished pique from those jowly cheeks. Still maintaining that initial handshake, she tugged me along the garden path. "Sikkim? Sikkim! Why, this is your most lucky day!"

"Glad to hear it, Mrs. Shaw, but why today?"

By now we had climbed to the front porch that extended across the width of her cottage. It was cluttered but cozy, with lush baskets of lobelia and tuberous begonias overhanging soft-cushioned wicker rockers.

"I can explain, I *will* explain," she rocketed ahead. "You would be lucky enough to get into Sikkim on any day. So few do, you know. How did you manage it, by the way? But, no matter, I don't mean to pry. Today your special luck lies south of the border, not north. In this very house!"

We passed into a bright front hallway. "Young man, do you have any idea who is sharing my hospitality? In the very room next to yours? Of course you don't. You couldn't, of course."

Mrs. Shaw led on to two adjacent doors at the back of the hall. With a theatrical dip, she threw open the one on the left. "It's dear old BM, His Majesty's Royal Tea Planter!"

I barely had time to set down my pack before Mrs. Shaw drew me through, past her billowing girth. A comatose male figure lay prone on the bed, a half-empty bottle of Scotch clutched precariously in one hand. Thankfully, he was fully clothed, though I couldn't help noticing he was still wearing shoes and socks.

Mrs. Shaw trumpeted, "Wake up, BM! Up, up! This young American wants to meet you. He's going to Sikkim!"

To his credit, my next-door neighbor showed remarkable grit. By sheer force of will, he roused himself to a sitting position. By stealth, the elixir miraculously disappeared. Momentum achieved, he continued upwards onto uncertain feet, both eyes now open, right hand extended. "BMW Dixon. Pleased to make your acquaintance."

His voice was deep and pleasing, the accent unmistakably British. Now vertical, Mr. Dixon stood six-feet-six. He couldn't have weighed more than 160 pounds. Despite his demonstrated capacity for spirits, he looked fit and his grip conveyed strength. With his close-cropped graying hair and creased leather cheeks, I put him in his mid-50s, 60 top.

Mumbling apologies for the intrusion, I introduced myself in return. Since Mrs. Shaw had already previewed my onward destination, I plunged ahead and mentioned my exasperating 24-hour visa limitation.

"Not to worry," he replied with a dismissive wave. "Cheeky Indian bureaucrats. Soon and simply corrected by His Majesty's Secret Service."

Things were moving faster than I'd dared hope. "How can I contact them?"

"Not *them*, him. Straightaway, on arriving in Gangtok."

"You know this official personally?"

"Good God, man, we're brothers in Rotary!"

Mr. Dixon strode past the two of us to a small writing desk. "A brief note will do."

He produced crested letterhead from a well-traveled satchel, jotted two sentences with a hefty fountain pen and tucked his message into a matching envelope. A flick of his lighter, a dollop of wax, the firm impression of a gold signet ring, and my benefactor handed over my *laissez-passer*.

With thanks for his extraordinary kindness to a stranger, I withdrew to let the gentleman recuperate.

That evening, over a gin and tonic, Mr. Dixon shared highlights of his remarkable career. Having survived commando service with the Chindits in Burma during World War II, he couldn't bear to return to "dank, snobbish" England. After a couple of false starts, he'd landed on his feet by responding to a royal invitation to revitalize Sikkim's tea industry.

In the ensuing two decades, he'd never looked back. Periodically, he dropped down to India for business or pleasure. On these occasions, he observed with a grin, Mrs. Shaw was invariably "energetic and understanding." Before we parted company, BMW graciously invited me to visit his Kewzing tea estate in Sikkim's Western District, en route back down from Gangtok.

I left Darjeeling the next morning clutching his note like a talisman. An honorable vintage Land Rover was pressed into taxi service. A half-day's jolting ride carried me north along a dry riverbed, past modest twin border posts, and up a sustained defile. The road surface varied from porous to non-existent. We passed few other passenger vehicles but numerous overloaded small pickups and lumbering military transports.

Reaching Gangtok, I proceeded immediately to the government compound to meet Mr. Dixon's fellow Rotarian. To my surprise, he wore the distinctive turban, full beard and steel bracelet of an Indian Sikh. It was inevitable, I surmised, that the Indian authorities would want to keep their finger on the security pulse in such a sensitive border enclave. But notwithstanding his plains origins, His Majesty's Secret Service quickly proved his mountain allegiance. As Mr. Dixon had confidently predicted, my visa-deadline impasse was swiftly dissolved.

"The Sunday Market," the Service declared.

I gaped my incomprehension.

"Straightforward, really. In order to advance Sikkim's potential interest in developing tourism, an influential foreign guest"—this with a conspiratorial cough—"must visit the unique capital bazaar. The Market is held only on Sundays. Unavoidably detained, the guest arrived Monday. A seven-day visa extension is therefore imperative." With a wink and a twirl of a date-stamp, he entered the extension in my passport.

After a week's adventures in and around Gangtok[3], on my way out of the Kingdom I detoured to visit Mr. Dixon's main tea plantation in Sikkim's southern foothills.

*BMW Dixon on his Kewzing tea estate. Sikkim 1969.*

---

3 The subject of the next tale in this collection.

Perched above the border's dry creek beds but below Gangtok's crystalline vistas, the Kewzing plantation was set in thick tropical forests. Cleared red soil had been shaped into giant symmetrical mounds, each the size of a small hill, now wreathed in cheek-clinging fog.

The tea bushes were planted in tight horizontal rows, circling each mound from base to crown. The dense bushes had been meticulously pruned into waist-high hemispheres to facilitate stem-tip picking of the choicest shoots. The pickers I saw were compact tribal women. Their hand-loomed rainbow kerchiefs and aprons stood out from black tunics and ankle-length skirts. Gossip, laughter and song wafted out of the swirling mists as the nimble workers plucked tiny leaves and filled inverted wicker cones strapped to strong backs.

After I'd nervously declined an offered ride on BMW's disdainful stallion, the planter gave me an informative walking tour of the grounds. We ended up at his weathered bungalow, another relic of the British Raj. The interior walls gleamed with aged teak. Solid furniture was covered with worn but comfortable cushions. The residual tang of wood smoke drifted from back-to-back stone fireplaces.

My angular host introduced me to his stunning Tibetan concubine, who supervised service of a hearty high tea on the broad veranda. We worked our way through welcome cups of Earl Gray, oven-hot scones, fresh butter, thick-cut marmalade and shortbread slices. A pair of brazen magpies hopped onto the railing, impatient for their turn. BMW broke out a pipe. I had no doubt this was one expatriate who had found his niche.

The shrill horn of the recommissioned Land Rover beeped an insistent tattoo. Regretfully taking my leave, I climbed in and looked back. As we braked down the steep drive through the dense rounded rows, the slim silhouette dissolved in the life-giving clouds.

# Almost Shangri-La

*Gangtok and Rumtek 1969*

Between Darjeeling and Kewzing, thanks to BMW's gracious intercession I was privileged to experience the special charms of Sikkim's national capital, Gangtok. In 1969, the town was more a way-station between the Himalayas and the plains than a significant center in its own right. At 5,200 feet elevation, it was pasted to the eastern wall of a narrow glacial valley. There were no paved streets, no hotels and no restaurants other than open-air tea stalls framing the main square.

With an introduction from his Majesty's Secret Service, I was able to secure lodging with a local Hindi-speaking family. After a wash-up and welcoming tea, I set off on a get-acquainted ramble.

On that first morning, traders and porters filled the stalls' rough-plank tables and benches. They called jovially for refills from huge, bubbling kettles of cardamom-flavored milk tea. In a week's time, on Market Day, I'd return to find this vast plaza totally occupied by peddlers' tarpaulins and awnings. Today it surged with Tibetan refugees, off-duty Indian border guards and jostling, pungent flocks of fat-tailed sheep.

I was struck by the unspoiled quality of the scene—not just the bright skies and thin air but the absence of modern earmarks. No billboards or logos, no television aerials or motor scooters. Throughout my week's visit, I would see no other tourists.

*Sikh peddler up from India for Gangtok's Sunday Market. 1969.*

*Gangtok Market tailor mending a monk's robe.*

As a relative novelty, I attracted stares and smiles, a few tentative greetings, but no apparent hostility. I felt like a time traveler deposited in a medieval hub.

Gangtok was a one- and two-story town. The buildings were constructed of wood or mud bricks, under flat roofs of corrugated iron. The prevailing tones were weathered browns and grays. Multicolored Buddhist prayer flags provided relief from this monotonous palette. At first I'd thought these were temporary banners announcing some rustic festival. However, I soon came to appreciate they were permanent affirmations of a devout population. Festooned on strings draped over city streets or tacked to tall bamboo poles at main pedestrian intersections, each bright cotton square was stamped with the pilgrim's safe-passage invocation, "*Om mani padme hum*" ("Blessed is the Jewel of the Lotus").

On my first night in my Gangtok accommodations, the father of my host family woke me well before dawn and led me silently up to a roof-top balcony. The black void was moonless. A thin mist dampened starlight. As my eyes adjusted, my host pointed upwards. High above, floating free in an ebony sea, hovered a vast triangular sail of increasing brightness, displaying a thrilling sequence of violet, lavender, pink and orange. Snow-capped Kanchenjunga, Sikkim's patron summit and at 28,000 feet the third highest mountain in the world, was heralding another day.

The next morning, I climbed angling lanes to Sikkim's royal palace, dominating a small plateau just above the town center. The views of surrounding ranges were magnificent, but the complex itself was unpretentious in scale and finish. It most resembled, and may once have been, a British District Officer's compound.

Mrs. Shaw would have been disappointed. The royal family was not in residence during my visit. She had set her hopes on my being granted an audience with the *Gyalmoh*, Sikkim's American-born Queen, whom the King had met while on graduate studies in New York. Despite her distant origins, the Queen had earned broad and deep public respect from the Sikkimese people for promoting women's rights and cottage industries.

Perhaps because of the monarchs' absence, I was invited by the gatekeepers to wander freely through the modest but well-maintained grounds.

Mid-way through the week, I was back in the Gangtok bazaar, watching a threadbare matron haggle creatively with a Tibetan peddler. An incongruous figure stepped in front of me, blocking my view. A preppy teenager in blue blazer, gray slacks and rep tie extended his right hand. "Hello, Sir, I am Tej Raissaly, aged 15 years."

*Tej Raissaly wearing his blazered best for our trek to Rumtek.*

Like an encyclopedia salesman racing the clock before the door slammed, Tej wasted no time in making his pitch. The eldest son of a successful Nepalese immigrant, he was home for the holidays from his fashionable Calcutta boarding school and growing rapidly bored with his dusty hometown and now-provincial chums. Tej offered his services as an "economical" guide.

Despite his adolescent need to impress, I enjoyed the boy's entrepreneurial verve and cheeky wit. I was also pleased to stumble upon an English speaker who could answer questions about the local scene.

Tej set the hook. He casually turned to point out the imposing complex on the valley's opposite slope. Its bold primary colors stood out against a beige background. Had I noticed Rumtek, the Tibetan monastery? I'd have been blind not to. Although perhaps three miles distant across the ravine, it was clearly the dominant structure in the region.

"I'd be happy to lead you there, Sir."

He didn't have to repeat the invitation. Young Tej had made a sale.

We set off early the next morning, fortified by glasses of scalding bazaar tea and trail snacks of dried apricots and sweet biscuits. On a steep, switch-backing trail, we hiked down the valley's eastern slope to the river, across a suspension bridge, then up the other side. It took us four demanding hours to log the 14 miles door-to-door.

Tej enlivened the trek with tidbits of monastery gossip. In his telling, Rumtek was ruled by a formidable abbot, locally admired for his courage and leadership as much as for his piety. In 1959, one jump ahead of the Chinese army sent to invade and occupy Tibet, the abbot had led his congregation of nearly 200 monks and attendants on foot and yak-back across high passes down into Bhutan, and from there to Sikkim.

This refugee caravan had reputedly rescued a "secret treasure" from certain confiscation by the pursuing Chinese. When I pressed Tej for specifics, he conceded that all he was certain had made it out were religious relics, vestments and scriptures preserving a monastic tradition stretching back centuries. But Gangtok gossip also insisted on gold and precious gems. Whatever his transportable resources, the abbot had managed to finance the construction of the Sikkim monastery, on a promontory donated by the King. The reason the compound sparkled so brightly across the valley was that it had been inaugurated only three years before, in 1966.

Upon reaching puberty, Tej confided, he and his next younger brother had been brought to the monastery for a coming-of-age blessing. Still as much children as adolescents, the boys had embarrassed their family and sponsors by collapsing into nervous giggles during the audience with the abbot.

"The abbot was not pleased, Mr. Russell, but he didn't shout at us. He just stopped the prayers and spoke quietly to Tulsi and me. 'Young gentlemen, you find something amusing? Then here's more entertainment. Watch my hat.'"

Tej grinned at the recollection. "Mr. Russell, this started us laughing again. Because the abbot's flat hat was like our toy monkey's. Flat and round. But we didn't laugh long. The hat rose straight up in the air. This far." He measured a six-inch gap between his hands. "Straight up. Above his bald head. And stayed."

"Tej, you're pulling my leg."

"No, no, Sir. I saw it. Tulsi saw it. We ran from the chapel."

Tej looked sheepish. "Of course, I'm too old for that now. Fifteen years. Next year, 16. Still, Sir, if you feel like laughing when you see the hat, better not."

The trail continued on up the long canyon. Finally, we climbed a short flight of stairs to the monastery compound. At the top, four young novices greeted us warmly. They looked younger than Tej. With shaved heads and beaming smiles, they fussed a bit with their yellow robes, as if they hadn't quite mastered how to hold their hands still.

*Rumtek Monastery.*

The novices escorted us across a main plaza to a small side courtyard, where we met a middle-aged monk. He told Tej he'd be pleased to serve as our guide. Like all Rumtek residents we were to encounter that day, the monk seemed to exude an intriguing blend of energy and repose. His maroon robe left one shoulder bare and was cinched at the waist with a woven-cord belt. He draped the excess fabric over one arm. It looked as if it could double as head covering in wind or rain.

The monk offered us plain cups of restorative green tea, silently served by the boys. With this diminutive quartet bringing up the rear, he led us on an informal tour of the stunning premises.

We started out by returning to the principal plaza and facing outward. The platform was cantilevered, as if soaring over the precipice. The massive structure marched in bold horizontal lines across the face of the cliff. Wide tiers were stacked like the layers of a giant wedding cake, each slightly smaller and set back from the edge of the one below, all fronted by wooden railed balconies.

The walls were made of stone and stuccoed brick. Despite the bulk and necessary weight, the effect was open and welcoming. Fanciful architraves ran the width of the façade. A portico of wooden columns led directly into open chapels. Tree-trunk beams, swathed in abstract serpentines and stylized clouds, supported the chapels' 20-foot-high ceilings.

Inside and out, the color scheme and carved decorations were festive, the antithesis of Western monastic restraint. Rumtek was brilliantly painted in red, gold, green and blue, an almost carnival palette.

The monk led us quietly into prayer halls where bronze Buddha effigies presided over altars stacked with white prayer scarves, trays of fruit and other offerings. Antique scrolls hung in the recesses. Notwithstanding the bold primary colors, even at mid-day these sanctuaries invited meditation. The interior light was muted, with shadows softened by the flickering illumination of hundreds of small butter lamps.

The entire complex was immaculate. Supervised novices were much in evidence, mopping and scrubbing pavements with buckets of suds. Our tailing acolytes looked thankful for their dispensation from these maintenance chores.

We climbed external stairways past stacked tiers of dormitories and classrooms. The pleasing drone of scriptural chanting was a mellow accompaniment to our stroll. In response to my question, our guide confirmed that the monastery offered non-resident religious instruction to local youths, as well as intensive training for novices entering orders. The novices were gradually replenishing the ranks of Rumtek's original Tibetan refugees.

On the top deck, hooded monks were blowing 12-foot-long brass horns. These ancient instruments were so heavy that their bells were propped on special carved wooden stands. Their deep bass tones resonated like musical foghorns. Our guide whispered that the roof-top trio performed the same function as a bell tower tolling key divisions in the religious day. Their solemn, penetrating notes must have carried for miles, to the faithful up and down the glacier-carved valley.

Informed that the abbot would see us now, Tej and I were ushered into an enchanting apartment. The front and side walls were pierced by red-framed windows, looking up and down the valley and across to snow-clad peaks. A half-dozen wicker cages contained buttery canaries and rose finches. Plump embroidered cushions covered most of the floor. Treasured *thanka* paintings hung on the interior wall, their fragile colors protected from direct sunlight.

I felt I'd been admitted to an intimate chamber for receiving foreign emissaries. I recalled Tej's comment that politics was a priority for this prelate.

The abbot was already in place, seated cross-legged, relaxed but attentive, on a slightly raised dais. His robes were saffron, his head shaven (and, thankfully, hatless), his eyes penetrating. I guessed his age to be about 50. He struck me as charismatic and centered, projecting power but also accessibility.

Seated slightly below the abbot was a senior monk drafted as Tibetan/English interpreter. The physical opposite of his superior, the interpreter was emaciated in the extreme. He came across as self-important, or at least totally absorbed by his privileged assignment. His rigid posture never wavered during the interview. I soon learned that his English was formal and antiquated.

The abbot welcomed me to Rumtek and inquired about my health and excursion. He implied he had some advance inkling of my nationality and touristic agenda. With a slight grin of recognition, he acknowledged Tej and asked about his younger brother and other family members.

"So tell me, Mr. Sunshine," the abbot quizzed with gusto, "what is happening in the outside world?"

"May I ask the Reverend Abbot if he has in mind America or Europe?"

"New Delhi."

Despite the necessary pauses for interpretation, we slipped comfortably into an exchange of impressions of Indian foreign affairs in the Himalayan region. His insights spanned a broad spectrum from savvy pragmatism to cloistered detachment. He ventured the prescient opinion that border tensions between India and China would escalate before they subsided, with Sikkim squeezed in the middle. He was resigned to the near-certainty that China would not soon tolerate a resurgence of autonomous Tibetan Buddhism. But he was taking the long view.

We chatted for the better part of an hour. Quietly signaling the end of our interview, the abbot asked me to lean forward. Cupping the top of my head in an expansive palm, he administered a sonorous blessing. Next he tied a maroon silk cord around my neck.

"So long as you wear this thread," he softly intoned, "no evil will befall you."

My '60s sensibilities tugged me in polar directions. The secular skeptic shrugged to dismiss the abbot's gift as a cordial but kitschy souvenir. The yoga novice shivered to embrace its mystical protection.

I wore that cord every day until it disintegrated after three harm-free years.[4]

---

4 I didn't fully appreciate until decades later that my tea-time host and interlocutor had been Rangjung Rigpe Dorje, the 16th Karmapa Lama. In this capacity, he was head of the Karma Kagyu or "Black Hat" School of Tibetan Buddhism, tracing its lineage to 1000 CE.

The 16th Lama began his own international travels in 1974, earning wide and deep respect in Europe, Canada and the United States for his spiritual enlightenment and cross-cultural aplomb. After founding satellite Dharma Centers in Dordogne, France and New York City, he died in Zion, Illinois in 1981 while on his last worldwide tour. The Lama's remains were repatriated to Rumtek for cremation.

# MR. MOON

*Manhattan 1969*

New York City cut me with cold. Not just the single-digit temperatures and gusts knifing through skyscraper canyons, but the natives as well. I couldn't believe how fast they walked, and how aggressively. More than once I was knocked off the curb by a sharp elbow or lowered shoulder. Never an apologetic word or wave, the locals didn't even break stride. The bitter weather might explain some of their determined rush, but the prevailing mood struck me as oblivious and even combative. So much for pre-Christmas cheer.

This was not what I needed on landfall in the United States. Leaving India had been wrenching. My two years on the Subcontinent had produced intense friendships, new priorities and perspectives. I'd been molded and reoriented by the remote sojourn. "Coming home" didn't accurately describe my reaction to re-entry. I felt unwelcome and out of synch. I could only hope that spending Christmas with my family in Los Angeles would get me back on a positive footing. But first, I had to get through what were supposed to be three upbeat transitional days in Manhattan.

I was desperate for a friendly face. David Moon was practicing law downtown, four easy subway stops south of my hotel. A surprise visit would probably amuse him. It would definitely give me a respite.

At law school in Berkeley, David and I had wasted no time becoming acquainted. For all but the most self-assured in our class, First Year was an intimidating rite of passage. The vast lecture hall reeked with the sweat of sharp-edged competition and mandatory recitation. The two of us were assigned adjacent seats across an intervening aisle. Since neither one was fast on his feet, sardonic instructors soon found they could inject a moment's levity into a flagging lecture by calling on us in tandem.

"No, that's not quite right, Mr. Sunshine. Perhaps Mr. Moon can shed some light on our problem?"

We soon learned to rally to each other's defense[5].

Touch football was another shared passion between interminable study sessions in the law library. By Third Year, we had drifted into the same cordial circle of beer-drinking, dance-party pals. I never got much beyond the Beatles. David was into the Stones. With his shoulder-length curls and hint of Jim Morrison wildness, he broke more than his fair share of hearts.

Despite our increasing infatuation with Berkeley culture and politics, we never forgot our common Southern California roots. By graduation, we'd grown close. I accepted a fellowship to India. David came East to join a blue-chip law firm. We kept up an irreverent correspondence between New Delhi and New York.

Now I was eager for even the briefest reunion. Just a few moments of West Coast warmth would help thaw Manhattan's needling chill.

Climbing out of the subway, I confronted One Chase Manhattan Plaza, a forbidding monolith of chrome and glass. I crossed the arctic expanse of its exposed forecourt and entered an intimidating atrium, three stories high. David's firm was featured on the brass-framed wall directory. The express-elevator ride to the 47th floor made my already nervous stomach clench. I couldn't remember the last time I'd taken an elevator, much less at high speed. There were no skyscrapers in Delhi—

---

5 David and I used to josh that, if another friend and classmate, Foster Knight, could be brought on board, then we'd only have to recruit a fourth partner named Day to start up a sure-fire entertainment-law practice in Hollywood.

we'd climbed stairs. The rapid deceleration compressed my remaining self-confidence. Maybe my friend would be tied up with a client. Or out of town. I should have called ahead.

The burnished metal doors slid silently open to reveal an unnerving void. Plush white carpet stretched into infinity. No partitions, no furniture, no flowers, no piped music, no bodies or bustle. It was doubtlessly some chic decorator's minimalist fantasy, but what popped into my head was Siberia. It was all I could do to force myself out into that deep pile.

Across the steppe, a veteran receptionist presided, suit severely tailored, gray hair pulled taut in a bun. Even at this distance, the non-verbal signals were unmistakable. The lady was inhospitable and unamused.

Tapered fingers arced on the pristine desk top. "What do *you* want?"

I froze in mid-stride. *Okay, maybe I do look a little strange in white cotton pajamas and a Nehru topcoat. The handlebar mustache and wire-rimmed granny glasses definitely aren't helping.*

She couldn't know that two years of pounding by back-alley *dhobis*, Delhi's ubiquitous laundrymen, had long-since demolished my American wardrobe. My version of South Asian business attire was what I could afford and Indian tailors could improvise. Thank God I wasn't wearing open-toed sandals.

As if reading my mind, the sentry scanned me from top to bottom, with a withering glare. "I said, what do you want?"

Direct response. Put her at ease. "Good morning, Ma'am. I'm here to see Mr. Moon."

The grim gatekeeper bristled.

*Jesus, she probably thinks I lifted David's name from the phone directory.*

She pursed her lips and stared me down. "And *whom* shall I say is calling?"

I exhaled with relief. I might be out of touch after two years abroad but this was one cross-examination I was uniquely qualified to parry.

"I'm Mr. Sunshine."

As soon as the words were out, I realized they'd made matters worse. The woman's shoulders tensed. Here hands retreated to the desktop's edge, grasping like claws.

I knew I had only seconds to salvage the interview. Stealing forward with a pasted grin, I tried mental telepathy. *I'm legit, I'm legit.*

No sale. As I drew near, she jerked her wheeled chair back from the desk. As if the zoned weirdo might try vaulting over the top.

"Wait over there!" she ordered, rigid tendons vibrating in a creped, veteran neck.

I meekly followed her pointing finger. Fashionably excruciating chairs flanked a cubic coffee table, with *Fortune* and the *Wall Street Journal* precisely aligned. This was one decorator who didn't know the meaning of compromise.

I stared out floor-to-ceiling windows at the East River directly below. On a sunny day, the view would have been spectacular. Today, under darkening skies, I was in despair. My spontaneous reunion was turning into a nightmare. A half-gainer with two twists would put us both out of our misery. If only I could figure out how to break through the double-paned glass without scattering unseemly shards on the carpet.

Her clipped subordinate's voice addressed the speaker-phone. "Mr. Moon, this is Miss Watson in 47th Reception."

I turned, mesmerized by her gaze.

"Mr. Moon, please accept my apologies for disturbing you when you are so busy. But there's someone here to see you." Her voice dropped an octave for the punch line. "And he's *extremely odd.*"

We both waited for David to digest that morsel. I strained without success to overhear his response.

Then my nemesis answered his question. "Well, that's the problem, Mr. Moon. At least one of the problems." And with a hesitant wince, "he *says* his name is... Mr. Sun-shine."

Her skepticism completed my deflation. I didn't belong here—in this quicksand carpet, in this uptight law firm, in this self-absorbed city, maybe even in this graceless country.

Miss Watson's frozen frown suggested that David must have hung up without further comment. Which left her and me in the same boat, but paddling in opposite directions.

She fixed me with a menacing glower. "Six short months to go until retirement," it seemed to convey. "You screw this up for me, Stoner, and I'll take you out on my way down."

Double doors split wide from an inner corridor. David burst through like the champion sprinter he'd been as an undergraduate. Now sporting close-cropped hair, custom tailoring and gleaming wingtips. Such a long, long way from Berkeley. Not to mention New Delhi. Had I made an appalling mistake by barging in?

Miss Watson sat poised with a confident smirk. It should take only a moment for David to administer my *coup de grace.*

I took a ginger step forward.

"Russell Babeee!" my classmate shouted, lifting me in a bear hug.

I hung on for dear life.

Past his shoulder, the heel of Miss Watson's palm slammed into her forehead. "Ieeeyahhhh!" came her anguished cry.

Home at last.

□ ⊞ □

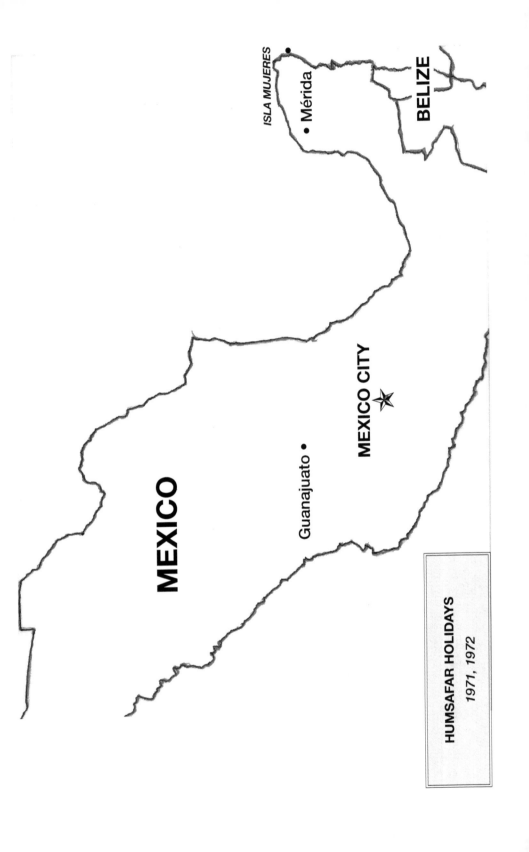

ISLA MUJERES

• Mérida

BELIZE

MEXICO

Guanajuato •

MEXICO CITY
☆

HUMSAFAR HOLIDAYS
1971, 1972

## CHAPTER FOUR

# FINDING A *HUMSAFAR*[6]

## So Much in Common

*New Delhi, Los Angeles 1969–70*

Jane Shetler was an excellent cook. The aromas of curry and spices emerging from her kitchen were making it difficult for me to concentrate on her monologue.

"You're a sweet boy, Russell B., but awfully stubborn. In this life, that's a guaranteed recipe for getting hurt."

Jane and I travelled in overlapping circles in the mélange of young expats and Indians that made up Delhi's lively international social scene. Now she was cooking me a farewell dinner as I dashed about tying up loose ends before flying to America.

"This has been your first long overseas stay," she continued. "You've heard about reverse culture-shock. Going home seems so natural, it should be easy, right? Wrong!"

Jane drove home her main points with a formidable wooden spoon.

---

6 In Urdu, the literal meaning of *humsafar* is traveling companion. Its figurative connotations include kindred spirit and soulmate.

"Your home country isn't even home any longer. You've both been growing apart."

I tried to get a word in but Jane was on a roll. "Look in the mirror. You're besotted with everything Indian—food, music, history, geography, politics, economics, castes, mysticism, you name it. Most Americans haven't a clue about any of that. More to the point, they couldn't care less."

A quick check on the curry, then back to the living room. "And while you've been devouring the Subcontinent, your American friends and family have gone their own way, leaving you behind. Pick any Stateside topic. Who won the World Series? Who'll be California's next Governor? Name the hottest TV show. You can't do it, Russell. Nothing wrong with that, you'll catch up. But you'll have to allow time to bridge the gap."

I jumped in. "Jane dear, you're selling my family short. They're not isolated rustics. My mother's still a British subject, for God's sake. They care about me, not the World Series. My brothers don't even like baseball. My relatives will all want to hear about my foreign adventures."

Jane's shrug conceded it wasn't a teachable moment. Over a delicious dinner and Kingfisher beers, she rolled out Plan B. "Okay, I can see we're going to have to let you fall on your face. Or some equally tender alternative. Take this bon-voyage token to cushion your landing."

She passed a small paper across the table. "Here's the name and phone number of a friend of mine from university days. The two of you have a lot in common. She spent a student summer in India. Now she's in LA working for CBS. I've alerted her to your pending arrival. Give her an SOS when no one else is responding to the magic of your temple bells."

"Jane, I won't need that number."

"QED: sweet but stubborn. Put the paper in your damn wallet and kiss me goodbye."

Three weeks later I was lapping up Mom's home cooking in my parents' Los Angeles dining room. Between the main course and dessert,

I had center stage, poised to deliver the climax of an irresistible Indian episode.

I glanced around the table at my captive audience. Dad was nodding off. My older brother Bob was peeking at his wristwatch. Younger brother Doug was glancing wistfully out the window into the backyard. Mother pushed back her chair to start clearing plates. Bob's wife Sylvia bounded up to help her.

This was some of my best material. And they weren't even listening. What was wrong with these people? How could they be so unappreciative? Claiming jet-lag fatigue, I excused myself from the table.

Upstairs in my childhood bedroom, I collapsed in a chair and sank into a sulk. My own family was treating me like a boring foreigner. We had nothing to talk about. And I hadn't even shown them my slides!

I looked over at my wallet on the dresser-top, recalling Jane's futile warning with chagrin. Crossing the room, I extracted a crumpled note and reached for the phone.

"Hello, is this Nancy Swing? I'm Russell Sunshine. Back from India. Jane Shetler encouraged me to give you a call. I was hoping you might be free one day this week for lunch and a chat."

In three years, we'd be married.

*Rehearsal Dinner before tying the knot. Sacramento 1972.*

# Señor Soonsheen

*Guanajuato, Mexico 1971*

"Señor, you are making a joke, no?"

The Tourism Officer set me straight. "It is Holy Week, 'Easter Week' you call it. In Mexico, this is the busiest week of the year for tourism. And for all of this week, Guanajuato is Mexico's busiest tourism destination."

Her hands came up in exasperation. "So when you walk into our office on Good Friday afternoon and expect us to find you accommodations for tonight, it is impossible. Not difficult, Señor. Impossible."

Nancy smiled and intervened. "But, Señora, your Mexico City colleagues didn't warn us. They just recommended we come to Guanajuato for Easter." She continued earnestly, "What can we do to solve this problem?"

"There's a six p.m. bus back to Mexico City."

Nancy's face fell. "Three hours from now?"

Her distress seemed to summon Latin chivalry in a man at the back of the office. He stepped forward and whispered in the female officer's ear. She nodded and looked up. "There may be one possibility."

She led us up ever-narrowing lanes to a house with a basement apartment. As we entered the front door, painters were dragging their drop cloths out the back. It wasn't the royal-blue walls that put us off. The lead-paint fumes would have killed us by morning.

Our escort walked us back in a mutual snit, no closer to a solution than when we'd first ruined her afternoon. I handed over my business card and asked her to keep on trying while Nancy and I squeezed in a pre-bus walkabout.

The stroll only intensified our disappointment. Guanajuato was a jewel of an eighteenth-century silver-mining hub. Its flamboyant architecture had been largely preserved or restored. Its university remained elegant. Its manicured plazas, now buoyant with celebrating families, eager vendors and resonant mariachi bands, were exactly what we'd hoped for. This was our kind of place. How grotesque that we'd made it all the way across the mountains on an under-sprung bus, only to have to turn right around because we'd picked the worst night of the year for a bed.

When we re-entered the Tourism Office, I thought I must be hallucinating. Our exasperated escort was now all smiles.

"Please have a seat in this lounge, Señor. Someone would like to speak with you."

"There must be a mistake," I blurted. "We've just arrived and don't know anyone here."

"Wait for the chime. I will transfer the call."

Nancy looked as baffled as I was feeling, but I picked up the receiver on the first ring.

"Seeeñor Soonsheen!" Honey flowed down the line.

"Señor Soonsheen, this is Alejandro Hidalgo Guadalupe, Director General of Tourism for the State of Guanajuato. On behalf of our humble corner of Mexico, permit me to welcome a distinguished representative of the State of California."

First he'd known my name. Now the California connection. I felt I had to set the record straight. "You are more than kind, Mr. Director, but I fear there's been a misunderstanding. I do work for the State of California, but only in a staff role."

Nancy poked my ankle with a persuasive toe.

"Too modest, Señor. We know the meaning of 'Senator' and 'Finance'."

123

The business card. It accurately identified me as a Legislative Aide. But in keeping with Sacramento protocol, the card gave top billing to my employer, Senator Anthony Beilenson, the Chairman of the Senate Finance Committee. The gold Capital dome in the card's background had probably been the crowning touch.

"Señor Soonsheen, I only wish we had known of your arrival in order to greet you in appropriate style. But I appreciate that you and your wife prefer to maintain a low profile."

Never a quick study, even I figured out this was not the optimal moment to reveal that Nancy and I were not yet married.

The Director General paused for dramatic effect. "I have taken the liberty of securing you accommodations at one of our most comfortable hotels."

I flashed on some harried innkeeper giving the bum's rush to irate guests who had made their reservations a year in advance. .

"It is anything but grand compared with your own San Francisco. But I think you will enjoy the top-floor view. Kindly pass the telephone to my colleague and I will issue the appropriate instructions."

Back up the hill, this time to a handsomely restored mansion fronting an elegant square. The huge doorman stepped forward to rebuff the presumptuous, blue-jeaned, young couple. But one steely glance from our escort converted his glower to a grin. He hefted our packs up the ornate stairway as if they were weightless. In the foyer, the primed front-desk staff received us at vibrating attention.

Our penthouse suite embodied tasteful elegance: polished oak, brass fittings, fresh bouquets and rooftop vistas. The hotel service was attentive but unobtrusive.

Unfortunately, only one of us was able to enjoy our good fortune. Perhaps the lethal paint fumes had been the trigger. Or the dusty bus ride. Whatever the provocation, Nancy spent most of that serendipitous weekend laid low by a sudden respiratory infection.

I'd venture out and return to share verbal snapshots—from the historical museum to smart craft galleries, even catacombs and a respectable performance of *Don Quixote* by the University Players. Local food was outstanding, the festival enchanting, preserved urban spaces a marvel.

Coughing and wheezing, Nancy lay propped up on our antique bed, good-naturedly making the best of a vicarious weekend.

*Señor Soonsheen making the tourist rounds. Guanajuato 1971.*

Back in Sacramento, my boss Tony was characteristically gracious and amused by our windfall. He wrote a cordial letter of thanks to the Director General, with that same imposing Capitol dome engraved on Senate letterhead. I like to imagine that the letter was framed by its hospitable recipient, and that he dined out on our Easter good fortune with as much gusto as we did.

# GRANNY GLASSES

*Isla Mujeres 1972*

Yucatan seemed the perfect honeymoon destination—exotic yet within reasonable air distance from our Sacramento base. When we could spare a moment from finalizing wedding arrangements, Nancy and I poured over guidebooks and maps. We were both eager to explore a new corner of America's closest southern neighbor.

Cancun was all the current rage—high-rise hotels, twice-daily flights from LAX, pina coladas and wet-T-shirt contests. Exactly where we wouldn't want to be.

Instead we opted for Isla Mujeres, short miles to the north and touristic decades behind. Reviews promised unspoiled beaches and "no-star" accommodations, just the ticket for a restful last stop after our animated itinerary across the Yucatan Peninsula.

Yucatan lived up to our high expectations. Mérida was a vibrant regional capital and our courtyard guesthouse, a small gem. Chocolate chicken was a bit of a stretch but the rest of Yucatecan cuisine was a delightful combination of novel and familiar. Mayan pyramids at Palenque, Chichén Itzá and Uxmal were dramatic centerpieces of once-sprawling metropolitan grids on now deserted plains.

Our short hop from Mérida to the coast was anything but tranquil. The small plane bounced all over the sky while the couple seated just opposite chattered obliviously. We were both relieved to emerge from the tempest and overlook glorious turquoise shallows as we skimmed the surf on our approach.

The rusting ferryboat across to the island confirmed that Isla Mujeres was not yet attracting other than lower-end tourists. The "private cabaña" plumped in the brochure turned out to be a thatched hut with bamboo cots. Still, we were pleased to be ahead of the high-rise curve, winding up our honeymoon in an unspoiled cul-de-sac.

The slow pace and privacy suited us perfectly. We had the long beach mostly to ourselves. A typical dinner was fresh prawns grilled over a wooden fire. We were even charmed by strolling guitarists. One memorable excursion took us out in a faded skiff. Plopping over the side, we snorkeled through lucid waters, trading nervous stares with rainbow schools. Our leather-skinned guide dove for giant conch shells. Extracting and pounding the meat, he added green onions, cilantro and lemon juice for a fabulous ceviche, dolloped unpretentiously onto glistening banana leaves.

Our last morning came too soon. We had just enough time for a final taste of that unspoiled beach. We trotted down to the sand outside our hut, staking out a perfect spot with our beach towels and bags. Even at mid-morning, the beach was almost deserted. Down the way, village women helped haul their menfolk's fishing canoes up onto the sand. Closer in, two small boys scampered in and out of the surf.

We strolled along the endless waterline in contentment, wading in whenever the sun's rays got too hot. Reluctantly, we returned to our towels.

I alerted Nancy before she got settled. "Sweetie, please be careful where you sit. I can't spot my specs where I left them on my towel. I don't want us to trample them into the sand."

She stooped for her bag. "Mine are gone too!"

Now startled and down on hands and knees, we patted our way over, around and under the two towels. Nada. Disaster. We each had only six inches of clear vision without eyeglasses.

Two pair was no coincidence. We'd left passports and wallets in the hotel safe. The small amount of cash we'd carried to the beach was still in Nancy's bag. So maybe the sole attraction had been gold-wire frames. The two tykes from the surf were nowhere to be seen. During our long-distance meander, we may have created an irresistible temptation.

At least I had a second pair back at the hut, with clear lenses for when I wasn't in bright sunlight. Nancy's glasses were photosensitive, combining regular and dark lenses. So she'd lost her only pair.

Annoyed by our carelessness but determined not to let this loss spoil our special holiday, we converted our plight to a game, plotting a holding-hands strategy for the homeward trek. Stuffing small suitcases demanded no visual acuity. Ferries were frequent and we already had our flight reservations back to California from Mérida.

The one challenge would be catching a bus from the coast to Mérida, since Nancy had insisted we not repeat that aerial roller-coaster ride.

We found a bus with little trouble and passed the journey in conversation, foregoing blurred scenery. Halfway across Yucatan, the driver pulled in for a snack and bathroom break. Perched on bar stools in a seedy roadside café, we ordered two Cokes and ran a shuttle to the toilets, passing our shared pair of glasses like a relay baton.

While Nancy took her turn, the bored barman exhausted his patience. "Señor, no eat, no sit."

In my halting Spanish, I asked what he had to offer.

His jerked thumb needed no translation. "Just read the board."

I lacked the vocabulary to explain that the menu's six-foot remoteness exceeded my range. So I surrendered my stool and resisted the beckoning nachos.

As we paid up and re-boarded, Nancy coined our nuptial motto. "If we can get across Mexico with a single pair of specs, the rest of marriage should be a snap."

The marital union launched on that blind-leading-the-blind honeymoon is going strong after 43 years. More important by far than our marriage's longevity have been its closeness and support. Without the nurturing security of that partnership, I doubt I could have sustained the international life that is the platform for these collected tales.

Despite matchmaker Jane's cheery confidence that our student stints in India gave us something in common, in other ways Nancy and I were not an obvious couple. She was an only child from rural Appalachia. She'd attended West Virginia University, huge, coeducational and state-sponsored. One of three brothers from urban LA, I'd gone to Yale, a small, private New England college then open only to male students. Her professional degree was in television production. Mine, in law.

But even before we met, we'd been forming individual interests and values that would draw and hold us together. Nancy's early exposure to international work and travel had not been limited to her Indian excursion. Just before we met, she'd returned from working with educational media in Afghanistan. In addition to my Indian sojourn, I'd travelled three times to Europe.

Complementing our shared enthusiasm for getting abroad were our values as members of the '60s Generation. Giving back to society through public service, especially to the less fortunate, was an ethic we had both internalized from John Kennedy, Sargent Shriver and our liberal-arts educations.

It also helped that the two of us were meeting and marrying relatively late, at 28 and 29. Having remained single through most of our twenties, we had a reasonable sense of who we were and what we liked. Having led active social lives, we were ready for a lasting partnership. Engagement gave each of us time to assess how well our needs and expectations were compatible.

Soon after we married, Nancy and I launched our joint international adventure. Our first stop was East Africa, followed later by Laos, Central Asia and Italy. Over time, we crafted a two-person nomadic family unit, pitching our figurative tent wherever work and travel carried us. In each long-term consulting assignment overseas, we (and mostly she) constructed a local homestead that offered sanctuary and familiarity in an unfamiliar environment.

In place of roots and relationships in a single geographical community, we cultivated and visited a global network of valued friends. We chose not to bring children into our grasshopper lives, instead cherishing the offspring of relatives and close friends.

Having Nancy as my lifelong humsafar has been a source of comfort in good times as well as bad. A kindred spirit and trail-mate with whom to share discoveries on the road. But also a trusted counsellor, confidante and nurse to help bear the burdens of inevitable overseas setbacks, conflicts, injuries and illnesses. Our congruent priorities made shared international life sustainable, nurturing mental and emotional health. (We have known other couples where only one partner relished the international path. This disconnect seldom worked out equitably or well.)

By no means have we been constant companions. To the contrary, we had divergent international disciplines, clients and projects. We frequently found ourselves working in different countries, even on different continents. This shared enthusiasm for independence, another legacy of marrying late, enriched our individual development and gave us marvelous opportunities for show-and-tell. We joke that spending so much time apart kept the honeymoon going for decades.

We have shared a two-fold blessing on this continuing journey. While marriage has secured and supported our international lives, international life has energized and enriched our marriage.

UGANDA

KAMPALA

KENYA

LAKE
VICTORIA

NAIROBI

RWANDA

SERENGETI

BURUNDI

LAKE MANYARA

Arusha •

ZANZIBAR

TANZANIA

DAR ES SALAAM

EAST AFRICAN
ADVENTURES

1973–1974

## CHAPTER FIVE
# EAST AFRICA: EARLY DAYS

Before our marriage, Nancy and I had agreed we would actively pursue an overseas posting. We were both keen to get back abroad. We sent out a flurry of résumés and decided to take the first attractive offer either of us received, provided it came paired with solid job prospects in the same location for the accompanying spouse.

The breakthrough phone call came from New York. The Ford Foundation was recruiting an American lawyer to work for two years in the East African Community's headquarters in Arusha, Tanzania. The Foundation knew me from India where they had co-financed my legal research. And I'd kept them apprised of my position in the intervening years as a Legislative Aide in the California State Senate. They thought these synergistic qualifications made for a good fit. Was I interested and available? I'd barely heard of the Community and couldn't have located Arusha on a map on a bet. But I asked for more details.

The Community was a fledgling experiment. More ambitious in scope and structure than its European equivalent, the East African version was not only a common market but also a functioning regional government. In addition to collecting customs duties and taxes for its three Member States—Kenya, Tanzania and Uganda—the EAC operated Common Services. Airways, railways, harbors, posts and telecommunications, agricultural and medical research were all integrated to serve East Africa's combined population of 30 million. The Community's Legal Department needed a Legislative Counsel.

Intrigued, I flew to New York City for interviews and briefings. Later, Nancy and I met my Arusha predecessor and his wife on home leave in Los Angeles. Both warmly touted their East African experience.

With Nancy's encouragement, I accepted the two-year position. We disposed of furniture, excess clothes, books and a goldfish named Sashimi at an exuberant Sacramento yard sale. (As a supportive local radio DJ trumpeted, "Come on, Folks, lend them a hand. The Sunshines are moving to Africa!")

My professional responsibilities at the Community proved technically and cross-culturally maturing. After an initially discouraging period of unemployment, Nancy landed an exhilarating assignment travelling all over back-country East Africa by bus, Land Rover, canoe and Cessna, producing a documentary film on the Lutheran Church's mission schools and hospitals.

In our periodic free time, we enjoyed low-budget safaris to surrounding game parks and climbed Kilimanjaro just down the road from our house.

## Two Fledglings

*Rome, Arusha 1973–75*

Settling into Arusha was comparatively free of drama. In fact, something of an anticlimax. After multiple delays, my new boss, the East African Community's General Counsel, summoned me to fly out from California within 72 hours to report for duty. On arrival, I was disappointed not to meet him. He'd been called away on assignment while Nancy and I were en route over the Atlantic. So my first week in Africa involved little more than reading dry regulations and helping Nancy to furnish our village bungalow outside of town.

I was plucked from this professional inertia by the Community's most dynamic personality. Al Noor "Nick" Kassum, the EAC Finance Minister, was a British-educated Ismaili Muslim of South Asian extraction. He had started his fast-track professional ascent as a protégé of the Aga Khan. Mr. Kassum won President Nyerere's trust and gratitude by uncovering foreign-investor skimming at Tanzania's diamond mines.

Recognizing his talent, energy and experience in dealing with powerful international interests, the Community's leaders had tapped Kassum to head up the new union's showcase project. As a symbol of East Africa's collaborative aspirations, the Community

*Julius Nyerere, Tanzania's founding President and hero of African independence, with EAC Legislative Assembly leaders. Arusha 1973.*

*Minister Al Noor Kassum leads Condotte's construction managers on EAC Headquarters site visit. Arusha 1973.*

conference center, secretariat and accommodations for the three national presidents when convened as the EAC's Executive Authority. The construction project's $25-million price tag[7] represented an unprecedented investment for the sponsoring governments. The prestigious Italian construction firm of Condotte had been selected as general contractor. The Community had secured expert engineering advice financed by Swedish development assistance. But Minister Kassum wanted in-house legal support to help him negotiate, monitor and enforce the construction contract with the Italians. Two days after our first meeting on his Arusha veranda, the Minister and I flew to Condotte's home office in Rome.

Condotte dispatched not one but two limousines to meet us at Fiumicino Airport, but we elected to ride together to the posh Excelsior Hotel on the Via Veneto, where they'd booked us into a VIP suite.

After a jet-lagged short night, we grabbed room-service coffees and breakfast pastries on the run before descending the elegant hotel staircase to our hovering transport. In lilting Mediterranean English, our polished escort in the front seat rattled off the first day's packed program. First, to Condotte's chrome-and-glass executive offices for a full morning of courtesy calls and an audiovisual presentation highlighting the firm's worldwide construction triumphs. On to a swank Tiber-side club for a Michelin-starred lunch. Then back to corporate headquarters for five straight hours of hard-nosed negotiations on contract terms and prices. Nick's wink confirmed my own impression that this whirlwind itinerary was no accident. It had been strategically choreographed to accomplish two objectives: playing up the wide gap between Condotte's international track record and the Community's comparative inexperience; and exhausting their visitors to lower our guard during crucial financial bargaining.

For my part, their Machiavellian strategy was a near-total success. I was intimidated by Condotte's show of power and numbed by too many wines and too little sleep. To his credit, however, Minister Kassum

---

7 Equivalent to $150 million in 2015 dollars.

was more than equal to the challenge. Never acknowledging a snub or miscalculating a subtotal, Nick took in stride every trick the Latins could throw at him. These were not the last Northerners whom I would observe underestimating this African representative. In his tailored safari suits and paisley ascots, Nick risked derision as a Bollywood matinee idol. But beneath that pomaded exterior lurked a razor mind and the guile of the souk. If the Italian engineers and accountants learned nothing else from that first day's marathon, it was that this equatorial peacock was a formidable client.

My personal hazing initiation came the next morning in the coils of Condotte's lawyer. After his receptionist kept me waiting for 45 minutes, I was admitted like a provincial petitioner to my counterpart's spacious chambers. Dottore Fabio Carlucci was a sleek serpent in bespoke pinstripes that must have cost twice my monthly salary.

"Mr. Sunshine—may I call you 'Russell'?—Welcome to my cubicle. I thought we could get acquainted while our principals are bogged down in boring figures."

Carlucci's office was a decorator's confection—inlaid antique desk, muted leather chairs and two sofas, paneled bookshelves of matched legal tomes, even a glass wall overlooking Roman pines and tiled rooftops.

My host waved me to the modest chair facing his elegant desk. "Tell me a bit about yourself, Russell. Where did you practice before landing your choice Arusha post?"

"I worked in the California Legislature drafting bills for Los Angeles's State Senator."

"How interesting." He lightly touched a graying sideburn to ensure no strand had strayed. "Was construction finance one of your specialties?"

"No, consumer and environmental protection."

A single "Ah," deftly spaced between pauses, sufficed to underline the gap between my Sacramento specializations and my Headquarters Project responsibilities. Then Fab Fabio effortlessly picked up the beat.

"California must be beautiful. I never got that far west after completing my Columbia LL.M. Had to rush back to Italy, unfortunately, to labor in the trenches."

Counsellor Carlucci's intercom buzzed regularly to relay incoming calls. Never instructing his secretary to leave him undisturbed, the lawyer paraded his multilingual skills and A-list clients.

"Henry, how's your Washington weather? ....Well, you knew he'd never let you outside when you accepted the job. May I call you back in five minutes? I have one small matter to dispose of."

I took the hint of extermination as my cue to withdraw. My host didn't explicitly identify the waiting party as President Nixon's Secretary of State, but the hint was left dangling for effect.

Minister Kassum and I returned from our Roman expedition with a fair and balanced construction contract in hand. During the ensuing two years of project implementation, we managed to continue to protect the Community's interests. As apprentice to the graciously delegating Minister, I acquired invaluable hands-on learning about construction contracts, financing and cross-cultural negotiation.

In an industrialized country like America, a relative novice like myself would never have been given comparable responsibility. In upcountry Tanzania, however, this young fish was the beneficiary of a much smaller pond. In addition to this specialized advising, I was able to maintain my full legislative-drafting workload for the Chief Counsel.

The Headquarters complex rose on schedule and on budget. Its facilities continued for decades to render service as the Arusha International Conference Center.

The Community, regrettably, enjoyed no comparable longevity. Although still in its formative period during my tenure, it quickly descended into a destructive spiral. With hindsight, blame for this deterioration can primarily be attributed to the 1973 OPEC oil-price hikes. Escalating petroleum prices imposed severe burdens on the three Partner States' foreign-exchange reserves. Nationalistic politicians panicked and seized Community assets—aircraft on the Nairobi tarmac, railway wagons in Moshi switching yards, telecommunications equipment in Kampala studios. Within months, the open border between Kenya and Tanzania had been sealed. By 1977, the young regional alliance was defunct.

During this terminal crisis, the conventional explanation for impending collapse was the ascendancy of Uganda's military dictator, Field Marshal Idi Amin. A larger-than-life figure caricatured in the British press as a harmless buffoon, this madman in fact did lasting damage to East Africa's most promising state. Soon after his coup, he began expropriating foreign investments in Uganda and driving out South Asian merchants. Before long, he was slaughtering so many political opponents that the Nile was literally clogged with corpses beneath Kampala bridges.

For the Community, his excesses had an operational chilling effect. All high-level Community boards and committees were required by Treaty to rotate their meeting venues around the three Partner States. In practice, this meant that every third session was scheduled for Kampala. After Amin executed a Minister with a pistol shot at a Cabinet meeting, many of our Ugandan colleagues were unwilling to return to that country, even when summoned by the furious dictator.

For me, this terror became personalized by an incident that began innocently enough in an Arusha parking lot.

After an informal Community committee meeting, I was standing around chatting with Emmanuel Wakweya while he waited for his driver to collect extra petrol. Wakweya was Uganda's Finance Minister, brilliant, already widely respected at 35. Tall and lean, he combined gravitas, modesty and judgment in a singularly attractive package.

"Even if he has to hunt for fuel in the bush," he joked about his trusted chauffeur, "I should still have time to catch the evening flight to Kampala."

We jumped back as a Community Land Rover screeched to a sliding halt at our feet. A uniformed security officer jumped out of the passenger seat, snapped off a Sandhurst salute and handed the Minister a sealed manila envelope. We exchanged a smile at this vestige of post-colonial officiousness.

Emmanuel's eyes widened when he skimmed the opened note. Air rushed out of his lungs as if he'd been sucker-punched. Out of the messenger's earshot, my colleague whispered details.

"No prying eyes could make heads or tails of this innocuous text," he confided. "But, coded or not, my batchmate has risked his life by sending it. Apparently the impulsive Field Marshal has lost patience with my vexing independence. The moment my feet hit the tarmac in Kampala, I'm to be taken into presidential custody."

And spotting my raised eyebrow, "There's no ambiguity. Russell, can you get me a telephone line with a direct Nairobi connection?"

By good fortune, Emmanuel's wife was on a brief shopping jaunt to the Kenyan capital with their two small sons. We rushed back inside where I prevailed upon the Community duty officer to patch the Minister through to his family's Nairobi hotel.

The visitors' extension was in a small alcove. There was no time or space for privacy. Emmanuel kept it short, his voice calm but unmistakably serious. "Dear, stay where you are. Don't try to go home. There's been a change of plans. I'll explain tonight. I'm on my way to Nairobi. Hope to see you at the hotel by eight. My love to the boys."

Outside again for a solemn handshake. Emmanuel climbed into his returned vehicle and his driver sped off.

I next saw him years later in the staff cafeteria at the World Bank in Washington, DC. A safe haven for the refugee.

The Wakweya family had gotten out. With no possessions beyond two suitcases, but with their heads still attached. Forced to start over, they counted themselves among the lucky ones.

# MUSHUMBUSI JUSTICE

### Arusha 1974

Saturday morning began routinely enough. Meetra, our Siamese cat, tried her high-wire act, leaping and scrabbling to the top of the kitchen door before losing her nerve. When her throaty dirge reached top volume, I gingerly lifted her down.

A shriek broke the routine. Nancy and I rushed outside to find Saidi's wife wailing as he came through the gate. His right forearm and wrist were covered in bandages, the limb bound across his chest by a tight sling.

Curiously, Saidi looked more satisfied than suffering. With our rudimentary Swahili, we discovered he was returning from the neighborhood clinic. They had diagnosed a badly sprained wrist and thumb. He'd been instructed by the medics to keep the arm immobilized for 10 days, a set-back for us all. As our gardener and handyman, Saidi needed daily use of both hands.

We asked him how he'd been hurt. Saidi blurted out that Shabani, our houseman, had struck him with a heavy stick and knocked him down.

Despite the commotion, Shabani and his family were nowhere in the yard. This was curious. Normally, he'd have made sure he was squarely in the middle of the conversation, interpreting and elaborating in clipped but comprehensible English.

Saidi went off to rest and we knocked on Shabani's door for his side of the story. Unusually querulous, he insisted he'd had nothing to do with Saidi's misfortune.

"He got drunk, Bwana. Yesterday you pay us. We walk to town. See friends, drink *pombé*. Saidi drink too much. After dark, we walk back. Saidi drunk. He fall down in ditch. He blame me because he ashamed."

Both our workers were nominal Muslims. However, like most Arushans we knew, they found the local home-brew irresistible.

Shabani seemed to sense our skepticism and upped the ante. "Saidi hurt me, I not hurt him."

"How, Shabani? You don't look injured."

"He put curse on me. Now bad things happen."

Nancy and I returned to our house and tried to make sense of this troubling incident. Shabani Shemtawa and Saidi Juma had always been cordial next-door neighbors in the staff quarters behind our bungalow. Their two wives shared a common cooking porch and seemed to get along fine. Their five kids filled the yard with squeals of laughter.

Shabani's prior job had been as safari cook for a big-game hunter. He bought most of our groceries, helped prepare meals and conscientiously cleaned our clothes and quarters, despite the lack of most simple appliances. Stocky and tidy, unfailingly cheerful, Shabani also demonstrated an uncanny prescience. He'd alert Nancy that I was about to return home from a field mission.

"Not until tomorrow, Shabani," she'd explain. "It's on the calendar."

"No, today, Memsahib. *Bwana* coming today." Sure enough, I'd drive up to the gate, ahead of schedule.

Spare, dour and shy, Saidi was more at ease with plants than people. He'd dug out a productive vegetable garden in our side yard, coaxing a bounty of tomatoes, cucumbers, watermelons, lettuce and onions from the rich volcanic soil. His flowerbeds raced into bloom. Blankets of purple morning glories and crimson bougainvillea met in the middle of our bungalow's tile roof.

These were our guys. Listening to other expats' carping complaints about local staff, we'd always counted our blessings. Now that domestic harmony had been disrupted. What had really happened? How could we find out, and what should we do about it?

I recalled that Mr. Mushumbusi, Chief Clerk in the Community's Legal Department where I worked, had served as a local magistrate under the British. Nancy and I agreed I should ask him if

*With Shabani Shemtawa and friends.*
*Arusha 1973.*

he'd lend his experience to unraveling our intramural knot. He graciously consented.

Mr. Mushumbusi rang our bell the following Monday afternoon. I opened the gate and shook his hand, trying not to show my surprise at his appearance. In place of his standard working attire of tired trousers and open-collared shirt, he now wore a smart suit and tie. But it was his bearing that denied familiarity. Erect and centered, a pillar of dignity.

At the office, Mr. Mushumbusi's posture was subtly hunched, nearly bowing when interacting with the Community's lawyers. The Chambers observed a two-tier hierarchy—lawyers above, support staff below. As Chief Clerk, Mr. Mushumbusi commanded the latter cadre. In this pivotal position, he controlled every administrative resource from the switchboard to the file room. So his deference to colleagues 30 years his junior like myself had struck me as an unattractive post-colonial holdover.

No shadow of comparable obsequiousness marked today's caller. "Mr. Sunshine, I believe we agreed on four-thirty."

I felt I was escorting a circuit judge along our canna-bordered driveway. Eyes peered from behind outbuilding curtains. Over tea in our living room, Mr. Mushumbusi succinctly reviewed his grasp of the quarrel's main points. Then he asked Nancy and me to summon the two adversaries. They appeared, spruced up in immaculate white shirts and traditional *kofia* caps, visibly impressed by the arbiter and proceedings.

Addressing the parties in Swahili and then translating into English, Mr. Mushumbusi led off with formal remarks. Describing, rather effusively for my taste, the professional contributions that Nancy and I were making to East African development, he reminded Saidi and Shabani that a stable homestead was vital to support our work.

With the tribunal's gravity unequivocally established, Mr. Mushumbusi next asked each man to describe what had happened. They replied, plainly but eloquently, confirming the richness of the East African oral tradition. No hemming or hawing from these two witnesses. They laid out their respective cases with conviction and self-confidence.

Which was exactly the problem from where I was sitting. Both accounts could not be true. The injury was a physical fact. Its cause was either a deliberate blow or an accidental fall. I dismissed the curse as Shabani's melodramatic embellishment.

The presentations dragged on. I grew increasingly vexed. At the brazen hypocrisy of the deceitful party, whoever he was. But also at my inability to penetrate the deception. Mr. Mushumbusi exhibited no parallel impatience. To the contrary, he somehow conveyed by his dignified attentiveness that the telling itself was valid and valuable.

When the second presentation wound down, the magistrate shifted gears. "What do you want?" he asked, taking all of us in with a sweeping glance.

My frown must have betrayed my confusion.

"How would each of you like this matter resolved?" Mr. Mushumbusi clarified. "What would be your preferred outcome? Mrs. Sunshine, may I ask you to begin?"

"We need harmony restored to our family compound."

"Mr. Sunshine?"

The American lawyer in me snorted exasperation. "Someone's lying. Either Shabani struck Saidi and is covering it up, or Saidi is embarrassed that he passed out and fell, and is trying to pass the buck to Shabani. The guilty party must be exposed and confess."

Mr. Mushumbusi continued his polling without acknowledging my emotional outburst.

"Mr. Juma?"

"I want Shabani to say he's sorry."

"Mr. Shemtawa?"

"Saidi must lift the curse."

With all cards on the table, the dealer started picking them up.

"Saidi Juma, if Shabani Shemtawa says he is sorry for your injury, will you lift the curse?"

"Not sorry for the injury," I interrupted. "Sorry for *causing* the injury!"

"Mr. Sunshine," the magistrate softly admonished, "why don't we permit Mr. Juma to decide what will satisfy him. Mr. Juma?"

"There is no curse."

"As you say. But will you promise that, whatever Mr. Shemtawa may have feared in the past, from this moment forward there will be no curse?"

"I will promise. But he must say he is sorry."

"Understood. Now, Shabani Shemtawa, are you prepared to say you are sorry for Mr. Juma's injury?"

"I not hit him. He drank *pombé* and fell in ditch." (By this point, Shabani's agitation was getting the better of him. He was no longer waiting for Mr. Mushumbusi's translations.)

"As you have stated. But if he lifts the curse, will you say you are sorry for his injury and never again blame it on his drunkenness?"

*Our Arusha bungalow where Mr. Mushumbusi worked his justice. 1973.*

"I will say it. If he lift the curse."

The magistrate paused to give us time to absorb the tacit bargain he had just engineered.

"Mrs. Sunshine, I believe these exchanged pledges will restore the harmony to your home that you requested."

He turned to Saidi and Shabani. "Let me be clear, Gentlemen. If I hear that either of you has re-ignited this foolish quarrel, I will recommend to Mr. and Mrs. Sunshine that they dismiss you instantly. And after that, as Chief Administrative Officer for the Community's Legal Department, I will personally ensure that you never again work for EAC staff."

The two disputants looked stunned, as if the full consequences of their domestic quarrel were at last sinking in.

Mr. Mushumbusi leaned in my direction, his tone moderated. Even this comparative informality left no doubt he was still pronouncing from the bench.

"Mr. Sunshine, that leaves only you. You have stated your

determination to resolve this dispute by exposing the guilty party. We have not done that. But all others in your compound have worked out an agreement. I would hope you could see your way clear to endorse it."

I begrudgingly accepted his disposition and muttered a few words of thanks for his intervention. Later, Nancy fairly described my expression as a pout. I was odd man out of this circle.

With Mr. Mushumbusi's guidance, the two complainants stood and shook hands. Then he asked Nancy and me to add our hands to this clasp. His own senior palms ratified the pact.

Even after I had simmered down, I was too green and too rigid to accept healing closure in place of "the truth." Shabani and Saidi had no comparable inhibitions. Putting their unfortunate fracas behind them, they basked in the Elder's blessing and resumed their cordial co-habitation for the remainder of our stay.

Nancy and I didn't want to insult Mr. Mushumbusi by offering him cash payment for his intervention. On our next trip to Nairobi, we procured a judicious silk necktie.

# SHORT HOPS AND LONG HAULS

## *East Africa 1973–74, 1983*

I was barreling along the highway from Moshi back to Arusha, too fast for the road but anxious not to be late for the appointment. My boss, Paolo Sebalu, the Community's Chief Counsel, was a stickler for punctuality, especially from his staff lawyers.

1:45. I could just make it by 2 p.m. I knew every stretch of this road after a week of daily back-and-forths, visiting Nancy in post-operative care at Kilimanjaro Christian Medical Center. Everyone napped during mid-day breaks under the equatorial sun. I had the entire 40-mile straightaway virtually to myself.

I was rehearsing what I anticipated could be an awkward interview as I raced over a rise. A blur of movement closed from my right. The dense vegetation had been cropped back from the shoulder to give motorists fair warning of darting game. This specimen had only two legs but was 10 feet long.

In the half-second it took me to realize I was going to hit him, my brain processed a spindly figure ferrying bamboo poles. I yanked the steering wheel to the right to cut behind him and screeched into a slide. With the stack on his left shoulder, the man's head was blocked so he never saw me coming. But the tires' squeal froze him in mid-stride and my left headlight clipped the back tips of his drooping bundle.

I stood on the brake, counter-steering to keep from rolling. In my mirrors, the man spun like a top. I skidded to a stop in the roadside gravel, switched off the ignition and jumped out, hyperventilating. The poles lay strewn across both lanes like a child's pick-up sticks. The gaunt figure sat in their midst on the burning pavement, broadcasting a high-pitched wail.

Expatriate consensus in Arusha counseled against stopping after any rural collision. Village crowds could turn violent when one of their own had been struck. It was more prudent for a *mzungu*, a white foreigner, to continue on to the nearest police station and send back assistance.

But out here at mid-day, I couldn't spot another soul. And I knew the sun-shriveled man hadn't been hit, although he was justifiably terrified. I wanted to help him to safety and then remove the lethal poles. They'd be as slick as an ice rink if another vehicle came over the rise at speed comparable to my own.

It was easy to lift my trembling victim by his armpits. He was all bones, no more than 70 pounds in his loincloth and four-and-a-half feet tall from cracked soles to bald head. He continued to howl as I guided him to what passed for roadside shade.

While he collapsed in a heap, I rushed back to drag the bamboo out of harm's way. By the time I turned around again, the legendary crowd had materialized out of thin air. I didn't need local dialect to grasp their escalating rage. Like an idiot lawyer conducting his own defense, I approached the villagers to explain.

A thirtyish man in an undershirt and faded shorts grabbed my arm to pull me aside. I shook him off before I realized he was whispering rapid-fire English in my ear.

"Sir, I too work at the Community. I have seen you there. The old man's relatives are angry. He complains he is injured. You will be also, if you stay here. Can you drive him to the clinic in Arusha?"

"Of course. Let's go. Please tell them I didn't hit him. Only the poles. He's more scared than scraped. But we need to get him checked over. Will you come with us?"

In Arusha, the clinic staff treated "Grandfather" with respect and insightful therapy. One large gauze bandage for a scraped elbow, a second for a bruised knee, two aspirins for swelling, a cup of cola for electrolytes. Most effective of all, receptive ears for his animated recitation.

With each retelling, the tale took on more drama. "My son always tells me, 'Father, look both ways before crossing the black strip. Then run like *swala pala*, the antelope.' But antelopes don't have to carry heavy sticks."

My contributions to his regimen included repeated apologies, coverage of the nominal clinic charges, an honorarium to compensate the victim for his trauma and return bus fares for him and his escort.

The old man began anew for the driver and fellow passengers as he boarded the bus on his kinsman's arm. "I was struck here, and here. The healers said I was very brave."

Other cars and other journeys animate many of my East African memories. Perhaps because settlements were so scattered and vistas so breathtakingly wide, it was the drives between destinations that often left permanent imprints.

Even though the Community had insisted that I rush out from America as soon as they'd confirmed the Ford Foundation's nomination, Nancy and I arrived to find our promised Arusha lodgings still occupied by their previous tenant. For the interim, the Community regretfully assigned us to quarters in the hamlet of Tengeru, 20 miles outside town.

Our purchased car was entwined in bureaucratic red tape on Mombasa docks. Twice a day, I would ride a Community van packed with other civil servants commuting to and from Arusha. With gymnastics I never did fully unravel, as many as 30 bodies were crammed into this 16-seat carrier. On the first few runs, I almost fainted from claustrophobia and assertive body odors. Within a week, I learned to sink into a trance like a resigned sardine.

At least I had mental stimulation and social contact at my office after this haulage. Things were much worse for Nancy, stuck in the village with no job, transport or telephone. (As previously mentioned, she eventually landed a super job that took her across the width of East Africa, by all modes of transport on land, water and air.)

Our own car, when finally delivered, was a plain but sturdy Peugeot 404 station wagon. We quickly had it "safari-proofed" by welding a steel plate to the undercarriage as an extra barrier against oil-pan or gas-tank punctures on rocky roads. For major excursions, a contingencies kit stored in the back contained, in addition to routine repair gear, a second spare tire, pump and patches, sand shovel, metal grids for traction out of ditches, towing rope, extra gasoline, lubricating oil and drinking water. Now we were ready to transport overseas visitors to Tanzania's National Parks.

Among our first house guests were Jane Shetler and her husband Richard Ross. She was the prescient matchmaker who had introduced Nancy and me after our separate sojourns in India. Despite now being well-along in her first pregnancy, Jane was keen to go on safari. So we loaded up and headed west. Our houseman Shabani came along to help with camp chores, delighted by even this tame sequel to past adventures as bush cook for a big-game hunter.

A half-day's journey brought us to Lake Manyara. Its backdrop, the Rift Valley escarpment, rose in sheer 2,500-foot cliffs, the most dramatic feature of a continuous fault line stretching from Turkey to Malawi.

Due to its overpopulation of free-ranging elephants, Manyara Park was open only to daylight visitors. We settled in for a light lunch at a cleared picnic area before setting off to search for Manyara's famous tree-lounging lions. It was an attractive glade—dense forest on three sides, a giant tumble of *kopje* boulders on the fourth.

Jane and I selected a downed eucalyptus log to double as seats and a table. As we caught up on mutual acquaintances from our days together in India, she raised a sandwich-filled hand to make a point. From behind her back, a silent shaft of fur and claws violently snatched the bread.

We shouted the alarm. The offending baboon, scarred leader of a foraging troop, answered our protest with a booming bark. He seemed huge, with a flared crown like a lion, and was definitely ferocious. He bared formidable canine teeth and puffed out his chest, daring us to try to retrieve his booty.

A blond-headed figure streaked across the clearing, arms pumping to intensify the challenge. "Wagh! Wagh!"

Jane, Richard and I stood in stupefied appreciation as Nancy jumped up and down to confront the alpha male. Shabani was much quicker on the uptake. He grabbed a downed branch and joined the *memsahib* in a dual threat-display.

For an instant, the cross-species contest hung in the balance. The baboon troop crowded forward to support their snarling leader. Then he dropped the contested sandwich and took a begrudging step backwards. The troop whirled and scampered away over the boulders. The leader covered their retreat, uttered a final frustrated bark and leaped to follow his entourage.

Nancy and Shabani shared whoops of triumph and a gleam of reciprocal respect. Calls of "Encore!" were demurely declined.

Late that evening, we pulled into the windswept campground on the bare rim of Ngorongoro Crater. Before setting up camp, we gazed down 2,000-foot walls at the magnificent intact caldera. One hundred square miles in area, the volcanic bowl was home to the densest permanent population of wild game in Africa.

We pitched our tent near a half-dozen others. One backpacking Scot made a show of touristic independence by camping at a distance from the rest of us. He paid a costly penalty for his hubris. In the pre-dawn, roaming Masai youths slit his tent, bopped him on the head and stole his wallet.

As he cooked breakfast, Shabani was happy to tell us how wise he had been to place his own bedroll inside the car. "No Masai hit *my* head. Can't get at it."

An embarrassed Park Warden came around to take the Scot's statement and warn us that incidents like this were distressingly on the increase. He explained that in traditional Masai culture, maturation was organized into seven-year phases. Boys eight to 14 guarded the nomadic tribe's herds of cattle and goats. Youths from 15 to 21 were armed *morani*, defending the tribe, raiding and fighting. Full adulthood was achieved by spearing a lion. Now that farmers' settlements and National Park regulations had constrained customary pursuits, the redundant warriors were reduced to snapshot-posing, panhandling and petty vandalism.

After a full day of game-watching inside the crater in a four-wheel-drive Land Rover rented from the Park, we returned to the rim for a feed and welcome rest.

Our own car's blasting horn woke us at midnight. We scrambled out of our tent to see more Masai racing away. Shabani lay sprawled and grinning across the car's front seat. He unlocked a door and jumped out, eager to expand his repertoire. "*Morani* make big mistake. Try open car doors. Very scared to see me inside." With due allowance for history being recorded by the winners, we were relieved Shabani had avoided injury and protected our gear.

Our safari party was ready to proceed to a more tranquil destination. We moved on to Serengeti and a cherished visit with paleontologist Mary Leakey. A mutual friend had provided a personal introduction. Mrs. Leakey had kindly extended an invitation.

Her field cabin in Olduvai Gorge was a spartan affair, but the wide veranda comfortably accommodated our visiting party and her six Golden Retrievers. Mrs. Leakey served tea. Nancy contributed a handsome tin of home-baked oatmeal cookies.

Our British hostess's hair and skin evidenced decades in the sun. She seemed to welcome the respite from solitude, even though we knew little of her specialization. Mrs. Leakey put in context the historic discoveries she had made with her late husband Louis, culminating in the 2.3-million-year-old hominid *Australopithecus*. Louis had received almost all the credit from the international scientific community. Every word of her narrative was self-effacing, but we knew that, in fact, she had been a full partner, reputedly even the principal discoverer, though without a status-conferring doctorate.

Mrs. Leakey asked her foreman to guide us into the gorge for a view of the key site. Nancy and I were both surprised by the bleached monotony of the parched creek-bed where the Leakeys had spent decades of digging. In this heralded repository, our untrained eyes could detect nothing distinctive. No vegetation, noteworthy geological colors or formations. I could barely make out the fossilized prints and fragments, even when our escort pointed them out. Somehow we'd expected more visual drama.

Driving out of the gorge gave us a different kind of excitement. The steep track and loose gravel roadbed really demanded four-wheel drive. The guide had had no difficulty negotiating the slope in his Land Rover. Since our modest Peugeot had no comparable traction, Nancy was designated pilot in recognition of her formative years in the Appalachians. The rest of us piled out to lighten the load as she made her run.

It was nasty going. The car fishtailed on the gravel, spinning wheels and nearing the precipice in one hairpin turn. Richard and I jumped behind to push and try to keep the car away from the treacherous edge. Twice Nancy stalled out and had to ease back to a relatively level spot. The third time, the tires caught. With a steady foot, our rally queen throttled to the top.

The long haul from Arusha to Nairobi was another signature itinerary of our East African sojourn. Through dense coffee plantations skirting Mt. Meru's fertile slopes, across the Kenyan border at Namanga, then due north on the crowded artery to Kenya's capital, Nancy and I made this four-hour trek every six weeks or so, forsaking Tanzania's socialist austerities for cosmopolitan capitalism.

In fact, our tastes were as simple as our budget was limited. We went north mainly for the change of scene, Cadbury's chocolate and staples unavailable on Arusha grocers' understocked shelves. A major splurge might be a dinner at Alain Bobbé's Bistro or lunch on the terrace of the historic Norfolk Hotel. Movies also lured us to the metropolis, as did magazines and paperbacks in the capital's bookstores.

These cabin-fever catharses were tame excursions compared to the manic dashes of colonial couples from Mombasa to Nairobi in the 1950s. They'd race 250 miles on the unpaved road up from the coast for a single theater performance.

During one Nairobi film matinee, Mel Brooks' *Blazing Saddles* was on screen, an irreverent parody of Hollywood Westerns. One marginal character, a pint-sized biddy with a barrel voice, hurled obscenities and racist epithets at the heroic black sheriff. Nancy and I were rollicking at the broad satire when we realized we were the only whites in the theater. Not only was no one else laughing, many local viewers were stalking out. They apparently hadn't realized the entire script was a spoof and were taking the racism literally.

Before we had time to react to the hostile stares, I had an eerie premonition and whispered to my wife. "Nancy, this isn't another gag, but I've got a weird feeling that someone's stealing our car."

"In broad daylight on Nairobi's main drag?"

"I know, it's crazy. But I still feel uneasy."

"Go check it out. It'll only take two minutes and make you feel better."

I dashed outside on a fool's errand. But not so foolish, as it turned out. Broad daylight or not, our car had disappeared.

The notoriously inept Nairobi police were blasé about our predicament. They explained with a collective shrug that organized gangs had their routine finely honed. Snatching parked cars in the city center, the thieves would spray paint them the same day before driving across Kenyan borders into Somalia or Uganda for black-market resale. We salvaged our mobility by renting a short-term substitution until insurance proceeds permitted purchase of a replacement.

Back in Arusha, neighbors shed more light on our lightening Nairobi heist. Peugeot had economized by cutting only six standard key patterns for all its cars exported to East Africa. So enterprising thieves with only six copied keys had ready access to the entire three-country fleet!

Fifteen years later, when my former Community department head,

Paolo Sebalu, was in private practice in Kampala, Uganda, a client asked him to confirm that a well-used vehicle he was being offered for sale had proper legal documentation. Paolo pulled the maintenance log from the glove compartment and laughed out loud. Faithfully recorded was the car's initial servicing in 1973, in Arusha, Tanzania, for original owner Russell Sunshine. After 180,000 miles traversing God-knows-what terrain, our faithful station wagon had emerged from the bush, still chugging along. What a challenge for Peugeot's Advertising Department! How to trumpet methuselan mechanical endurance without revealing the firm's complicity in cross-border car-jackings?

My final East African road trip took place in the 1980s, again in the company of now Tanzanian Cabinet Minister Al Noor Kassum. I was back in the region on a World Bank consultancy. Nick had to inspect the former Community Headquarters in Arusha on behalf of the Tanzanian government. He invited me to accompany him south from Nairobi.

The journey was deeply depressing. With the border long closed between Kenya and Tanzania, this once-vital artery had been virtually abandoned. In the old days, the thoroughfare had hummed with commercial trucks, buses, official vehicles and private cars. Now it was a ghost strip. In four hours of high-speed driving, we saw no other vehicle moving in either direction. Tumbleweed rolled across the cracking pavement. Giraffes crossed at a walk, cattle and warthogs dozed insolently on the road. It evoked a Hollywood scenario of post-Armageddon decimation.

With Nick's driver at the wheel, the two of us were free in the back seat to chat and catch up. His family was thriving, mostly emigrated, but East African politics and development continued to deteriorate. Nick's tone was less buoyant than I'd remembered, his hair now predominantly gray.

As our car approached Tanzania, my former client warned me to remain silent at the border. Even when the highway had been bustling, border-crossing had always been a bureaucratic hassle for private vehicles.

But diplomatic license plates had guaranteed smooth and swift passage. Now, with the border sealed to all but infrequent official vehicles, the Tanzanian government had economized by mobilizing teenage militias to man the frontier.

At Namanga, swaggering 14-year-olds with Kalashnikovs thumbed our passports upside down, as illiterate as they were surly. My Cabinet Minister could not assert his rank because these juvenile sentries had no concept of a national capital. They held us for an uncomfortable hour while Nick's driver affably distributed cigarettes.

In Arusha, Nick kept his appointment and I walked through the impoverished town to our former residential compound. The splendid garden where I'd greeted Mr. Mushumbusi was now scoured of all vegetation. A felled coconut-palm had sliced our house roof in half, dragging with it dead bougainvillea strands. The whitewashed compound wall was battered and breached, with bricks from whole sections chipped loose and carted off. Seven families squatted around the once-tidy porch of Saidi and Shabani. I leaned on the rusted gate and choked back tears.

With the ebb and flow of historical tides, today the East African Community is re-emerging. Surviving elders recognized the grave error they had made by allowing, and even fomenting, the original disintegration. To right this wrong, the founding trio of Kenya, Tanzania and Uganda officially revived the Community in 2000, adding neighboring Burundi and Rwanda to strengthen the partnership. Membership is also in the pipeline for the fragile new nation of South Sudan. In addition to a customs union, a common currency, regional services and a Community legislature, now full monetary union and even political federation are being seriously contemplated.

As a prime beneficiary of the EAC's reconstitution, our sleepy agricultural market town of Arusha has mushroomed into a diplomatic metropolis of 500,000 population.

Forty years ago, we lived a dream of regional integration and shared prosperity. Those once-flattened hopes are getting a second chance.

# In-Between

*Worldwide Short-term Consultancies 1980–1987*

After returning to the United States from East Africa in 1975, Nancy and I continued to work in our chosen professional field of international development, but from an American home base. During this Stateside interlude, we lived in Washington DC and then Central Virginia.

For the first four years, I served as Executive Director of the Investment Negotiation Center in Washington. Co-sponsored by Georgetown and Columbia University Law Schools, the INC offered in-service training to lawyers from 60 developing countries.

By 1980, I was hanging out my shingle as an independent consultant. My chief clients in the latter capacity included the World Bank, the United Nations and the International Development Law Institute in Rome. Short-term assignments during this period carried me to the Caribbean, Africa, the Middle East and Asia.

Nancy meanwhile was undertaking short-term projects in Guyana, Egypt, Somalia and Pakistan, chiefly under the sponsorship of USAID and the US Department of Agriculture. Simultaneously, she completed her PhD degree at American University's School of International Service.

The travel tales in this collection resume in the late 1980s when I began long-term engagement in China.

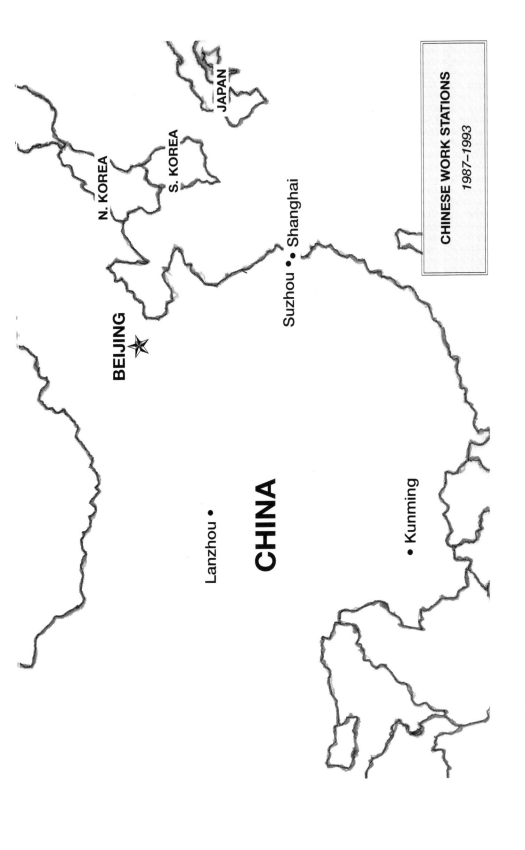

CHINESE WORK STATIONS
*1987–1993*

## CHAPTER SIX
# CHINA: WAKING THE DRAGON

### SQUEEZING A LEMON

*Suzhou 1987*

"Russell, you're going to love this." The teasing tone on the phone was not the one I'd come to expect from Richard Bumgarner, the World Bank's normally dour Senior Project Officer for China. "I'll bet it's the shortest fax ever received at the Bank. 'SEND SUNSHINE.' We must make a copy so you can frame it for your office."

We shared the laugh, but I was genuinely excited. After months of hints and hesitation, here was the green light.

The Bank and the Chinese government were still in a preliminary phase of their courtship dance. The twin suitors circled and bowed, advanced and retreated. The assertive international organization was impatient to get its foot into Asia's largest door. The proud, isolated Peoples Republic was desperate for foreign know-how and capital but determined not to compromise its sovereignty or self-esteem.

Our proposed project was one small but potentially influential step forward in this development-assistance minuet. The government sought World Bank financing to construct a refrigerator-manufacturing plant in the provincial city of Suzhou. The Bank was keen to lend the requested funds but insisted that the Suzhou Municipal Authority engage an experienced global engineering firm for design-and-construction oversight. Recruitment of the foreign firm would have to comply with the Bank's procurement guidelines requiring international competitive bidding. Since I had helped write those guidelines as a consultant to Bank headquarters in Washington, the Bank recommended my qualifications to the Chinese for offering in-country advice on compliance.

Determined not to let this pioneering invitation evaporate, I relaxed normal professional caution. Within hours, I booked the most direct connections from Washington to Shanghai. Within days, I stuffed a briefcase with background materials and boarded a 747. As if gulping a high-risk cocktail of hubris and naivety, I was agreeing to fly half-way around the world with no visa, no pre-paid air ticket, no consulting contract and no agreed fee amount or payment schedule. Legally speaking, I was totally exposed.

Richard's parting words drove home my vulnerability. "Russell, it goes without saying that the Bank is pleased the Chinese have accepted our referral. But you'll be on your own out there. Working for them, not for us."

He made "out there" sound like the far side of the moon.

The hand-lettered cardboard square teetered above a sea of black hair at Shanghai International Airport.

---

### WARMLY WELCOME

### Mr. Sun    (Mr. Shine)

---

I pressed forward towards the homing beacon through the surging throng. My reception committee looked as relieved as I felt. Physical contact at last.

Laboring to make herself heard above the din, the bespectacled interpreter introduced her three colleagues. Her idiosyncratic pronunciation of English would have been a challenge for me even without the competing clamor. At least I managed to catch their institutional affiliations. The short, older gentleman with the pockmarked face represented the Suzhou Municipal Authority, owners of the planned refrigerator factory. The tall thin fellow was a factory manager. Much younger and visibly self-assured was the Beijing-based lawyer from the supervising national Ministry of Industry. I struggled but failed to imprint names on faces within the monochrome Mao-suited quartet.

During our 90-minute ride to Suzhou in an ancient van, engine noise and mutual self-consciousness kept our conversation to a minimum. I stared out the van window at the early dusk of approaching winter. Clusters of weathered huts sagged on embankments above desolate fields and drainage ditches. Dented trucks and buses clogged the road. The few visible dogs and cattle were striped with protruding ribs. Drained by jet lag and the marathon trans-Pacific flight, I couldn't wait to collapse into bed.

Finally reaching Suzhou, we pulled up to the austere concrete block of the government guesthouse where I'd be staying. Its faded lobby resembled a half-vacant warehouse—no directional signs, wall decorations or a single potted plant. The unventilated air was musty, with a residual odor of cooked cabbage.

As I registered at the bare reception counter, my escorts split in half. The Authority representative and factory manager took their leave. But their two younger colleagues seemed to catch their second wind. Taking my suitcase in hand, the Ministry lawyer led me up the stairwell with the interpreter scuttling behind.

My surprise escalated to claustrophobia when they followed me into my room. The metal bed and wooden desk left the three of us barely enough space to stand without bumping. I felt cramped and wrong-footed by my hosts' intrusion. I unlocked my bag and popped it open on the bed to send a non-verbal request for privacy.

The lawyer peered over my shoulder at the contents and shouted something in Chinese. "Why do you have so many clothes?" came the translation. The question's decibels and bluntness were jarring. I hadn't been sure how much I'd be moving about within China. So, when packing at home back in Washington DC, I had purposely kept my travel wardrobe simple.

"So many?" I repeated.

The lawyer marshalled his evidence. "You have two jackets and three trousers."

"Well, yes. I'm here for 15 days."

"I have one suit. I am here for always."

*What's this turkey up to?* I wondered. *He doesn't seem to be joking. Maybe trying to demonstrate from the get-go that he isn't intimidated by the privileged foreigner?*

Whatever his problem, I hadn't the energy to defend decadent capitalist consumerism. I just wanted to finish unpacking and hit the sack. So I held my tongue and the zealous prosecutor chose not to pursue his sartorial cross-examination.

By shuffling forward in the narrow space, I gave the duo little choice but to back out into the hallway. With a brusque good night, I closed the door and got ready to crash. I was unsettled by the lawyer's crass intrusiveness. Despite my exhaustion, I thrashed about on the hard mattress for an hour before falling asleep.

My biological clock, still on Washington time, jolted me awake at 5 a.m. I rang the guesthouse switchboard but no one picked up. I still couldn't feel any central heating. So, throwing on trousers, a shirt and my topcoat, I walked down the hallway stairs to see if I could rustle up a dawn snack.

Downstairs I found the front desk deserted and the cafeteria closed. I strolled out into the guesthouse garden. Its paths were swept clean but the few shrubs seemed as undernourished as I felt. Hints of human waste wafted through opaque mist. Clutching my coat collar against the chill, I shuddered in near-panic. What the hell had I gotten myself into? How was I going to make it through two weeks?

Back inside the now-stirring cafeteria, I downed a cup of scalding green tea to boost me out of my funk. Then up to my room to make myself presentable.

The shower had no hot water, but the cold spray chased the cobwebs. When I turned off the tap, the pipes continued to rattle. No, the persistent knocking was coming from outside my room. I wrapped an inadequate towel around my dripping waist and opened the door to make clear I was all tea'd up.

In the hallway stood a dozen wide-eyed, Mao-suited officials. Bravely beaming, the interpreter informed me that the Suzhou Municipal Authority's Executive Committee was ready to start my day.

I stammered my appreciation for the generous size of the welcoming delegation. I blundered on with an apology for my lack of appropriate attire—in fact, any attire, I realized, but didn't elaborate.

When we'd pulled up to the guesthouse the previous evening, my escorts had pointed out the Authority's offices just down the road. Now anxious to get past this excruciating encounter, I asked if we could reconvene there in an hour.

"That won't be necessary," the interpreter assured me. "We're staying here."

I prayed she didn't mean the hallway, "In this hotel?"

"We've all moved into the guesthouse so we can spend more time with you."

My negotiation training recommended a fallback. "Great idea. Can we meet downstairs in, say, half an hour?"

"The Committee will wait here."

*You're doomed, Sunshine. She had meant the hallway.*

I scanned the chair-less corridor and suggested that her superiors might be more comfortable seated in the downstairs lobby while I was dressing.

"This is no problem. They will stand."

The dripping pool was expanding around my feet. The towel was heading south. Cutting my losses, I retreated with a grin in place of a grimace. But I couldn't get the door shut. It was jammed open by the interpreter's determined toe.

*She can't want to watch?*

Clothes snatched at random with my one free hand, I backed into the bathroom to throw on an extravagant suit.

Over breakfast of more green tea, barely boiled eggs and steamed rice, my clients laid out their expectations for my assignment. Their surface agenda was straightforward. My task was to help them draft bidding documents for hiring an engineering firm, documents that would pass World Bank muster. Beneath the surface, I could sense a cold current of resentment, even through the filter of translation. The Chinese needed the Bank's money to build their factory. To get their hands on that financing, they needed to hire foreign engineers. To hire those engineers, they needed Bank-approved bidding documents. To produce those documents, they needed a foreign draftsman. The bottom line—maybe my input was unavoidable, but they didn't have to like it.

As I intuited my clients' reservations, my own concerns were piling up. These Suzhou clients had zero familiarity with the World Bank or its procedures. The learning curve would be steep. If they wanted to participate in drafting the legal documents, our time frame would be tight. The pace would be slowed by the Municipal Authority's insistence that all key decisions be taken by its full Executive Committee. Language would be another drag. No one on the Chinese team had much English beyond the three interpreters. And even that trio lacked relevant vocabulary. To add insult to injury, my Beijing-based wardrobe critic was missing no chance to belittle his country cousins.

We were all in for a rocky ride.

"What is competition?"

The question hung suspended over the table like a dinner guest's faux pas. Someone's phlegmy throat-clearing filled the vacuum, doubling my discomfort. A quick glance around the circle convinced me that the glaring questioner wasn't a maverick—just bolder, or perhaps more senior, than his nodding colleagues.

Interruptions like this gave "back-to-basics" new meaning. At this rate, we might never get to my planned topics for this seminar session, particularly with the lag of bilingual interpretation. But instinct told me my best route to building trust and rapport led through frank dialogue, even if those exchanges produced detours and delays.

"Competition is a contest, Chief Engineer Wang." I reached for an example where China enjoyed world prominence. "Like a table-tennis tournament."

The Chief's rigid jaw asserted his personal stake. "We are serious professionals, Mr. Sunshine, not athletes. Why do we need competition among engineering firms? The Municipal Authority should just assign this project to our own Engineering Department."

His gored ox was self-evident, but I respected his candor. "These are good questions. I believe you're really raising two points. Why competition at all? And why let foreign firms participate? Do I understand you correctly?"

"Yes, two points."

"Let's take them in order. Why competition? It generates higher-quality proposals from contractors and lower prices for the client—in this case, the Municipal Authority. If interested firms know they have to outscore rival bidders to win a contract, they'll sharpen their pencils. Sole-sourcing has the opposite effect. As a contractual monopoly, it invites careless proposals and higher prices."

Alert posture and scattered nods around the table suggested at least some of this was getting through.

"Now for your second point. Why foreign participation? Globally-experienced foreign engineering firms can introduce fresh approaches to your project's design and management challenges. As the client, you stand to benefit from a variety of dishes on the menu."

"We prefer Chinese noodles. We just need more pork!"

I welcomed the jibe from the wit with longish hair to my left. The rolling chuckle confirmed I wasn't alone.

Only the Chief Engineer seemed annoyed by the levity. I sensed his remarks were addressed to his peers as much as to me. "Foreigners cannot possibly know as much about China as our own engineers."

"True enough. But you can teach those foreigners about Chinese conditions and practices. In return, the guests can help you adapt proven international techniques to suit your local needs."

"Harrumph!" The glowering Engineer was giving no ground. But my message, like his, was for the whole group.

During our first working week, I was repeatedly thrown off-stride by these large team meetings. In place of the lean drafting team I'd envisioned as my core counterparts, I was being introduced to two dozen or more contacts per session. Worse from my viewpoint, each session brought mostly new faces, requiring multiple repetitions of the same elementary Q&As. I felt like an exotic zoo acquisition on display for a parade of curious locals.

With my days taken up by these familiarization seminars plus factory site-visits and interviews with senior management, my drafting and lawyer-mentoring obligations got shunted to early mornings and evenings. The Chinese have an expression—squeezing the lemon. If they had to import expensive foreign expertise, they'd make damn sure to extract every drop of juice. They assigned relays of counterparts to pump me with questions and record every response. This tutorial assembly line operated at full-tilt for a solid fortnight, in fourteen-hour cycles.

My sole breaks came on Friday afternoons. The Committee implied that it was using these pauses to caucus and confer with higher echelons in Shanghai and Beijing. I leapt at the chance to get out and about. I was finding the marathon interaction wearing. Besides, when doing advance reading for this mission, I'd been enchanted by Suzhou's cultural pedigree.

The city was celebrated for its Wu Kingdom glory in the third

*Modern replica of Admiral Zheng He's flagship. Nanjing 2005.*

century CE and its Ming Dynasty re-flowering in the early years of the fifteenth. Comparing its urban canals to his own Venice, Marco Polo had reputedly marveled at Suzhou's "1,600 stone bridges under which a galley may pass." Classic gardens were another local signature. Poets and minstrels had entertained imperial courtiers in intimate pavilions overlooking rock-framed, carp-filled pools.

For me, the city's most exciting legacy was as home port for Admiral Zheng He. For his first expedition in 1405, this bold explorer had commanded an incredible fleet of 200 junks from the deck of his leviathan 1,500-ton flagship. Zheng He sailed with 20,000 men to Java, Sumatra, Ceylon [Sri Lanka] and India. His six subsequent voyages, over a 30-year period, reached Zanzibar, Madagascar, and, according to some modern historians, West Africa, the Americas and Australia.

But on grim streets in 1987, even a romantic had to strain to reconcile that fabulous heritage with present realities. No trace remained of the magical fleet's anchorage. Between them, the Japanese Occupation and the Cultural Revolution had destroyed much of the city's historical center and gardens. Carp pools were drained. Canals had deteriorated to open sewers. Suzhou's artistic reputation as the paragon of silk hand-embroidery was suffocating in State-owned workshops churning out kitschy kittens and neon butterflies. As a foreign-investment specialist, I was convinced that this city had dynamic potential as a magnet for cultural tourism. But that would be a distant tomorrow. Today's walls and tunics were unrelievedly gray.

As our consultation advanced, I was drawing some preliminary conclusions about my complex clients and our awkward give-and-take. My hosts were very bright, well-grounded in technical theory but comparatively lacking in practical skills or experience. Cut off from most information beyond China's borders, they lagged behind my prior advisees in other developing countries. But they were racing to overtake. And in marked contrast to those other clients, the Chinese seemed to be vigorously promoting talented female colleagues to positions of responsibility.

My chief concern was that collective discipline was depriving my Suzhou clients of individual initiative. In our rolling group conversations, personal opinions were seldom expressed, and never at variance with official positions. I sensed that anonymous Party watchdogs were ever-present and monitoring.

Nearly as troubling was a pervasive, chip-on-the-shoulder, provincial resistance to change. Like the Chief Engineer, most of the local big-shots were self-interested custodians of the status quo. They seemed to perceive new ideas, particularly from offshore, as a destabilizing threat.

The refreshing exception to this reactionary phalanx was the planned refrigerator factory's designated Managing Director. A compact fireplug in his late forties, Director Ling had scarred, muscled hands that confirmed his long tenure on the shop floor. This go-getter's comments and questions were consistently thoughtful and confident. His determination was palpable. His position seemed to grant him license to reveal personal enthusiasm and a sense of humor. This was an executive who appreciated setting goals as well as achieving them. I came to believe that he saw this construction project as his ticket to recognition and promotion.

During our second week of candid interaction, the Director returned exuberant from a Shanghai exhibition of Japanese home appliances.

"Tall refrigerators! Home freezers! Can you imagine them, Mr. Sunshine? Lime green. Peach pink. Gleaming black. Mirrored chrome."

Caught up in his exhilaration, I asked the Director if these foreign models inspired his vision for his own production.

He chafed with impatience for the translation. "You misunderstand my enthusiasm. I admired those machines as foreign fancies. I touched them all. I opened and closed their sealing doors until the exhibitor had to ask me to stand aside and give others a chance. But they have no practical value for me. None for China."

"What do you value, Director Ling?"

"White boxes. Small boxes. Half a cubic meter[8] in volume. Sturdy frames. Simple motors. Scratch-resistant surfaces. Dependable for five years of daily use—ten years, if possible. My 'market', as you Americans call it, is Suzhou Municipality. Then Jiangsu Province. Cold food, safe and healthy, for the people."

He paused and smiled, "Chinese people."

And then, with all seriousness, "They have earned a better life, Mr. Sunshine. Step-by-step. Bicycles yesterday, television sets tomorrow. Refrigerators today. Suzhou refrigerators."

"No colors?"

"No limes or peaches. White boxes."

---

8 Roughly equivalent to three feet by three by two.

Our collaboration rushed to conclusion. We crafted a full set of the required legal documents in English for me to hand-carry to World Bank headquarters in Washington. While I traveled, a Chinese-language translation would be produced in Beijing. The Chinese version would make the documents accessible to a wide circle of State institutions. With appropriate adaptation, our prototype text could become a valuable template for other planned projects requiring foreign expertise and financing.

On departure, Director Ling paid me the courtesy of a personal escort to Shanghai Airport. En route out of Suzhou, we stopped by the Municipal Bank to collect my consulting-fee payment. My prior inquiries about telegraphic transfers or cashier's checks had elicited awkward silence. Now, at the bank, a belated explanation was tacitly forthcoming.

After two hours of introductions to tiers of bank officers, countless cups of green tea, stair-climbing, signatures and inked stamps, I was discretely handed an unmarked plastic sack, just like a grocery bag. A peek inside revealed bound bundles of small-denomination U.S.-dollar bank notes.

I was charmed but disconcerted. How would I explain this quaint carry-on to U.S. Customs? "Oh, no, Officer. Not drugs. Refrigerators."

In the airport departure lounge, the full Executive Committee lined up to say goodbye. I wondered if their smiles recalled, as mine did, a hallway rendezvous and a dripping towel. I moved down the queue of now-familiar faces, shaking hands, no longer tone-deaf to local names.

How well had we done together? Would our encounter prepare the Suzhou team for effective partnering with the foreign engineers? Could I have been less didactic? More empathetic? What had I learned about working for Chinese clients in their own backyard?

I wanted to open more doors. Not merely on refrigerators.

# BOYS' NIGHT IN

## *Beijing 1990*

We first made contact high above the Sea of Japan, en route from Tokyo to Beijing. Our 9:00 p.m. take-off had been delayed, but it was too short a flight to settle in for a full night's sleep. As seatmates do, we introduced ourselves, exchanged business cards, and got acquainted over drinks and snacks.

Mr. Miyoshi was a stimulating neighbor, atypical of most reserved Japanese executives I had met. Early in our chat, he disclosed that he'd done an MBA at Stanford. That California exposure went a long way towards explaining his English-language confidence and accessible warmth on first meeting.

Now in his fifties, Mr. Miyoshi had a hugely important job (although he never boasted), leading the China-market penetration team for a major Japanese multinational. He'd been based in Beijing for over two years, commuting home monthly to see wife and kids.

During this same period, I'd been shuttling in and out of China on a regular basis, assisting the Chinese Ministry of Public Health with its Vaccine Production Project.[9] Although development assistance and vaccine production were a far cry from Mr. Miyoshi's own priorities or expertise, he nimbly extracted analogies.

9 That advisory assignment extended, on an intermittent basis, from 1988 into 1993.

The landing came quickly. When we parted in the Beijing terminal, my traveling companion cordially suggested we get together over dinner when our schedules permitted.

As with most casual airborne encounters, I doubted there'd be actual follow-through. So I was surprised to find his message at my Beijing hotel before the end of the week. When I returned his call, Mr. Miyoshi invited me for a relaxed evening at his apartment. I was flattered by this special courtesy, knowing that Japanese executives almost invariably entertained at restaurants. I accepted with pleasure.

My surprise increased when my host greeted me at his door. The car and driver he'd sent to collect me, the posh neighborhood and penthouse were only de rigueur for someone in his elevated corporate position. What I hadn't expected were the other guests. Despite their casual attire, the four gentlemen introduced by Mr. Miyoshi were the country representatives of the top tier of Japanese multinationals doing business in China.

Sensing my slight unease, Mr. Miyoshi made light of this VIP roster. He explained that his coterie of "involuntary bachelors" convened every fortnight. Tonight was his turn to cook. In fact, two demure waitresses served all the food, flitting in and out like silent moths. The host poured the first rounds of drinks, all premier labels. His friends helped themselves to refills, confirming the group's familiarity. Never a fan of hard liquor, I opted for the treat of chilled Kirin beer.

A passing remark made it clear that Mr. Miyoshi had not only paid close attention on the airplane to my personal profile, he had also shared highlights with his chums. My increasing suspicion that I'd been invited for more than refreshments was soon confirmed.

Our host shifted gears from movie banter to shop talk by confiding that he and his friends shared frustration at failing to get their corporate feet inside Chinese buyers' doors. After months, even years in some cases, of meeting phalanxes of bureaucrats and making state-of-the-art promotional presentations, not one major Japanese deal had been signed.

"Sunshine-san, it's been all talk and no action," he concluded, playing on our California backgrounds.

Through his interpretation or in their own less-proficient English, Mr. Miyoshi's pals chimed in with congruent complaints. Chinese contacts missed deadlines and commitments and kept shuffling representatives. They handed over incomplete, obsolete or unreliable data, then stalled and reneged. There were escalating rumors of key officials' double-dealing and bribe-seeking.

My host had the last word. "We have nothing concrete, or even promising, to show for our long postings here. Several of our firms are considering pulling us out. That would be most unfortunate—for our companies, and for ourselves."

I was struck by their candor. Letting one's hair down on a drinking-night-out with the boys was standard procedure in Japanese business culture. These undisciplined sessions forged workplace bonds and suspended corporate hierarchies. But to admit a foreigner to such backroom intimacy was all but unheard-of.

Now I understood why I'd been invited. The discrete choice of venue also made sense. I was expected to sing for my supper.

There was no way I would betray my Chinese clients' confidences, much less in a bull session with fellow "foreign devils." But I tried, in the spirit of the evening's camaraderie, to offer a few generic observations to help explain the snail's pace of Chinese-government decision-making. Ad-libbing, I also mentioned a related topic much on my mind—the government's fierce determination to master foreign technology, rather than continuing to merely import foreign products.

My bland response seemed to disappoint my host. "Sunshine-san, we would, of course, never ask you to disclose inside information. Just talk to us as an American. That's what we want to hear."

"Miyoshi-san, why would an American perspective on the Chinese be of interest to you and your friends? You Japanese are one hundred times better informed."

"Because your two cultures are so alike!"

I tossed discretion aside and burst out laughing. "You're kidding, right? The Americans and the Chinese? With all respect, from where I sit, if any culture closely resembles China's, it must be Japan's!"

Guffaws erupted around the room. With our host as arbiter, the opposing sides to this mostly comic debate paraded their arguments. Which nationality was the closer match with our Chinese partners? Who was better-qualified to decode Chinese behavior towards foreign business?

The Japanese team jumped in first, each member taking his playful shot.

"Chinese are just like Americans! Unsophisticated and aggressive in international relations."

"Their speech sounds harsh and grating. Every gesture lacks nuance and restraint."

"They have schoolboys' obsession with competitive sports."

The jibes came from all corners. "In negotiations, the Chinese stake out extreme positions and then never budge."

"Yet for prices, they have a street haggler's fixation on discounts."

"And a vulgar preference for quantity over quality."

As the Japanese side paused to catch collective breath, it occurred to me that either they were well-rehearsed or smarting from common slights. Our boisterous parlor game was gathering momentum. It was my turn.

"Gentlemen," I began, you are trotting out trivial stereotypes. And distortions to boot. In the process, you're ignoring the more valid Chinese and Japanese parallels.

"Any experienced American businessman trying to operate on the Chinese mainland could tick off close similarities to the Japanese. He'd complain that the Chinese never show their cards. Saving face is more important to them than admitting their problems, even when frankness could cut through an impasse.

"He'd point out that the Chinese stifle individual initiative in the classroom and in the workplace, demanding subservience to hierarchy and consensus. No surprise, then, that institutional decision-making takes forever and produces dull, conservative compromises.

"If you were still listening, the American CEO could tell you that signed Chinese contracts are not honored when conditions change. As they always do. What is worse, he'd conclude, the Chinese are suspicious of lawyers and foolishly keep them away from the bargaining table. In sum, Chinese and Japanese business cultures are not merely cousins. They're twins!"

Mr. Miyoshi was the first to laugh. Soon we were all doubling over. After another round of drinks, however, our postmortem started creeping towards seriousness. It wasn't the game's cheap shots at absent Chinese that had produced surprises. Although those salvos had been crude, we agreed that most contained a kernel of truth.

More unsettling had been the unintended revelation, if only through the Chinese prism, of a glimpse of how Japanese and American business communities saw each other. As the rhetorical dust settled, I sensed we were all as much embarrassed as amused. Leaving well enough alone, we turned to the safer terrain of baseball.

On the ride back to my hotel, I reflected on what I would never be comfortable telling Mr. Miyoshi and his friends. My Chinese clients had affirmed that the roots of mainland resistance to Japanese trade and investment were historical, not economic. Strictly in business terms, Japanese firms offered China unparalleled advantages—close proximity, superior products and processes, favorable financing, and outstanding service networks. The stumbling block was the Japanese government's refusal to officially and publicly apologize for atrocities committed in Manchuria and during World War II Occupation. Confronting and rectifying those historical humiliations was a matter of principle for the Chinese side. The Japanese authorities were equally adamant. Responding to their own nationalistic constituencies, they refused to accept receding responsibilities. So despite my dining partners' best efforts, Chinese doors were unlikely to open wide any time soon.

Leaving all of that unsaid, I had found this evening as enlightening as it was entertaining. In most international transactions, national delegations tend to carefully conceal from outsiders the bedrock values and perceptions underpinning bargaining positions and tactics. What each party prizes most dearly. Which prejudices and stereotypes distort its judgments.

Thanks to mutual curiosity and liquid lubrication, tonight those curtains had parted for a peek.

# High Stakes

*China 1988–1993*

Clammy fog soaked our clothes as we climbed the nearest stairway to the Great Wall. The sprawling parking lot at the main viewing point north of Beijing was deserted in early winter. What a contrast to the hordes clambering off tourist buses when Liu had brought me here two summers ago. Now he flashed government identification to the surly gatekeeper who reluctantly let us through. On top, the paving stones were slick with mist. We stepped with care along the dragon's undulating spine.

Liu walked in silence, then began speaking as if we'd already been in the middle of a conversation. "Russell, why are the Dutch behaving this way? Can they not see they are poisoning our working relationship before we even get started?"

"Liu, that's your Chinese long view. My guess is that these guys are strictly focused on the coming six days. With contract signing fixed for next week, they're having a last-minute panic attack and grasping for better terms."

"How can they expect to do better than a $30-million fee? Even for Westerners, that must be a fortune."

"Sure it is. That's the prize that lured them to bid on your project in the first place. That, plus preferential entry into China. But now they've been selected and are being called on to perform. It's your proverb—'be careful what you wish for.'"

"You are saying they are afraid they cannot do the job."

"Damned right they're afraid. To be managing the largest public-health project in the world? A fixed-price contract with the World Bank guarding against cost overruns? Live vaccines that can maim Chinese children if not safely produced? Guaranteed quality and quantities? Quantities one thousand times larger than anything the Dutch have ever manufactured at home? They'd be crazy not to be intimidated."

Liu pulled his collar up against the chill. "If they are having second thoughts, why not just admit they overreached and withdraw before contract signing?"

"Greed. Arrogance. And they don't want to be mocked by their global competitors. Better to claw for every advantage during negotiations and confront you at the eleventh hour with demands to restructure the entire deal. If you cave in, they've reduced their risks by 90 percent. If you balk, they can blame you for the talks' collapse. They think they've got you boxed into a corner. Either way you react, they win, you lose. For them, it's strictly a zero-sum game."

"So what do we do?"

"That's for you, Dr. Yin and your team to decide. You're in charge."

My client flinched. "I know that. I accept my responsibility. Yin accepts his. But I am asking for your advice."

"Liu, please excuse my impoliteness. I'm just focused on our predicament."

He waved me to continue.

"What you must do is stare them down. Tell them it's the original deal or no deal."

Liu's irritation flared again. "You make it sound so easy."

"Exactly the opposite. 'Easy' would be to capitulate to their demands. But if you surrendered, the Dutch would squeeze you for advance payments, make excuses for performance delays, and then slip away in the night leaving the job undone. You'd never get your production facilities or your vaccines."

I turned to face him. "You must call their bluff."

Liu gestured with gloved hands. "We have no fallback bidder. If this negotiation collapses, China will lose five, even ten, years before producing our own vaccines that can meet international standards."

"Liu, I understand China's stakes. That's why I owe you my best professional judgment, regardless of consequences. Besides, even at this crunch point, I'm not overly concerned. If you reject these Dutch demands, they may stomp and shout but they won't back out. They've invested too much in this competition. And they've been counting on this revenue to finance their firm for the coming decade."

"What if your confidence is misplaced?"

"Then you'll still be better off. No-deal is always better than a rotten deal. The World Bank is lead financer. They will help you regroup."

Liu shoved his hands in his overcoat pockets and started the trudge back. "I don't share your certainty. But I agree with you. I will speak to Yin. He and I must explain to our team and win their concurrence."

*Clearing skies. Great Wall walkabout with*
*Liu Peilong. Beijing 1990.*

By any measure, China's Vaccine Production Project was a historically ambitious undertaking. Its goal was no less than to inoculate all Chinese children against a cluster of dreaded diseases—poliomyelitis, measles, diphtheria, pertussis and tetanus. From its Beijing headquarters inside the Ministry of Public Health, the Project encompassed production facilities in Shanghai, in north-central Lanzhou, and in Kunming in southernmost Yunnan Province. With co-financing from the Chinese government, the World Bank and the Rotary International Foundation, the budget exceeded $100 million.[10]

The Chinese government's main Project objective was to acquire world-class live-vaccine production know-how, rather than continuing to rely on inferior, domestically produced vaccines. This technology-transfer agenda made the Project a prototype of pioneering significance for China's economic-development strategy.

*Vaccine Project colleagues take a break from our negotiation training seminar. Lanzhou 1990.*

Over three intermittent years, my role in this contracting marathon had steadily expanded—from legal draftsman, to bid evaluator, to the Chinese delegation's senior advisor on contract negotiations. On an evolving basis, I came to liaise between the government and its international funding agencies. Gradually, I'd become a trusted de facto member of the Chinese team.

---

10  Roughly double that in equivalent 2015 value.

The morning after our walk on the Wall, Liu Peilong, Director of the Ministry's International Loans Department, and Dr. Yin Suiya, Director of the Vaccine Project Office, assembled their negotiating team in the Ministry's large meeting room. In physical appearance, these two leaders could hardly have been less alike. Yin, tall and gaunt, bearing deep smallpox scars. Liu, short and solid, with a trace of personal style surviving from student years in Europe and the States. In their analysis and instincts, however, the odd couple smoothly meshed gears.

Twenty-five nervous bodies gradually took seats around a cracked conference table. The government's Project team included top bosses from the sponsoring Ministry and the three participating Biological Products Institutes. One and sometimes two interpreters helped me to grasp the gist of the free-flowing discussion. I could smell the sweat of agitation, though the room was brutally unheated.

Dr. Yin briefly recapped the state-of-play. I was asked to describe, without comment, the Dutch team's latest proposed contract amendments. Mr. Liu drew the bottom line—to accept or reject that restructuring ultimatum. Then discussion was thrown open to the floor.

The ensuing caucus consumed two hours. At first, the delegates were stunned to realize the negotiation was teetering on the brink of collapse. That prospect produced near-panic. Then several administrators grasped at straws, pleading that capitulation might not be so bad. Mr. Liu set this record straight, leaving no doubt that scrapping the contract's performance guarantees would leave the Dutch no incentive to achieve our required vaccine-quality and -quantity results.

At this point the scientists chimed in, reiterating their stale mantra that China didn't need foreign technology in the first place. "Let them go!" shouted one senior biologist. "We don't want them."

Dr. Yin softly reminded his peers that their self-assessment was not endorsed by the authorities. China could no longer afford to continue denying that its process know-how lagged decades behind.

In the end, with much grumbling and visible trepidation, the roundtable endorsed their leaders' recommended plan. The Chinese side would reject the Dutch demands and take the consequences. The possibility of a collapse was so intimidating that, for the first time in three years, the team opted not to meet the Dutch as a full delegation. They sent Yin, Liu and myself as their proxies.

We went directly from the bleak Ministry premises to the Oriental Hotel's atrium lobby, resplendent in mauve and gold. The Dutch team had commandeered two sofas across a large coffee table. Tygo Jansink, the Dutch engineering firm's Project Director, waved us expansively over.

With him were his two senior colleagues. Norbert Vann was the firm's contract lawyer, a quiet but tenacious advocate in rimless eyeglasses and an unvarying black suit. Andries Spijker, the consortium's lead scientist, headed up the team's technology-transfer and training unit.

Mr. Jansink was all smiles as we approached, but his sweat-beaded forehead was a giveaway. "Dr. Yin, Mr. Liu, so good of you to come. We'd have been happy to travel to the Ministry, as usual, but this venue gives us an opportunity to offer you tea."

I didn't react to his excluding me from his greeting. Mr. Jansink divided his world into patrons and peons.

As hotel waiters served refreshments at his nod, the Dutch team leader delivered his sugar-coated set piece. "Chinese friends, after all we've all been through together, the end is in sight. The lawyers have arm-wrestled over adverbs and semicolons. But we three," with a bow to Dr. Yin and Mr. Liu, "have kept our sights on the larger common ground.

"I am truly sorry if we've inconvenienced the Chinese side by proposing late contract clarifications. But my Board of Directors insists on realistic limits to their corporate exposure before I am authorized to sign. I hope your arrival here this afternoon confirms that you have reached the same conclusion."

Dr. Yin set his cup down. "Mr. Jansink, the Chinese side has carefully considered your latest demands. We have regretfully concluded that those demands are unreasonable. They would destroy the agreed foundation of our balanced relationship."

Mr. Jansink's fixed smile evaporated. Norbert Vann began taking notes.

Dr. Yin's deep bass continued. "You are an engineer, Mr. Jansink. I do not have to remind you this is not a conventional engineering contract. It is a guaranteed technology transfer. We must have successful results, for the sake of Chinese children and our country's scientific independence."

"I don't understand."

Mr. Liu took his cue. "Mr. Jansink, I believe you do. You knew our requirements from the beginning. The Bid Documents were unambiguous. We require three facilities producing three live vaccines in agreed quantities and qualities. Any failures to reach those targets and standards will be the Dutch party's responsibility, to be corrected, at your expense, without financial limit. And without contract amendments."

Mr. Jansink's hands were both on the table as he leaned forward for emphasis. "And if we refuse to withdraw our amendments?"

"Then we have no contract to sign."

Mr. Jansink flushed and rose to his feet. He was small but towered over the seated group. "And then where will you go, Director Liu? You have no other bidders. Where will that stubbornness leave you?"

Dr. Yin took back the gavel. "In that case, Mr. Jansink, you would no longer be our partner. It would be for us to decide on next steps."

"Well, fuck you!' Fuck all of you!" The obscenity came with flying saliva, silencing refined atrium buzz.

Mr. Jansink threw down his crushed napkin, rattling the immaculate tea service. He pivoted to his companions. "We're done here, Gentlemen. Andries, check us out. Bert, call KLM and get us on the next flight home. We've wasted two precious years, only to have the goddamned door slammed in our faces."

Left alone in our seats, for a long moment we said nothing. Dr. Yin was very pale.

Mr. Liu was controlled but plainly insulted. "Violent oaths are demeaning, but revealing."

After the storm, I felt eerily calm. "Not pleasant, I know. But not unexpected. Please don't overreact to Jansink's tirade. The Dutch delegation will come crawling back. As soon as their leader gets his high blood pressure under control."

Dr. Yin was more pessimistic. But he didn't hesitate to shift into action. "Mr. Sunshine, I am sending you to Washington on tonight's flight. I do not want the World Bank to hear a distorted account of this unfortunate confrontation."

"Doctor, who will you send with me from our team?

"Go alone. We trust you to represent our interests. The World Bank recommended you to us in the first place. So they trust you too. You're the best person to persuade them to help save our Project."

While I made rushed travel arrangements, Yin and Liu administered first aid to their distressed delegation.

At World Bank headquarters in Washington, I worked with the Bank's supervision team to honor the Chinese government's project goals while allaying the Dutch contractor's concerns. Together we crafted a win/win compromise that we thought could dissolve the negotiators' impasse. The government would retain its contractual guarantee that the Dutch must produce all required vaccines, in the specified quality and quantities. But the Dutch firm would be granted a moderate financial ceiling capping potential penalties for performance delays.

While this Washington salvage operation was still in progress, a chagrined Mr. Jansink telephoned Dr. Yin from Hong Kong. He apologized for his atrium outburst, attributing it to lack of sleep and the stress of protracted negotiations. He'd decided not to continue on to the Netherlands. He would lay over in Hong Kong and hope to receive a renewed invitation to Beijing.

After a cooling-off period during New Year's holidays, the two parties accepted our suggested compromise. All the principals returned to Beijing for contract signing on January 25, 1990.

Smile firmly restored, Mr. Jansink was pouring belated champagne. My glass tasted sour with apprehension. The parties had made it to the wedding. Staying married would be another matter.

Dr. Yin took me aside for a private toast. "Friend Sunshine, you know that, for centuries, we Chinese have called foreigners 'barbarians.' Not always in jest! I want to be sure that you also know I give frequent thanks you are *our* barbarian!"

Today China is the world's largest manufacturer and exporter of refrigerators, as well as myriads of other industrial and commercial products. Despite entrenched historical grievances, she has pragmatically accepted Japan as her largest trading partner.

After its rocky start, the Vaccine Production Project remained operational for a dozen years. It was probably inevitable, given both parties' cross-cultural suspicions and inflated assessments of their own capabilities, that the Project never fully achieved all our ambitious goals. That said, the collaboration became a pioneering conduit for the modernization of Chinese bio-technology, accelerating the Republic's emergence into the global economy.

My personal involvement in this historic transformation was doubly privileged. First, I was invited in early, before the economy's dramatic take-off. During that pivotal threshold period, the Chinese knew they needed foreign know-how but not how to get it. Second, to help plug their learning gap, I was engaged to advise Chinese negotiating teams on how to deal effectively with multinational corporations. This singular intimacy set me apart from virtually all other international consultants then operating in the country. Those consultants, and the clients they represented, were outsiders knocking on the Chinese door. This barbarian stood inside, defending that door.

My China bore no resemblance to today's sparkling Shanghai skyscrapers. It was glaringly impoverished and underdeveloped, even in privileged strata. My senior counterparts, despite their high rank, still lived in spartan dormitories. They and their compatriots were driven by fierce national and professional ambition.

I witnessed close at hand the pervasive inferiority complex that constrained so many Chinese interactions with foreigners. Schooled since childhood about the imperialistic abuses of occupying powers— Europe and the United States in the nineteenth century, Japan in the twentieth—Chinese leaders and representatives were obsessed with reclaiming international respect. This determination led them repeatedly to harm their self-interest by digging in their heels with extreme bargaining positions and by taking offense at perceived slights. Catching-up was a national fixation, in laboratories and on factory floors in addition to sports arenas.

Without doubt, authoritarianism cast an inhibiting cloud over my efforts in China. In my first Beijing days, my local contacts had to debrief government security agencies' "foreign watchers" after our conversations. However, few of my Chinese colleagues or clients were committed ideologues or even much interested in politics. They tolerated Party monitoring as an unavoidable intrusion. But ingeniously they found ways to exercise an increasing degree of personal freedom.

The authorities, for their part, were sufficiently shrewd to ensure that at least most urban families shared in the improving national economic conditions. I inferred, as outside pundits also observed, that the controlling regime was offering its subjects a tacit social contract: unprecedented individual and family participation in a rising standard of living, in exchange for social and political stability (i.e., no tolerated dissent.) In the first surge of accelerating prosperity, few paused to consider whether this pragmatic but precarious bargain could be sustained, especially if growth were to lose momentum.

CHINA

BURMA

HANOI

Luang • Prabang

VIETNAM

VIENTIANE

THAILAND

L A O S

BANGKOK

**LAOS AND
ITS NEIGHBORS**

*1990–1993*

CHAPTER SEVEN

# LAOS:
# OPENING LONG-SEALED DOORS

In 1990, my international consulting career carried me to Laos, the landlocked Southeast Asian country sandwiched between Thailand and Vietnam. Laos was desperately poor in economic terms but rich in the gentle and dignified Buddhist culture of its citizens.

The nation had suffered a tragic modern history, ironically cemented by its victory in the Vietnam War shared with its allies and patrons, the Vietnamese. After December 1975, when the dominant Lao Communist Party seized unilateral control of the national government, retaliatory international isolation was swiftly imposed. The bulk of Laos's skilled workforce—civil servants, professionals and entrepreneurs—fled in a mass exodus. Many of the unlucky remainder were sent to punitive "re-education" camps.

National economic productivity drastically contracted. Even subsistence agriculture was crippled by the plague of lethal ordnance carpeting the landscape. (The American military had dropped more bombs on Laos during the Vietnam War than it did globally during World War II. An estimated one-third of those weapons remained unexploded, rendering vast fertile areas out-of-bounds for cultivation.)

Educational services collapsed, replacing already frayed remnants of French colonial curricula with socio-political propaganda. By default, Laos's external contacts were basically limited to the Soviet bloc. Market-oriented learning and skill-building were taboo. The study of Western languages was actively discouraged, even though (or because) French had been the working tongue of the Lao elite for 100 years. The Lao People's Democratic Republic subsided into 15 years of stultifying hibernation.

Finally, the pragmatic, if still Marxist-Leninist, national leadership decided that enough was enough. Launching an "Open Door" policy in 1989, the Lao government reached out to the United Nations to help guide the country's re-emergence into the global economy. I was chosen to head up one of the first teams to go in. Our mission was to help Laos attract private foreign investment without getting trampled in the process.

I approached this assignment with curiosity and excitement, but also no small degree of trepidation. In China, I'd been working as an individual technical advisor. In Laos, I'd be leading a large multinational squad. Most of those experts would be economists. I was a lawyer. Most would be European. I was American.

The consulting firm that was hiring us was Paris-based. And most of the senior Lao officials I'd be advising spoke French rather than English. I'd minored in French Literature at Yale 25 years before, but my accent had never progressed beyond Californian.

UNDP (the United Nations Development Program) was sponsoring this Project. But the World Bank had direct supervision. These two agencies were known to have diametrically-opposed institutional cultures and a prickly operating relationship.

All in all, no small basket of reservations to juggle on my way in to Southeast Asia.

Thankfully, as things worked out, our intervention was remarkably productive. Our experts designed and drafted a legal framework for doing business in the new Laos that received international kudos for its transparency and competitiveness. The Project organized familiarization trips to Thailand and Malaysia for our Lao-government colleagues to observe successful investment-management precedents on the ground. Having helped to identify economic sectors where Laos enjoyed a potential comparative advantage (including ecotourism, small-scale export agriculture, hydro-generation of electricity and mining), we hosted investment-promotion forums in Vientiane, Sydney and Paris. The forums' message to responsible investors was that Laos deserved a fresh look. To drive home the point, we publicized the new Friendship Bridge across the Mekong being financed and constructed with Australian aid, and the East-West Regional Highway planned with Vietnamese support. Laos, the landlocked backwater, was strategically positioned to assert a new role as a land-linked hub.

During the three years of our UNDP Project presence, Laos attracted $1 billion in new foreign investment. More per capita than booming Vietnam next door.

Markedly less successful were our team's efforts to transfer sustainable investment-management knowhow to our Lao professional counterparts. With hindsight, this disappointment was probably inevitable. When we'd arrived, there reputedly remained in post-diaspora Laos only seven university graduates, in a population of four million citizens. Here, as elsewhere, impatient donor agencies like the Asian Development Bank and the World Bank were financing technical-assistance interventions of only two years' duration to address capacity-building challenges requiring 15-20 years of sustained support. Equally debilitating, potent commercial and political interests within and without the country were maneuvering to undermine the Open Door and its associated level playing field.

The combined effect of these constraints was to sap investment-promotion momentum soon after our expatriate advisory team withdrew. Bureaucratic inconsistency and protracted delays replaced prompt, even-handed business-licensing. Bribery and misprocurement became all too common. Foreign-investor confidence and commitments accordingly plummeted.

Twenty-five years on, Laos has enjoyed a series of years with national economic growth approaching 8%. China and Vietnam are contesting for economic domination and political influence. Reasserting a claim to regional hegemony, China has been showering Laos with scholarships, aid and infrastructure investments. The first segment of the planned Chinese railway linking Kunming to Singapore was recently inaugurated in Vientiane. Counterbalancing this trend, the latest Party leadership shuffles suggest Laos may be tilting again towards Vietnam. If so, this could have profound implications for Chinese-promoted initiatives including hydropower and Mekong development. As always, the reticent but resilient Lao are maneuvering to avoid getting trampled by neighborhood elephants.

# LAYERED LAO

*Vientiane 1991–93*

From the moment I set foot in Vientiane, I was intrigued by the Lao temperament. Intrigued, but also baffled. I found the Lao harder to read than any other culture I'd worked with, even the "inscrutable" Chinese. My preoccupation was more than pop anthropology. As UNDP's Chief Technical Advisor in charge of attracting foreign investment, I needed to understand local perceptions and perspectives in order to effectively counsel national decision-makers and train host-country counterparts.

On the surface, there was much to admire. The Lao were unfailingly pleasant and gracious in their social interactions. Smiling, soft-spoken, neat as a pin, graceful in posture and movement, the locals seemed intuitively to maintain dignity and decorum.

Yet even in my earliest days, I began to find this unwavering gentility curiously off-putting. Was I observing Buddhist equanimity, tropical lethargy, or some distinctively Lao combination of the two?

The Minister of Economy was graciously hosting a reception at his home for our Project's visiting specialists. Now his living room had been cleared for after-dinner entertainment. A small orchestra of traditional stringed instruments started up and the senior officials and their wives led the *lam vong*. The couples formed two large concentric circles, ladies within, gents without. The circles wheeled in opposite directions to a hand-drum's slow beat. The dancers advanced, turned to face the other circle, then continued on their way.

The figures were relaxed but poised, with no movement of torsos or hips. Dancers raised their arms, elbows bent, hands in front of the chest. With fingers extended in graceful arcs, the hands flowed up and down in alternation, wrists and palms rotating. The stylized gestures paid tacit homage to classical Indian and Khmer inspirations from centuries ago.

As the twangy melodies rose and fell, Ministry staffers invited the expatriate guests to join the rotations. We did our best to fit in and imitate the movements. Our Lao hosts were smiling, some almost playful, but no words were exchanged in this courtly mime. At the end of each number, couples rejoined and saluted each other with the palms-together *nop* greeting.

One foreigner's *sotto voce* aside neatly captured my own first impressions. "It's charming and sweet. But if they moved any slower, you couldn't call it a dance."

A snail's pace on the dance floor was eccentric. In the workplace, it was debilitating. Cynics at the Australian Club mocked torpor as a national ailment. "The Vietnamese cultivate rice," went the jibe. "The Lao watch it grow."

I reserved judgment on this sneer, but indolence was not my sole concern. The Laos' unshakeable restraint, even when provoked, seemed to me to approach the pathological.

Our progress slowed to a crawl in Vientiane's morning traffic. In the back seat of my UNDP sedan, I looked up from a file.

"An accident, sir," Khun Kham, my driver, anticipated my question. "Girl knocked off bicycle."

In the middle of the crowded intersection, a young woman sat dazed on the pavement, her bike knocked from under her by the car stopped just beyond. One sleeve of her white blouse was soiled, the elbow torn and bloodied. Both her palms looked nastily scraped. She rolled to her knees and stood up, demurely readjusting her wrapped tube skirt.

The offending driver stepped out of his car to inquire about his victim's injuries. Through my window, I could see the woman's reassuring smile. She gave him a slight bow, fingers steepled in a *nop*, scooped up her papers and wheeled her dented bicycle to the curb.

To me, incongruous incidents like this seemed to symbolize the daily conflicts between traditional culture's inculcated reserve and modernization's intruding stresses. I couldn't but wonder which tide would prevail.

*With my cross-cultural mentor, Sipraseuth Chanthapanya. Vientiane 1991.*

Now in close working contact with Lao colleagues and clients, I continued to puzzle over those imperturbable countenances. What lay behind and beneath? It defied logic that an entire nationality could be serene to the core. But, if not, what explained such resolute cordiality?

By good fortune, I had daily access to an insightful tutor. Sipraseuth Chanthapanya, my Executive Assistant, was a development-assistance veteran. She came highly recommended for her diligence and initiative. What I valued even more was her perceptivity. For three years we sustained a rolling seminar.

"Seuth, why are our Lao counterparts so passive? I get so frustrated. Why don't they show some enthusiasm? I don't need them to agree with me, just to react."

"Lao are always guided by what you don't see," she would patiently explain. "First and foremost, the leadership's resistance to change. You're a foreign advisor. You're expected to critique the way things are here, to propose new ideas. Your Lao colleagues dare not take that risk. Safer for them to let you stand in front. Stand or fall."

Or in the same vein, "Russell, your counterparts are all permanent staff within the Ministry of Economy. Just seconded to you for the brief duration of our UNDP Project. When you leave, they will have to squeeze back into the roster. Prudent for them not to be seen too close to you. Okay to join your study tours, take your training courses, pocket your per diems. But without burning bridges."

I asked Sipraseuth about her countrymen's remarkable sangfroid. "*Bo pen yang*" ("Not to worry") seemed the national motto.

She issued a caution. "Buddhism and elders teach us composure from childhood. But do not think we are saints. Smiles conceal deep feelings." And without naming names, she'd recite sagas of extended-family vendettas that spanned generations.

If more complexity were needed, I became aware of extreme conservatism in Lao social and sexual values. A marked reserve characterized every public interaction, even among intimates. Physical contact in public was virtually non-existent. When Nancy asked a close Lao acquaintance why even spouses never embraced at the airport when one of them was returning after a long absence, the response came instinctively, with a shudder. "Only dogs do it in the road."

From my reading and observations, I learned that psychological strata were not the only Lao layers. This nominally egalitarian Marxist-Leninist society enforced strict hierarchies. Each Ministry, of course, had its bureaucratic ladder, patrons and protégés. But behind and above the government, the Communist Party's Central Committee and Politburo exercised total control. Invisible to foreigners, the Party placed monitors within every government agency, tracking and enforcing strict adherence to its directives.

The military had its own power base. Virtually independent, it generated vast revenues through ownership of the largest State-owned Enterprises. Seldom seen in Vientiane, the top brass controlled and exploited vast provincial tracts and natural resources. Their rapacious logging of tropical hardwoods was notorious.

Privileged families constituted still another hierarchy. Decades after the dissolution of the royal court at Luang Prabang, these aristocrats and former landowners retained educational advantages, prestige and influence, secured by offshore wealth, relatives and remittances.

With so many masters and watchers, it was no wonder that mid-level functionaries kept their cards close to their chests.

"How does one get anything done?" I asked my cross-cultural tutor.

Her answer came with a wink. "Watch Boun Omme."

My main national partner, Mr. Boun Omme Southichak, was the senior civil servant in charge of foreign investment. This diminutive colleague had a towering public stature. Boun Omme's professional experience and judgment were well-respected by compatriots and foreigners alike.

In his youth, he'd been spotted by the French colonial authorities as a promising talent and whisked off to Paris for legal training. He'd remained abroad during Laos's protracted military conflicts, rising in United Nations service to a responsible position in Geneva. Then drawn by patriotism, he'd returned to serve national recovery.

Now in his mid-50s, he'd been tapped by the leadership to help usher the announced Open Door Policy to operational reality. I welcomed his measured legal analyses and grace under pressure.

What puzzled me at first was his self-effacement. I knew Boun Omme to be a bright problem-solver, far sharper than most national officials and foreign visitors he was briefing. Yet he always held back, deferring to titles, voicing opinions only when invited, often channeling his inputs through principals so they'd get the credit.

Gradually, I came to appreciate this low profile and indirection as "locally appropriate technology." From the back of the room, Boun Omme was masterfully working the system.

Through his example and those of other respected Lao colleagues, I began seeing through local eyes. On my best days, I could even emulate their approach.

An American businessman was throwing a high-volume tantrum at the front desk of the Lane Xang Hotel. "Get me the General Manager! This bozo's trying to cheat me," jabbing an indignant index finger in the face of the imperturbable cashier.

Passing through the lobby, I winced for my Lao lunch guests at this tirade. I decided to risk an impromptu intervention. "Excuse me, Sir, what seems to be the problem?"

"Who are you, Buster, and why's it any of your business?"

"I live and work here. Perhaps I can help."

"These guys are trying to stiff me for two Kraut beers out of my mini-bar. Their scam won't work. I only drink Bud."

"Is there anyone else in your party?"

The foreigner swiveled to confront a heavy-set woman stepping out of the lobby gift shop. "Madge, have you been raiding our room bar?"

"For Christ's sake, Harry, after 30 years I'm supposed to ask permission? Just be glad it wasn't champagne."

I spoke softly to the approaching Manager. "Mr. Vieng, I believe the gentleman is now ready to settle his account."

Of course, I wasn't Lao but American. So I retained a deep-seated preference for directness. This predisposition led me to seek out and admire rare examples of Lao assertiveness.

One paragon in this context was Madame Khempheng Pholsena, the Deputy Minister of Economic Planning. An incisive decision-maker, she was never afraid to speak her mind. She helped me to navigate past bureaucratic impasses on a half-dozen occasions. In Ministerial debates, she consistently prevailed over male counterparts by marshaling quick wits, superior preparation and insightful analysis. To be sure, her bargaining position was not weakened by her high-ranking family pedigree.

Another forceful pragmatist was my main client, Investment Minister Phao Bounnaphol. I asked him on one occasion when we were alone in his office if he were struck by the irony of our pairing. Here was the former Commander-in-Chief of the Pathet Lao Air Force engaging an American citizen as his confidential advisor.

"Mr. Sunshine," he grinned, "so long as you continue to give me sound advice and keep it between the two of us, I don't care whether your passport is red, green or blue!"

And in another, more somber exchange, "As far as the War of Liberation is concerned, we will never forget. But if we are to move forward, we must forgive."

At this time, America was skillfully represented by a gifted Ambassador, Charles Salmon. Savvy and sociable, Charlie had served with distinction in a half-dozen posts across the Asia-Pacific Region. But in Laos, his talents were restrained by Washington directives that required him to focus bilateral relations on searches for the remains of MIAs and drug interdiction. Laos's glaring development-assistance needs were largely being addressed by other bilateral and multilateral organizations.

Perhaps because of his military background, Minister Phao, alone among my official Lao acquaintances, was not averse to engaging in public confrontations. At a get-acquainted assembly in Bangkok hosted for my Lao colleagues by the powerful Thai Board of Investment, the presiding Thai Minister made no effort to conceal his disdain. "We will try to enlighten our Lao cousins with the lessons of our success," he assured in his toast. "Although you must permit me to observe that the gap between our respective levels of development may make those lessons difficult for you to absorb."

Minister Phao, our Lao delegation's leader, didn't miss a beat. "Excellency, we will do our best to give your lessons diligent study. You may permit me to observe that I anticipate we will find the failures as enlightening as the successes."

# Royal Capital

*Luang Prabang 1991*

The Fokker Friendship was the most reliable aircraft in the Lao Aviation fleet. And its Scandinavian trainer-pilots were uniformly respected. But this afternoon, our plane was bucking like a mustang. Spiraling down into the bowl of hills surrounding Luang Prabang was an adventure even in smooth air. In severe turbulence, it was a nail-biter. Out the passenger windows we couldn't see the airport directly below. What we *could* see was a swirl of sheer green cliff-faces far closer than we cared to measure. As much as Nancy and I had been itching to get out of Vientiane, we were having second thoughts about our timing.

Despite Laos's declared Open Door Policy, the cautious national government was still severely restricting foreigners' in-country travel. As a United Nations Project Manager, I could and did move about freely on official business. But private individuals like Nancy needed a *laissez-passer* merely to step outside Vientiane. And for all non-official in-country travel, foreign residents and visitors alike were required to use the services of government-owned Lao Tourism.

The firm's four-wheel-drive Toyota truck met us now at the Luang Prabang Airport. The single runway and bare-bones terminal were of modest proportions. Our driver and guide would remain with us as attentive escorts during virtually all of our five-day visit.

On this first excursion to Luang Prabang, I was wearing two hats. As a vacationer, I was keen to glimpse the city's layered heritage before things really opened up to tourism. Luang Prabang had been the Lao Kingdom's royal capital and religious center from the late fourteenth century CE until 1975 when the Communists had seized unilateral control of the government. It had also been the headquarters of the French colonial administration from the mid-nineteenth to mid-twentieth centuries. Under my second hat as the government's Resident Foreign Investment Advisor, I wanted to gain an on-the-ground impression of the city's potential to attract up-market tourism.

Our guesthouse provided immediate evidence relevant to both hats. The *Villa de la Princesse*, as its name implied, laid claim to past occupation as the personal residence of a member of the Royal Family. Now it was a modestly attractive 11-room inn in which our second-floor room and balcony overlooked the town and ridges beyond. The town setting was optimal, on a peninsula at the confluence of the Mekong and Nam Khan Rivers. Those mountains, which we'd first experienced in the plane, were impressively steep, sharp and green. Nancy dubbed them "sleeping stegosauruses", and they contributed an appreciated contrast to Vientiane's flat alluvial plain.

On the downside, as we soon discovered, municipal electricity was only operating from 6 to 10 p.m. and from 4 to 7:30 a.m. Priding ourselves as developing-country veterans, we promptly adopted a daily program of evening showers and froze water bottles in our fridge every evening so they'd slowly melt during the day. We took advantage of those same electrified evening hours to run our room air-conditioner, after which open windows, frequent rains and the town's elevation kept us reasonably cool for a good night's sleep.

After unpacking and freshening up, we visited the town's best-restored Buddhist temple. (Thirty of 60 original temples and monasteries within the city boundaries were still standing, though many in disrepair.) Wat Xieng Thong had been constructed by the King in 1560 CE. A strikingly handsome white-walled structure with steeply-tiered orange tile roofs, the temple featured stylized *naga* snakes at each roof corner and a metal parasol on its crown signifying royal patronage. Inside, a gold-painted statue of Buddha 15 feet tall dominated the central space, flanked by smaller chapels and statues. The temple's interior columns and ceilings were decorated in gold designs on vermillion backgrounds. The sanctuary's atmosphere was peaceful, mystical and welcoming.

*Wat Xieng Thong Temple complex. Luang Prabang 1991.*

*Guardian images. Luang Prabang 1991.*

The Royal Palace had been converted to a museum but mostly stripped of its original furniture and trappings. Its bare, mold-stained walls were a melancholy testament to neglect.

Our next three days took us outside Luang Prabang on a series of itineraries tightly programmed by our Lao Tourism handlers. Although Nancy and I were normally fiercely independent travelers, on this occasion, since we both planned to return, we went along for the ride.

Our first excursion was a two-hour, 20-mile jounce over rough unpaved roads to Kuang Si Falls. Our driver, through the guide's interpretation, confirmed that all regional roads were in comparable terrible condition. Apparently as the result of governmental budget constraints, equipment shortages and a lack of skilled labor, no major road upgrades were yet being undertaken. The falls, though, were lovely. They descended in tiers for perhaps 300 total feet, with vibrant fern-filled grottoes at each stage. UNDP had established a modest park at the bottom with picnic tables and trailheads. But the lack of any toilet or clean-water facilities underlined that this was a work in progress.

Our second-day's destination, up in the mountains on an even worse road, was the only truly negative experience in this vacation. Our government guide had enthusiastically promoted this visit to a hill-tribe village—to see "authentic" rural life and purchase distinctive handcrafted textiles. The distasteful reality bore no resemblance to this oblivious PR. The Hmong village was a dispiriting cul-de-sac of poverty and ill health. With the male villagers away working in the fields, we met mostly women and children. They were lethargic and passive and, not unreasonably, seemed to resent being exploited as exotic fauna on display. Nancy spoke with the schoolteacher, through the interpreter, about health, education, nutrition and desperately needed development assistance. But the villagers' prospects were obviously grim. Perhaps again due to governmental resource constraints but also, I feared, because many Hmong had fought against the Communists in the Civil War, these desperate rural dwellers were at the bottom of the pecking order.

More pleasant was our next-day's boat ride on the Mekong River.

Even with the river level 20 to 30 feet below its post-monsoon crest, there was considerable water traffic in both directions. At Pak Ou Caves, thousands of Buddha statues from one inch to six feet high filled a series of grottoes climbing steeply up from the riverbank. The whole site was shabby and run-down, but still-standing iron-grillwork gates gave evidence of its former luster. Our guide explained that the king had once paid annual visits to bless the site. A platform remained from this ceremony. We were told that the Australian Embassy planned to rehabilitate the site.

In between excursions, we made time to wander Luang Prabang streets, especially admiring surviving structures from the French Indochina Empire. Laos's Communist and patriotic regime lacked enthusiasm for restoring and celebrating the country's colonial architecture. But my Project colleagues and I were convinced this legacy was a major drawing card for *Indochine* buffs, if the political hurdles could be cleared.

We also sampled and enjoyed diverse cuisine, embracing both homage to French traditions and fresh local fare. Imported wines were inferior but not prohibitive. Beer Lao, as always, was delicious.

On our last night, we were treated to a natural sound-and-light display that was the highlight of the entire trip. An operatic storm struck with buffeting winds and artillery-barrage thunder. The main act was an hour-long lightening extravaganza, with strikes flashing in sheets, ground-to-air and air-to-ground. Most stunning were the horizontal bolts, like visible electricity racing along a high-voltage line. Our hoteliers assured us this was not an exceptional tumult. We were thrilled and fascinated but glad to be watching the production through the windows of our room.

On our last day while waiting for our on-again-off-again departure flight back to Vientiane, we climbed the 328 steps to Phou Si Hill in the town center, topped by a golden stupa and fabulous 360-degree views.

We came away charmed by even the neglected remnants of Luang Prabang's noble heritage. And more than a little concerned about the city's vulnerability to future tourism development.

*In our Vientiane garden before the new arrival. 1991.*

# Un–Pet

*Vientiane 1991*

I was reading a book on the garden swing. Khamsing approached across the lawn.

"Sir, man ask for Madame Carroll."

Carroll Long had been the UN Country Representative before Ameerah Haq. She had lived in the Vientiane house we now occupied and people still sometimes called for her.

"Khamsing, did you tell him Madame Carroll is no longer in Laos?"

"Yes, but he want to speak with you."

At our gate I found a forty-something Lao man still sitting astride his bicycle. Through Khamsing's interpretation, I explained that Madame Long had moved on to another country. The reply seemed a non-sequitur.

"He asks, Sir, if you want to buy the animal."

"I don't understand, Khamsing. What animal?" The bicycle was empty except for a crumpled scarf in the front basket.

"Monkey, Sir. The man's friend found it in the forest."

The man may have understood some English because he seemed to take Khamsing's explanation as his cue. Dismounting and setting his kick-stand, he gave a light tug with his left arm.

I now noticed his wrist was attached to the scarf by a light string.

Like a conjuror's trick, the scarf rose in accordion sections and climbed out of the basket. On the ground stood a baby gibbon, two feet tall from toes to crown.

I thought it was one of the most beautiful creatures I had ever seen. With the same limbs as people or other primates, but proportions that seemed like an alien fallen to earth. The animal's body was smaller and lighter than a housecat's. But its arms and legs were incredibly long. The lack of fat on these slender appendages made this elongation even more exaggerated.

The gibbon's fur was a lustrous black. The only exception was pale-beige mutton-chop whiskers on a small, triangular mannish face, with black, deep-set eyes. The animal stood silently, grasping the bicycle-man's hand.

"Khamsing, it's only a baby. Where is its mother?"

"Gone, Sir. No mother. Baby only."

Nancy and I knew that wild animals were often hunted and trapped in the forests. Or scooped up after trees were flattened by logging operations. We also knew that bush meat was considered a local delicacy.

"What does he want from me, Khamsing?"

"Buy, Sir. Buy and eat."

By now, Nancy had observed the conversation from the house and joined us at the front gate. The two of us held a hushed family caucus to weigh our ethical dilemmas. Our best solution would have been to take the animal and then arrange to have it returned to the wild. But the government prohibited foreigners' travel outside Vientiane without a special permit. This mission of mercy would not pass muster.

Monkeys and gibbons had been kept as pets for centuries in Southeast Asia. The idea of this defenseless creature being dismembered for a neighborhood cook pot was repugnant to us both. We had no experience with primates but had fostered puppies and kittens.

We told the man we'd think it over and he said he'd come back later. He worked at the Swedish Embassy nearby so he'd have no trouble returning.

Nancy and I knew an American who had worked for years in Thailand and Laos. George was an agricultural and livestock specialist, so we thought he might be able to tell us about the practicality of caring for a gibbon. It was a longshot but we wanted more information before washing our hands of the orphan.

As luck would have it, when I was out at Wattay Airport that same afternoon to greet some short-term experts arriving to join my Project team, I bumped into George. To my surprise, he was strongly encouraging. Gibbons, he assured me, were highly intelligent, a quick study and easily domesticated. Their diet was a simple blend of readily available fruit, nuts and vegetables. Despite their emaciated look, they were hardy and not highly susceptible to infections. You could keep them on a lead clipped to a fixed wire. A cardboard box with a soft towel could serve as sleeping quarters. Unlike a doghouse, however, you should put the box high off the ground where the animal could feel safe when it rested. George thought Nancy and I should give it a try.

*Nancy and our houseguest getting acquainted. Vientiane 1991.*

When the man passed by our gate again in the late afternoon, we took in a boarder.

Our first purchase was a soft dog collar. With this as a belt, the gibbon could have maximum freedom of movement. In the outbuilding behind our house, there was an open room at the end—roofed but allowing in fresh air on the side and front. Khamsing and I bolted a wire to the walls eight feet up. It stretched ten feet from side to side. We clipped a thin linked chain like a bicycle chain to the wire, attaching the other end to the animal's belt. The room had a wide shelf just above the wire and there we placed a sleeping box. An extra wooden ladder would give the gibbon a conduit up and down if it needed it. A waist-high countertop was ideal for food and water bowls. We were in business.

The gibbon was as curious about its new quarters as we were about the gibbon. The animal was incredibly agile, with nimble fingers and toes. It obviously found the chain confining but we hoped this unfamiliarity would be temporary.

My research at the UN Country Office library revealed fascinating background information. Our guest was a member of one of several gibbon species native to the mountains straddling Laos and Vietnam. As we'd already witnessed, gibbons could walk bi-pedally, with arms raised for balance. They excelled at tree-top locomotion, swinging like trapeze artists in 50-foot leaps at up to 35 miles per hour. What made this performance possible was a unique ball-and-socket wrist joint. This flexibility reduced stress on shoulders, upper arms and torsos. Gibbons were social animals, preferring companionship, and were strongly territorial. More disturbing, all 17 species of gibbons across Southeast Asia were listed as endangered, due to loss of habitat from agriculture and forestry.

Nancy and I agreed to spend as much time as possible with the young ape during its settling-in period. I sat with it three times a day, early morning, mid-day and late afternoon after work. I was strongly attracted to its sensitivity. The animal would chatter when I approached and then watch me intently with large eyes. Often it would climb down and sit on my lap. Sometimes it groomed my forearms, scratching or nipping without breaking the skin. What I most liked was when the gibbon napped in my arms.

Trying not to be sentimental, I felt an inarticulate connection to this fellow creature. From the outset, the gibbon never exhibited fear. We would watch each other for long moments, occasionally touch each other, or mostly just be together.

What upset me was its sudden screaming whenever I left. I had no choice but to keep on with my life. But the cries were piercing and wrenching.

Nancy too had intended to sit regularly with the animal, mornings and afternoons while I was at the office. But a severe respiratory infection keep her bed-ridden for two weeks. We later wondered if this would have made a difference. Probably not. The household staff were also fascinated and attentive, so the animal got lots of company.

Contrary to our expectations, the gibbon grew more, not less, uncomfortable and unhappy. The key obstacle to its adjustment seemed to be the chain. Unlike a dog, and perhaps because of its supreme flexibility, the gibbon never adjusted to the lead. It tied itself in knots to the point of immobility, especially when anxious after I left it alone. I'd often return home to find it tangled and trapped, exhausted from its struggles. I'd try to calm it with soft words while I slowly unraveled the links. The animal would let me tease out the knots and not fight me or struggle. But then the cycle would repeat itself every time I walked away.

After a fortnight of frustration and discouragement, Nancy and I reluctantly concluded our well-intended experiment was not working out. Happily and unhappily, we found the gibbon a better home. Through a mutual friend, we met a Frenchman who worked on an irrigation project in northern Laos. He was very fond of animals and hosted several of them on a 35-acre project plot outside the provincial capital of Oudomsay.

He collected the gibbon in our garden and placed it in a small cage with padding and water during transport. They travelled together by helicopter to the site, the only way to get there in the rainy season. There the animal would be able to range free in a protected area, with an attendant to feed and look after him. This, after all, had been what we'd hoped for from the beginning, though we hadn't been able to figure out how to make it happen.

Nancy's letter to our Stateside families only hinted at our ambivalence. "We are sorry to see him go, but it's much better for him. And for us too, I guess."

# Family Funeral

*Vientiane 1993*

Saddened co-workers at the Ministry of Economy, where our UNDP Project Office was located, informed me of the passing of Boun Omme's father. Like my own father, he had died at the age of 83, after a long illness. I asked Sipraseuth if there'd be a funeral and whether it would be appropriate for Nancy and me to attend. Boun Omme was becoming my cherished personal friend, as well as a valued professional colleague.

She explained that there would be a cremation in three days' time. But first there'd be a vigil at the extended-family's compound. She encouraged me, as Boun Omme's senior foreign counterpart, to visit the home to convey my condolences.

When I arrived at the substantial residence, I joined the stream of mourners taking off our shoes on the front porch and stepping over the threshold. The two main ground-floor rooms had been cleared of all furniture. In the closer one, the deceased's body lay on a simple floor mat, surrounded by creamy lotus blossoms and glowing oil lamps. The mourners knelt and silently communed before continuing on into the adjacent chamber.

There Boun Omme and other male relatives were seated cross-legged on the floor, receiving condolences. My colleague looked exhausted, almost drowsy, his deep-set eyes puffy. Gone was his unvarying professional uniform of Western suit and tie. He was dressed in a simple shirt and traditional sarong, folds of fabric covering his bare feet. Around the walls of the shadowed room, female relatives softly keened.

The funeral was scheduled for a Saturday, so working folks could attend. Sipraseuth reminded Nancy and me that white was the color of mourning in Asia. A white blouse or shirt worn above a dark skirt or trousers would be our appropriate attire.

We drove to her house to pick her up and she brought out a white scarf for Nancy. Sipraseuth helped her to drape it over her right shoulder and tie it at the waist on the left side, with the ends hanging down. Seuth wore a similar emblem herself.

We stopped to buy for each of us a small bouquet of flowers tied with incense and small candles. We then met the cortege which had started earlier from the deceased's house, proceeding to the temple three or four miles away. Non-family mourners were expected to join the procession en route.

At the head of the slowly moving column walked monks from the temple, as well as close male relatives of the deceased who had elected to become temporary monks for a minimum of three days. Their public commitment was a gesture of respect for, and gratitude to, the deceased. All these men wore saffron robes, with one shoulder left bare and their heads freshly shaven.

Next came the rest of the family, men, women and children, all dressed in white, rough-woven sackcloth. One young-adult relative was shooting video footage of the proceedings.

The bier was transported on the back of a flat-bed truck. It was constructed in tiers to resemble a small stupa, and was vaguely reminiscent of an American wedding cake. This box was covered in white paper with an overlay of stenciled gold designs. It was draped with palm fronds, flowers and "trees" of bamboo with attached leaves made up of banknotes.

Behind the bier, we joined friends of the family, some walking, some on bikes or motorbikes, others in cars.

At the temple grounds, pallbearers carefully lifted the bier off of the truck and deposited it on a cement platform with logs and kindling stacked underneath.

The flowers and money trees were placed around the bier, and a thick white cord was looped from the bier to a nearby roofed pavilion. The monks and immediate family members sat on mats under the pavilion. Seuth softly explained that the cord was to link the living to the dead during final prayers.

We were escorted to a second nearby pavilion with wooden benches to accommodate special guests. I recognized Ministers and other top government officials among the one hundred or so attendees. Their presence, we were told, honored the Southichak family for their remembered role in "National Liberation." Only a handful of expatriates were present. As soon as the three of us found seats, we were offered soft drinks. Other guests remained standing between the two pavilions and some sought elusive shade beneath the adjacent *peepul* tree.

The monks led family members in short chanted prayers. Senior relatives removed the white cord and poured water around the cremation platform. Sipraseuth said this libation was to appease the spirits of the soil. I was reminded of the Lao mélange of pre-Buddhist and Buddhist traditions.

The guests were then invited to place our bouquets on the bier, along with perfumed resin provided by the family. With *nop* salutations, we bowed slightly to convey formal condolences to the family. At this moment, Boun Omme reached out to grasp my upper arms with both hands. I was moved by his spontaneous gesture. Even modest public contact was exceptional in Laos.

After everyone had had the chance to contribute their offerings, the family members posed in front of the bier for a videotape portrait to commemorate the passing.

Senior male relatives then removed the money trees and handed them to the monks as a temple donation. Wreaths previously delivered to the house, including ours, were now placed around the bier, while the deceased's framed photo was lifted off and safely preserved.

Liquid fuel was poured over the bier. Each male relative, starting with Boun Omme as the eldest son, touched lit tapers to the bier to ignite the cremation fire. In short minutes the blaze was consuming bier and flowers, incense and all.

With the fire still fully active, another male relative stepped forward into the space between the two pavilions. He carried a platter mounded with small banknotes wrapped around sweet rice cakes. The man tossed these good-luck tokens into the air and neighborhood children who'd been waiting for this bounty grabbed them almost before they hit the ground. Young members of guest families leaped into the commotion. We were told that this gift-giving was a traditional signal that the ceremony was over and it was time to disperse.

As we prepared to leave, I approached Boum Omme and put my arm around his shoulders. He knew of my own parents' recent passing. We shared a moment of silent commiseration.

# 20/20

*Vientiane 1992*

Michael and Monique were sitting in our living room, sharing drinks and snacks before dinner. The Manns were among our favorite friends in Vientiane. Australia's dynamic Ambassador, Michael was helping his country to pivot from British Commonwealth affiliation to Asia/Pacific engagement. In Laos, he was overseeing major foreign investments in mining, plus financing and construction of the Lao-Thai Friendship Bridge across the Mekong, just south of the capital.

Monique's grace reflected her dual French/Lao heritage. A China specialist and Mandarin speaker who also worked at the Australian Embassy, she quietly enlivened every foreign-affairs discussion.

Michael was playfully grousing. "The bridge is aging me by the week."

As the oldest person in the room, I only half-sympathized. "Stop complaining. You're in the full bloom of youth."

Michael refused to be flattered. "Monique and I have an upcoming anniversary that will mark the end of the youth phase."

Nancy turned to Monique. "Where were you married?"

"In Phnom Penh. Michael was Vice Counsel at the Australian embassy. My father was a Colonel in the French Military Mission. How about you?"

"Sacramento, California. We were married in our back garden."

I was curious about the timing. "Michael, you said 'upcoming.' What's the date?"

"October seventh."

"No way! Are you serious?"

Nancy explained my reaction. "That's our anniversary too. How many years have you been married?"

Monique smiled with contentment. "Our twentieth."

Now Nancy was excited. "That's really amazing! It'll be our twentieth as well."

Michael was on his feet. "We all got married on the same day in the same month twenty years ago, on opposite sides of the Pacific?"

Nancy confirmed with a toast. "To October 7, 1972. Long may it wave!"

The four of us were as pleased as kids. We agreed we had to commemorate the coincidence with a party. Our first idea was a "Come As You Were" costume party, if people could dig up '70s outfits. Then Michael injected a somber note. "Seriously, Guys. Twenty years ago was not a happy time for Laos. The CIA was still bombing and most of the current government's leadership was fighting out of caves. We need another theme."

Nancy restored the roundtable's levity. "We could always run off to Hong Kong."

Michael met her half-way. "Right. One thousand miles, give or take a few. Do we walk or swim?"

I warbled in my wife's defense. "*That's what planes are for....*"

The conversation moved past the joke and we agreed on a Vientiane party for the night of the seventh. Suits and ties and short party dresses would be safer than costumes. Michael graciously offered the use of the embassy and its first-rate kitchen staff. We'd keep it small, close friends only, and Monique would see if she could organize engraved invitations for the special occasion.

It was only on the Saturday before the seventh that I returned to the topic with Nancy. "I'm still thinking about Hong Kong."

"Sweetie, it was a joke."

"I know, I know. But 20 years is nothing to sneeze at. How many of our friends' marriages have lasted that long? I keep thinking we all deserve something more special than another Vientiane dinner party."

Again we were off and running, this time to the Manns' residence, because its phone lines were down. Michael and Monique were enjoying mid-morning coffee and playing with their young daughters, Nathalie and Alexandra.

Nancy broke the ice. "Russell doesn't want to leave Hong Kong off the table. He thinks our special occasion deserves more special observance."

Monique was again amused. "We've been teasing out the same idea. We can't let go of it."

I decided to test the waters. "Just suppose we got serious. Could we pull it off?"

Michael looked at his mental calendar. "Monique and I are up to our elbows with the Bridge. But by good luck, things are out of our hands for a few days. We have to wait for the next set of drawings."

Monique had more positive news. "Monday October twelfth is a Lao holiday."

Nancy played her hand. "I'm submitting the Vientiane Guide to the printers on October 1."

That left me. "I've been finalizing plans for the Sydney Conference. But that's reached a plateau."

Michael asked a follow-up. "Do you have any accrued leave?"

"I get 30 days a year. It's October and I've used only ten. This is kismet. How often are all four of us available at the same time? For that matter, how often do Ambassadors and Resident Advisors get to disappear? Legally, of course."

Michael cheered. "We can do this! It's our second honeymoon!"

Then he grinned and closed the deal. "I've got a great contact at Royal Thai Air."

Wheels still turning, he moved on to another detail. "What about the girls?"

Monique calmly replied. "They'll come along. Alexandra's just turned three months. It's time she sees Hong Kong."

And so she did.

The party was a treat. The Bridge contractors gifted Michael and Monique with legs of lamb airlifted from Australia for roasting. Nancy baked an angel food cake with chocolate-mousse filling.

*The Mann family on tour: Monique, Nathalie, Alexandra, Michael. Hong Kong 1992.*

Quick next-day packing and we were on our way. Our rooms at the Hong Kong Mandarin were lovely, with water views. We arrived in time for dim-sum tea. Nancy shared a cherished memory of first eating these Hong Kong savory snacks as a college student nearly 30 years before, while en route to India for her summer work-study program.

A fish dinner that same night at the Tai Pak Floating Restaurant. Shopping on Saturday, for long lists of items unavailable in Vientiane. Monique and Nancy were surprised to find fewer quality goods and bargains than in Bangkok. Next, a dress-up dinner that evening in the Mandarin's best dining room.

The Star Ferry to Kowloon on Sunday. And as we boarded the boat, "My God, it's Nancy Swing!" Another coincidence on a trip full of them. The surprised fellow-passenger was a friend, neighbor and colleague of Nancy's when they'd worked in Washington DC years before. Now Massachusetts-based, she was homeward-bound from a tour on the Chinese mainland.

The unanimous verdict: our best anniversary yet.

In later years, our two families re-united in Vietnam, Italy and Thailand. We missed out on spending our fortieth together. But we're counting the days to 2022.

# LEAVE-TAKINGS

*Vientiane 1993*

"Good morning, Counselor. I hope I'm the first to offer congratulations."

It was indicative of the UN Country Director's utter lack of pretension that when she wanted direct contact she dialed her own phone calls.

Ameerah Haq was the most competent official of an international-development organization I had ever worked with. In Laos, she coordinated the in-country work of 20 United Nations-affiliated agencies and project offices with calm attentiveness and a light touch. She unfailingly supported my efforts and those of other project managers with effective collaboration, never micromanaging, withholding information or stealing the credit for our field successes. In the macho milieu of development assistance, Ameerah was often underestimated, due to her diminutive stature and female gender. But she invariably got the job done, without tooting her own horn.[11]

"Ameerah, it's always a pleasure to earn your approval. But what's the occasion?"

"Aha! He doesn't know. Russell, I just heard from the Ministry of External Relations. You're going to be decorated by the Lao government."

11   In an unusual instance of quiet talent receiving due recognition, Ameerah was eventually appointed an Under-Secretary-General of the United Nations.

I thought she was enjoying a mid-morning jest. "Do I get to choose the colors?"

"All decided. A red and blue ribbon with a dangling medal. The Order of the Friends of Laos."

"I've never heard of it."

"That's because it's so rare. They routinely hand them out to ranking diplomats like me when we end our tours. But that's mostly protocol. It's never awarded to an individual expert. This is exceptional."

Boun Omme Southichak protested but beamed when I later insisted the recognition belonged to our entire team. "*Non, non, cher* Sunshine. It is a personal honor. We are all proud for you."

The ceremony was set for Friday morning at my host Ministry. I was permitted to invite a few friends and colleagues in addition to the government's official guests.

The Director of Protocol escorted us into the Ministry's main chamber for receiving large foreign delegations. It was seldom used and the drawn curtains made the space dark and close. Things were getting off to a slow start and the room was still virtually empty. After three years in-country, I knew not to expect punctuality. The delay gave me a chance to greet my invitees as they trickled in, introducing them to my government colleagues.

Boun Omme led in a sizable delegation from our Foreign Investment Management Agency. Flanked by his lieutenants, Houmpheng and Boun Nhang, for once my self-effacing partner was willing to stand near the front. Not so the shy staff, unaccustomed to this elevated company. They retreated to soft-cushioned sofas ringing the chamber walls, as if hoping to avoid attention.

I glanced around the swelling circle who had shared so much. It was especially gratifying to spot two favorite mentors. Governor Bousbong from the Central Bank resembled a provincial French uncle, complete with wire-rimmed eyeglasses and rumpled waistcoat. He had the keenest financial mind in the country. Vice Minister Khempheng Pholsena was circulating deftly, utilizing the occasion to conduct informal business.

*Ministerial award ceremony. Vientiane 1993.*

Ameerah Haq had kindly brought with her Renata Locke, our UNDP Project Officer, to share the observance. Dear friends Charles Salmon from the United States and Australia's Michael Mann represented the ambassadorial corps.

At a nod from Boun Omme, the guests gathered around in an arc for the ceremony. I was honored that my former client, Phao Bounnaphol, had come across from the Prime Minister's Office to present the award. His successor now heading up External Economic Affairs, Minister Khamphoui Keoboualapha, invited Phao to convene the proceedings. A gracious gesture, I thought. In his other capacity as Deputy Prime Minister, Khamphoui was the ranking official present.

What meant most to me in Minister Phao's presentation was not the recitation of Project achievements under my tenure—laws enacted, investments attracted, publications launched, conferences organized, counterparts trained. I knew he was reading from prepared remarks. Instead, I was touched by his departure from the script.

"Mr. Sunshine, my colleagues and I value the respect you have shown us and our country. This, not the medal, is what makes you a true friend of Laos."

I accepted the honor on behalf of our multinational team, foreign experts as well as Lao partners. We'd made solid progress together. I closed with an optimistic wish for Laos's sustained foreign-investment attraction, after our Project folded its tents.

Our household staff softly approached Nancy and me after breakfast. Khamsing, our gardener, Khetmani, our housekeeper, and Khun Kham, my driver, never appeared in consort without advance planning. "The Three Ks" were hesitant but determined. Khamsing had the best English. He spoke for the trio.

"Sir and Madam, Khun Kham, Khetmani and me, we would like to give a *baci* to say goodbye."

The *baci* was the Lao tradition Nancy and I most cherished. An ancient ritual with Hindu origins, it offered a blend of prayers, blessings and good wishes at times of transition. Buddhism had preserved and absorbed this primordial rite. But the custom's deep roots antedated that religion's seventh-century arrival in Southeast Asia.

It turned out that my office staff would be co-hosting the event. As we prepared to leave Laos, Nancy and I were being feted at a series of official banquets and receptions. But somehow this more personal gathering moved us more deeply.

On the afternoon of the evening ceremony, the Ks spread palm-leaf mats in a makeshift carpet across the width of our living-room floor. Pride of place in the center was reserved for the *khan*, an imposing silver chalice kindly lent by Sipraseuth's extended family. This embossed vessel supported a cone of banana leaves, anchoring an elaborate bouquet and long, thin candles. Around its rim were stacked food, fruit and coins, symbolic bounty for our onward journey. Khun Kham assured me he'd tucked in a crisp banknote.

As the guests gathered for the ceremony, Nancy and I were guided to the front row directly facing the urn. Everyone sat on the floor in concentric circles, feet tucked demurely under to avoid giving offense.

The presiding elder, the *mohphon*, wore a blue-and-white striped sash

*The* mophon *begins the* baci *ceremony.*
*Vientiane 1993.*

across his chest. I wore the same. Nancy's was white. The elder was not a priest but a layman highly respected for his piety, confirmed by several years spent as a monk. He lit the candles with a stick of fragrant incense that he then stuck into the urn. He took his seat on the floor in the front rank directly opposite Nancy and me. The *baci* was ready to begin.

Clearing his throat to command attention, the *mohphon* steepled his hands in a *nop*. Then he launched into a rapid chant, invoking the gods in a sonorous blend of Pali and Lao. Occasionally, the gathering would repeat key refrains.

Long white cotton strings dangled from the urn. After a pause, the chanter rose from his place to hand the end of one string to me, the next to Nancy, and on around the inner circle. We each took our string and grasped it between joined palms. Guests seated farther away lightly touched those in the front row. We were now all connected.

At the end of the prayer, as we'd been instructed, Nancy and

*Reaching out to the* khan. *Vientiane 1993.*

I dropped our long strings, raised our left hands to our cheeks and extended our right hands palms up. The *mohphon* rose to deposit tangible gifts in our palms to nurture our onward journey: an egg, fruit, a roasted chicken leg, a sprig of blossoms, a foil-wrapped sweet.

The elder now lifted short white strings from the urn's bottom tier. Kneeling in front of Nancy and me, he recited travelers' blessings. Gently, he tied a string around each upturned wrist. To preserve each wish and give it more potency, he rubbed the knot above the pulse.

Now well-wishers stepped forward to lift more strings from the *khan*. They knelt before Nancy and me, knotting their own blessings. Each wish was whispered, securing personal connections. Soon all four wrists were covered in a soft white cuff. Then others received blessings in turn, from each other and from us.

I looked up to see Nancy's cheeks wet with tears. We were joined to this circle even as we let go.

"Wear your strings for three days," the *mohphon* admonished. "Think of the givers," Sipraseuth translated. "When you are ready, untie the strings with your fingers. Do not cut them. Do not break the bonds."

The strings are long gone. The bonds are intact.

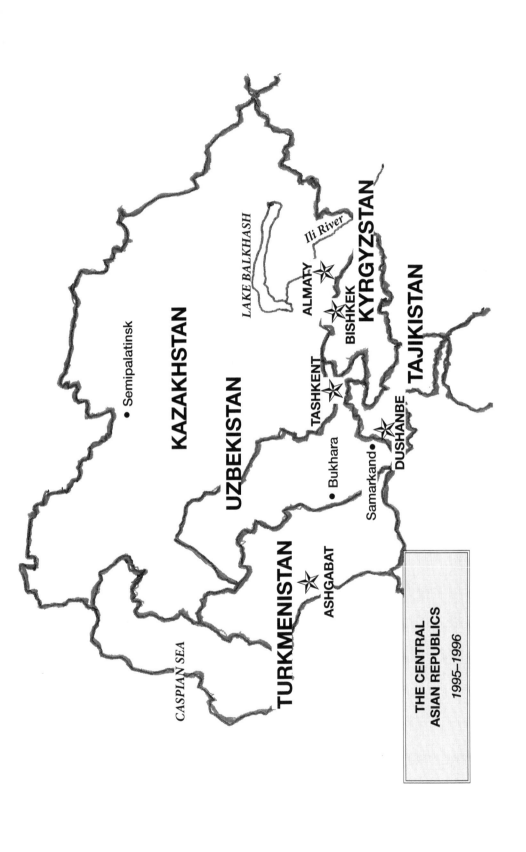

THE CENTRAL
ASIAN REPUBLICS
1995–1996

## Chapter Eight

# CENTRAL ASIA: AFTER THE FALL

When the Soviet Union collapsed in December 1991, almost nobody saw it coming. It was "Here today, gone tomorrow" on a transcontinental scale.

The chief victims of this seismic shift included Russia's satellite republics. For 70 years these diverse states had been bound to Moscow in tight political, economic and social dependency—a quasi-colonial empire. The five Central Asian Republics—Kazakhstan, Kyrgyzstan, Tajikistan, Turkmenistan and Uzbekistan—had demarcated that empire's southern flank. Their contiguous land mass sprawled from the Caucasus to China, 1,800 miles across. The Union's implosion cast these remote Asian protectorates adrift in a destabilizing independence for which they were sorely unprepared.

The ensuing political and economic vacuums were filled by the boldest opportunists. In the Central Asian Republics' governing councils, seasoned Soviet apparatchiks cynically swapped "red hats for green", securing their incumbency by morphing from Communist loyalists into nationalist patriots. The Turkish mafia rushed in to seize control of lucrative trade in alcohol, tobacco and luxury goods.

Multinational corporations from America, Britain and France were no less quick to open negotiations for Central Asian oil and gas concessions.

On the geopolitical front, the American government launched a multi-pronged diplomatic offensive, asserting its claim as Cold War victor to displace Russian hegemony. This ambitious agenda encompassed promotion of foreign (i.e. American) investment and trade, locking down Soviet nuclear weapons, forging military alliances against Islamic extremism and encouraging Central Asian democratization.

This democratic-transition initiative was coordinated by the U.S. Agency for International Development. USAID contracted with private American consulting firms which hired individual experts. I was recruited by Chemonics of Washington DC to manage the largest of these efforts.

Our Rule-of-Law Project served all five Central Asian Republics, championing parliamentary and judicial development, public access to legal information and the emergence of grassroots non-governmental organizations (NGOs). The Project's professional staff numbered 25 full-time locals and expatriates, supplemented by a pipeline of short-term specialists. Our $8-million budget supported offices in Almaty, Bishkek, Dushanbe and Tashkent, backstopped by Chemonics's Stateside headquarters.

Despite these generous resources and our reformist energy, our team swiftly confronted formidable obstacles. The Republics' national leaders had no intention to permit, much less promote, political pluralism or dissent. Authoritarianism was what they had inherited. Authoritarianism was what they were determined to sustain.

More surprising to us, at least initially, was the inertia we encountered from local clients and even colleagues. Decades of Soviet-enforced isolation had instilled in these provincial elites a distorted impression of international development and a vested interest in resisting change. "Arrogant ignorance" was the cruel cliché coined by expatriates to describe encountered attitudes.

Compounding these hurdles, our sponsor, the American government, was juggling incompatible objectives—trying to win oil-concession agreements from corrupt oligarchs while simultaneously undermining those dictators with democratic reforms.

For our dedicated Project team, these systemic conflicts made for two frustrating and stressful professional years. Between headaches, however, we were able to plant and nurture some transformational seeds. Across Central Asia, we encouraged and empowered more than 60 NGOs. Their objectives spanned human rights, women's development, independent media development, and environmental conservation. We established Legal Information Centers giving citizens unprecedented access to laws and legal protections. Simultaneously, we launched promising international careers for gifted local professionals within our own Project ranks.

*NGO leaders from the five Central Asian Republics celebrating at a Project convocation. Almaty 1995.*

On a personal level, I was able to visit and work within all five Central Asian Republics, at times sharing overloaded Tupolov cabins with butting goats and protesting chickens. I survived an armed insurrection and near-evacuation in Dushanbe.

Nancy and I set up housekeeping in Almaty, Kazakhstan, in an eccentric Russian colonial dacha. Building on her Vientiane experience, she spearheaded the publication of an Almaty Guide for foreign residents and visitors. On vacation, accompanied by her 85-year-old still-adventurous father, we travelled along the historic Silk Road to enchanting Samarkand and Bukhara.

## OUR CHERRY ORCHARD

*Almaty, Kazakhstan 1995–1996*

The stench was gagging, even in the sub-zero morning. Detecting our pallor, Roza Buldekbaeva, my new Executive Assistant, explained that Kazakh migrants to the capital often hauled freshly butchered sheep carcasses back with them in the trunks of their cars after visiting rural relatives. In the apartment building selected for Nancy and me by our local Project staff, tenants had dragged their protein bounty up the stairs for grilling on high-rise balconies. When apartments were privatized after the Soviet Union's collapse, no one accepted responsibility for maintaining the common spaces. So even in this upmarket tower, spoiling sheep blood, cooked cabbage and stale urine competed in a nauseating miasma.

Not the welcome we'd looked forward to after an all-night flight from Frankfurt. I felt sandbagged by Chemonics's headquarters recruiters. They'd assured us that our pre-selected Almaty living quarters were outstanding. "Spacious," "great views," and "prime location" were the amenities that rang in my ear.

From the ice-slick curb where we unloaded our bags, the concrete monolith that confronted us was a brutish Soviet block. Inside was worse. Apart from the reek, the grim lobby was unlit and unheated, with dank, soiled walls. The cramped elevator rattled like a B-movie cage, yet our seventh-floor destination made walking up out of the question.

The front door to our apartment looked solid enough but we both spotted the four separate locks. We crossed the threshold into a tired, tacky suite. I sank into a demoralized sofa and surveyed the peeling wallpaper. Nancy stood in the kitchen door-frame, taking in stacks of thin metal pans and plastic plates.

The poorly plumbed bathroom belched sewage vapors. The two-foot-wide balcony would only accommodate a laundry rack, and not before warm weather. For Almaty's six-month winter, sagging clotheslines suspended from the hallway ceiling would have to serve as proxies.

My beaming Kazakh associates made it clear they considered these quarters palatial for a family of two. But as soon as they'd departed, my wife and I pledged that we'd escape from this depressing den at our earliest opportunity.

Living and working in another culture, however stimulating, is often wearing. Nancy and I always tried to create a household sanctuary overseas, not just for our personal comfort but for entertaining colleagues and visitors. We made a point of avoiding self-absorbed expatriate enclaves and ostentatious suites. Our threshold criterion for an in-country domicile was always a local house in a local neighborhood. Settling into such a niche invited welcome community contacts and cross-cultural immersion.

Our first morning in Almaty revealed that our normal homesteading approach was going to be difficult to implement. As we made get-acquainted rounds at the American Embassy and USAID, obstacles started piling up. Orientation briefings emphasized that current political, economic and social conditions in Kazakhstan were turbulent. The rude withdrawal of the Soviet safety net of social services had made basic survival a struggle for local citizens, especially in literally killing winter temperatures. Crimes against property were accordingly rampant. One consequence was that the Embassy's Security Office was insisting that all U.S. nationals based in Almaty, whether publicly or privately employed, must reside in pre-vetted apartments within a one-mile radius of the Embassy. Hence our pungent bastion.

Nancy and I struggled to come to terms with this stacked deck. Additional factors soon complicated our housing search. No market for leasing residential property had yet taken root in Almaty, so there were no commercial listings and no published prices. Apart from rumors and cocktail-party gossip, it was impossible to find out what houses and apartments might be available. Properties "suitable for foreigners" were exorbitantly priced and in appalling condition. Restored apartments were the choice of most expatriates we met, although suburban nouveau-riche villas were also coming on stream.

We were determined to find a traditional house and garden. On our first ride in from the airport, we had spotted a number of charming pre-Bolshevik wooden structures, fancifully decorated with gingerbread eaves and pastel siding. "Forget it," we were told by Embassy veterans. "They're mostly high mucky-mucks' trophies or locked shrines to Revolutionary heroes."

While I was concentrating on setting up Project operations, Nancy and Roza scoured the metropolis for livable quarters. After we rejected garish, jerry-built "palaces" and teetering rural sheds, one morning Roza tipped us off to a possible new prospect. Off we rushed through an intact neighborhood of surviving smallholdings. The quarter was called "*Kompot,*" Roza grinned. "Preserved fruit," in honor of its venerable cherry orchards. Careening along rutted lanes, my driver swerved into a nondescript cul-de-sac and pulled up at a metal gate. Stepping inside, we got our first glance of a quirky relic.

This eccentric bungalow may once have evoked Chekhov or Dr. Zhivago but now it was down on its luck. Rusted supports for the front-porch roof and crumbling stucco testified to neglected maintenance. Sasha, the owner, personally conducted our walk-through. In his late 30s, Sasha reminded me of a lean and lanky Joel Gray. On first meeting, he exuded the manic optimism we later came to recognize as his default mode. We marveled that such a volatile non-conformist had withstood the crushing pressures of this statist backwater. He spoke no English but peppered his bursts of Russian with the occasional inapt French phrase.

Through Roza's translation, Sasha explained that he was the third generation of his family to occupy this dacha. His grandfather had come out from Leningrad in the 1920s to organize the new Kazakhstan Republic's Ministry of Mines. Sasha proudly showed us family heirlooms retained from that historic relocation. Framed golden icons, now permitted again in the accelerating Orthodox reassertion. A silvered samovar, an inlaid wooden sideboard, a massive dining table and matching suite of 12 chairs. Most winsome was a hand-painted upright piano with hinged candle sconces. Hardwood floors had also miraculously survived.

The other furniture, unfortunately, was modern and shabby, cobbled together from veneered pressboard. High-gloss wall colors spanned a garish spectrum from emergency orange to algae green. Sasha assured us these saturated hues were traditional Russian solutions to interminable winter gloom. In a lax moment, he later confided he'd "gotten a good price" on marine enamel. Not a big seller, we surmised, 1,500 miles from the nearest port.

The kitchen was refreshingly white, but tiny, unhygienic and primitive. In the adjacent bathroom, the toilet had been shoe-horned into a separate closet so cramped its door wouldn't close when occupied.

The surrounding yard presented a challenge of a different order. A midden stacked eight feet high with the detritus of 70 years, the entire half-acre was a porous mound of rusty pipes, chains and wire, moldy timber, random chair legs, chipped bricks, detached wheels and axles. In an economy of severe scarcity, nothing had been discarded. Every ruin was zealously hoarded for cannibalizing on a rainy day.

Nancy and I found this stubborn survivor irresistible, a symbol of Soviet hardships and post-Independence potential. After wearing down an Embassy security officer already fed up with our search, we won approval for this unprecedented lodging experiment. The bureaucrat only insisted that we erect a 10-foot perimeter fence. Since we were paying

*Sasha's Dacha. Before renovation must come demolition. Almaty 1995.*

a full year's lease in advance, we in turn insisted that Sasha clear the grounds and replace the Captain Nemo boiler in the basement before we risked occupancy.

We repainted with softer tones, squirting Italian pigments into a white base. The results, mostly to our satisfaction, included a subdued peach for the living room and muted yellow for the study. Sasha was disdainful of these "timid" choices. We preferred them to nautical neon.

Nancy and her friend Saulya combed Almaty shops and bazaars in pursuit of modern appliances and comfortable furniture. Most sofas on offer were overstuffed, covered in plush brocades and exorbitantly expensive. However, if one didn't ask too many questions about provenance and had cash in hand, one-off treasures could be snapped up from as far afield as Korea and Spain. After weeks of stalking, they procured a stove, fridge, and clothes-washer, plus a functional couch with two matching chairs. They even located drapery fabric free of the baroque flourishes that appealed to local tastes.

*Looking better: the cleared veranda.*

Nancy fitted out the upstairs room as her study, delighted by the southern exposure. She soon discovered that winter frost and summer heat made the space uninhabitable. So she shifted to the small den downstairs next to the front door. With blankets, space heater and two locally acquired long-haired cats, she created a nook for writing Almaty's first expatriate guidebook.

The wizard who crafted extensive household repairs and renovations was our gifted handyman, Valodya Federov. A professional engineer with two university degrees, Valodya was employed by a bottling plant but had not been paid for six months when we met. Working half-time for us, he demolished and installed, wired and painted, nailed and drilled. As strong as an ox but with a kindly disposition, Valodya became a close friend, introducing us to his handsome wife Ludmila and daughters Katya and Juliya.

Inside the house, our favorite room became the enclosed veranda with windows on three sides. At one end we used Kazakh tribal rugs, saddlebags, cushions, and painted chests to evoke a traditional floor-seating area. An embroidered *yurt* cinch circled the ceiling. This sunlit bubble became our chief living space from June through September.

Outside we labored to convert the cleared junkyard to flower and vegetable gardens. Valodya laid pathways of round river stones he and Nancy had gathered on the banks of mountain creeks. He built benches and painted them robin's-egg blue to match the woodshed door.

The spring thaw revealed a precious gift in the form of ancient peonies. With exotic colors half-way between rose and magenta, as a bonus they emitted a heady perfume. Nancy added nasturtiums, day lilies, pansies, iris and impatiens. Burpee seeds hand-carried from America rewarded us with giant sunflowers on 12-foot stalks.

Sasha had never taken interest in his grandfather's marvelous fruit trees—cherries, apples and pears neglected for decades. Our landlord's idiosyncratic attitude towards his arboreal inheritance was brought home to us by the cherry-tree saga. One afternoon, just as Valodya was leaving the garden after a full day's work, Sasha came running around the corner of the house, parading a large cherry-tree branch heavy with fruit.

"Nensi! Nensi! Look what I've brought!" This, in the broken French that was our chief channel for direct communications.

Nancy was pleased by this pruning windfall. She set aside an editing task and began to pluck cherries off the branch.

Then Sasha brought another. And another. Valodya helped Nancy fill plastic bowls and a larger washbasin, for sharing between our two families. Branches soon filled the yard, crushing just-sprouted grass into mud. When the shuttle showed no signs of abating, Nancy walked around the house to trace the assembly line to its source.

Our landlord was hacking down an entire cherry tree, the only shade outside my home-office window. Nancy registered vain protests, trotting out multiple objections.

"*Je comprends, je comprends,*" was Sasha's only reply. But the woodsman's ax kept falling.

The venerable specimen, planted by Sasha's pioneering grandfather, was soon totally destroyed. At first we were baffled by Sasha's unrelenting assault. Valodya shrugged that Sasha was an "*artiste*", an ironic Russian put-down describing someone too daft for the real world.

Eventually, the three of us thought we'd puzzled out our landlord's convoluted rationale. Sasha was preparing to install a new exhaust pipe for our house's heating system. And he wanted to protect the tree from the welder's sparks, so it didn't ignite and burn down the house. His solution was to move the tree out of harm's way. By chopping it down.

The only upside to this sorry tale was the distribution of the rudely harvested fruit. Valodya's family received bushels that they converted to *kompot*. Other friends and office colleagues were thrilled to be showered with delicious cherries. Nancy made cherry pies, cherry-oat pudding, and preserved bottles of brandied cherries that enhanced ice cream and cakes for months to come.

Unharvested fruit of all varieties had been dropping in the yard for decades. They'd fertilized the soil, making it rich for planting once cleared of debris. Newly exposed to sunlight, our flower and vegetable gardens produced like champions.

The main function of our vegetable garden was to supply us with foods not reliably available in local markets—broccoli, acorn squash and Chinese snow peas. We also took pleasure in growing our own eggplants, lettuce, spinach, zucchini, and Valodya's gifted strawberry sets.

House and garden became a warming haven. Staff parties for my Project team lowered barriers between expatriates and locals. On half of an oil barrel filled with charcoal, we grilled *shashlik*, chunks of local mutton marinated overnight in wine and herbs. My Kazakh co-workers preferred *bishbarmak*, stewed horsemeat heaped over wide noodles. Potato and eggplant salads, coleslaw, fresh fruits and home-made pastries rounded out a typical feast. With wine and beer for the foreigners and vodka for the locals, singing soon filled the shaded grounds.

One less-mellow memory emerges from my mental dacha archive. After one long evening celebration, I was helping to tidy up by emptying a bathtub full of chilled Chinese beer. Losing my grip on a slippery

*My Project staff gathered in our home. Almaty 1995.*

bottle, I managed to grab it in mid-air. But my arm's forward momentum carried hand and bottle into the exposed plumbing pipes. The thin glass shattered and blood sprayed the tile wall.

Nancy and I couldn't stanch the flow. It was 10 p.m. on a Sunday night so we anxiously rang Dr. Basset, the missionary doctor who doubled as our family physician. He graciously agreed to come out and take a look. In halting Russian, Nancy dictated the route to his driver.

The doctor's inspection revealed I had severed small blood vessels and nerves in the smallest finger on my right hand. Commenting sardonically that our kitchen was more hygienic than any local hospital, Dr. Basset set up a sterile field on a kitchen counter. With light from a desk lamp and my wife's calm assistance, he sewed me up with a dozen stitches. I recuperated from this potentially serious accident with no infection and full use of my pinkie.

Madame Aitbaeva, our next-door neighbor, was a widow who had served the Soviet government faithfully for four decades. With the collapse of the Union, she'd seen her pension savings devalued with the stroke of a pen when Kazakhstan's newly independent government refused to convert Russian rubles. This ailing elder lacked adequate clothing or heating. Like millions of others, the widow was barely enduring the mismanaged transition. She scraped by with remittances from her son in Moscow, as well as quiet gifts from other friends and ourselves. We shared cordial moments over tea and cakes. When we left our household after two years, Madame Aitbaeva came in tears to our door with her own parting gifts. She had knitted a traditional woolen cap for me and indoor "booties" for Nancy.

Our cottage restoration became a precedent for other expatriates in Almaty. More families took the risk of fixing up dilapidated traditional houses, escaping from dispiriting Soviet apartments. Foreign embassies relaxed and precious structures were saved. Sasha's pioneering grandfather would have been gratified to again lead the way.

# Book Cop

*Dushanbe, Tajikistan 1995*

The Dean and his entourage hovered as expectantly on the Law Faculty's front steps as a proud family welcoming a godfather to a christening. His 200-watt smile confirmed that my visit capped a successful campaign.

Our Rule-of-Law Project's original intent had been to sponsor only one Legal Information Center in Tajikistan, within the National Academy of Sciences in downtown Dushanbe. The Education Minister and the American Ambassador cut the ribbon on national television. From Day One, this modern facility, humming with trained librarians, on-line databases, and multilingual treatises and periodicals, attracted appreciative clients.

We were delighted by this ground-level affirmation. Our premise was that citizens of the newly independent Central Asian Republics had to know the law in order to assert their legal rights. Legal academies and libraries had existed under the Soviet Union. But they were deliberately closed institutions, accessible only to vetted Party faithful. Our proposal, at once modest and revolutionary, was to throw those doors open wide.

Even before that inauguration, Tajikistan University officials across the river were demanding a parallel installation for their campus. We'd already equipped them with computers for legal research, electronically linked to the downtown hub. But the proud academics insisted on their own book collection, allegedly for their students' convenience but primarily, we surmised, for professorial prestige. We gladly complied and the stocked satellite center was up and running. The proud Faculty had been requesting my on-site inspection of the new operation for several months, but commitments in other Republics had postponed my return to Dushanbe. Now the elaborate printed invitation confirmed they were pulling out all the stops.

If the Dean was the daddy of this literary offspring, the Law Librarian was unequivocally mama. Madame Oblova pushed to the front of the welcoming delegation, her prominent bust barely contained by a heroic bodice. Hennaed hair, a prominent cheek mole and two sets of spectacles dangling from chains completed her operatic ensemble.

I'd been briefed in advance that the Librarian's Party connections had secured her appointment, as well as the license to ignore traditional academic protocol. Now her body language spoke volumes. This inspection tour was her production and no listless professors were going to pull rank. With a pre-emptive lunge, the diva seized my arm and led her chorus back up the steps and into the Law Faculty's foyer.

I'd have much preferred a low-key walk-through. The Dushanbe temperature was 104 degrees Fahrenheit and my afternoon flight back to Almaty left only three times weekly. But the bountiful refreshments table, hovering photographer, scrubbed students and printed program announced that my hostess had grander ideas.

After sips, nibbles and grinning group photos, at last we were permitted to inspect our donated books. I followed the posted sign towards to the Main Reading Room. Madame Oblova overtook me like a highway patrolman and redirected my progress into her outer office. Two imposing armoires filled an entire wall.

"Honorable Dr. Sunshine," the lady's presentation began, "on behalf of our Vice Chancellor, esteemed Law Faculty Dean and accomplished professors, our heartfelt thanks go out to you, the Rule-of-Law Project, the United States Agency for International Development, the

American Embassy and countless benefactors beyond Central Asia who have collaborated to bring precious legal materials to our neglected institution."

My interpreter was hyperventilating to keep pace with this florid recitative until I whispered that the gist would suffice.

"Your gift will link our remote Pamir caravanserai to a new Silk Road of scholarship stretching beyond the horizon. And here are the treasures." With a flourish, the Law Librarian hoisted formidable keys on a ribbon from their privileged sanctuary. Twisting twin locks, the diva signaled her supernumeraries to throw open the doors. Five hundred legal treatises stared back at us, each as pristine in publishers' cellophane wrappers as a stamp collector's first-day-of-issue acquisitions.

I barely succeeded in muting my shock, but my eyebrows soared.

Madame Oblova placed a plump hand on my forearm, emboldened by what she apparently mistook for speechless admiration. "Distinguished Doctor, you must have thought we lacked professional standards in this back-of-beyond. Certainly, you could be excused for assuming that progress had passed us by. But some of us still carry the torch. Some still safeguard the sacred flame of knowledge."

The soloist pivoted for her aria's climax. "Here I stand, your trusted Chief Steward. Regard! Four months in our care and not one volume stolen. No single page torn or soiled. We know how to respect intellectual value. Your entire collection un-despoiled and intact. We have honored your treasures as today we honor you!"

Not one book borrowed. Not one page turned. Not one word read. For four months the book cop had hoarded her cache like a miser. Conscientious to a fault, Madame Oblova had guaranteed that no vulgar law students would lay greasy fingers on her virgin texts.

Our Rule-of-Law Project staff had labored half a year to select, purchase and import these costly legal materials from Moscow and London, Geneva and The Hague. Curator Oblova had been no less dedicated in ensuring the collection was not defaced or diminished.

I didn't know whether to laugh or cry.

# Silk Road Safari

*Samarkand and Bukhara 1995*

As a boy, Nancy's father had dreamed of retracing the Silk Road, the ancient caravan routes linking China to the Mediterranean. During his working adulthood, World War II and the Cold War had put that wish beyond reach. But in retirement, the fall of the Soviet Union and his daughter's presence in Central Asia gave Leonard a second chance. So, at age 85, he flew from South Carolina to join us in Almaty and got ready for a close look at history.

Our ten-day loop from Kazakhstan to Uzbekistan and back was the brainchild of my Tashkent Project Assistant, Alisher Kasymov, who hailed from the fabled Fergana Valley. Three and a half years after the Soviet Union's implosion, a professional tourism industry was not yet ready to organize foreigners' travel between the Republics of Central Asia. Never-better-than-utilitarian Russian Intourist hotels had fallen into disrepair. Simple on-arrival tourist visas that should have been pro forma when entering one Republic from another instead required navigating an all-day bureaucratic gauntlet. So interactions with the authorities were best kept to a minimum.

Alisher tapped into his personal network of contacts to coordinate a do-it-yourself tour. Every local person he mobilized was moonlighting. Our hosts, drivers and interpreter/guides were all talented individuals working overtime to make ends meet. For example, Rafzhan from our Tashkent office and Sasha from our Almaty office earned extra income by utilizing accrued leave to drive us around. In this as in other sectors, Central Asia's informal economy was responding spontaneously to bubbling demand.

Modern private-sector ingenuity and traditional Uzbek hospitality were both on display during our first hours in Tashkent. We flew into Uzbekistan's capital from Almaty. Alisher led us to a *chai-khana* (teahouse) for a delicious welcoming dinner of grilled dishes of lamb, chicken and beef. He'd arranged accommodations at an aging but clean and comfortable boarding house where Leonard, Nancy and I shared a two-bedroom apartment with private bath. Breakfast was served in a parlor paneled in wood and brocade. We sat on modified camel saddles and watched CNN News!

In Tashkent we visited a well-endowed Islamic Arts museum, an old mosque and *madrasa* (Islamic religious school), and the huge central bazaar. This roofed but open-sided market filled a city block. Strolling through mounds of spices in a medley of inviting colors and aromas, we bought pistachios and saffron for pennies.

The next day, we invaded the separate wholesale bazaar to stock up on bottled water, snacks and sodas for our onward drive to Samarkand. Before we left Alisher in Tashkent, his uncle prepared us a feast of Uzbek *plauf* (rice, meat and vegetables), accompanied by fresh fruits and flatbread. We sat on a traditional raised platform with a low table in front of us. When I tried to stand up after a leisurely afternoon of good food and conversation, I was sure everyone could hear my protesting knees.

Our four-hour drive to Samarkand in the cool of early evening took us past irrigated fields of cotton and food crops. This was Uzbekistan's livelihood but the diverted water was literally killing the Aral Sea.

Half-way along our route, Rafzhan pulled into a roadside *chai-khana* so we could sample some more local fare. Nancy and I were a bit nervous for Leonard's sake. This facility was the definition of unimproved. No electricity, chipped crockery plates sluiced in a bucket, and unspeakable bathrooms. But her father seemed to relish the skewered-lamb *shashlik* and puffed flatbread cooked over squat charcoal grills and washed down with tea. It was not difficult to envision similar stopovers serving Silk-Road travelers for a thousand years. And the full moon didn't hurt.

When we arrived in Samarkand near midnight, Emma, our bed-and-breakfast hostess, showed us into our apartment directly across the hall from her own. An ebullient Russian widow, Emma was a larger-than-life cousin of Zorba's Bubalina. Irrepressibly effusive, she took a shine, I think, to Leonard and asked me softly during our visit if he were still married. When I replied that he was a widower, her beaming smile revealed gold teeth.

Emma was a fabulous cook of Russian and local dishes. She fed us three generous meals every day of our Samarkand stay. Nancy's breakfast favorite was *Aladdin* (pronounced "all-ah-deen '"), a small pancake made with yoghurt and sprinkled with powdered sugar, then topped with homemade jam.

We'd all read about Samarkand's layered history as the "Crossroads of World Cultures" and were eager to sample its architectural legacy. The city was most famous as the fourteenth-century CE capital of Timur, better known in the West as Tamerlane (from "Timur the Lame"). Samarkand had also hosted much earlier residents, including Alexander the Great who occupied it in 329 BCE and renamed it "Marakanda." In between, Samarkand had been the main base of the Persian Sogdians, who dominated Silk Road trade with China from the second century BCE to the tenth century CE. These Zoroastrian practitioners protected Buddhists, Manicheans and Nestorian Christians within their walls.

To show us some of the historical highlights, Alisher had engaged the services of an English-speaking guide, Valentina, whose day job was on the faculty of the local Institute of Foreign Languages. On our first day she escorted us to Gur i Amir, the mausoleum of Timur and his family. The pleated blue-tiled dome capped the structure like a snug turban. Inside, severe, rectangular marble tombs ranged in size from the heroic to touchingly small for children.

Valentina reaffirmed that Timur's complexity mirrored that of Central Asia as a whole. A Turkic Mongol determined to restore the empire of Genghis Khan, Timur basically succeeded in achieving his grandiose ambition. By the time of his death in 1405, he had conquered Egypt, Syria, the Ottoman Empire, northern India and everything in between. Only fatal illness halted his military advance, knocking on China's door. Still regarded today as a military genius, Timur was also feared and cursed as a ruthless slaughterer.

Yet this same cruel destroyer was also a cultural creator and patron of the arts. Timur imported architects and artisans from across his empire to beautify his capital of Samarkand. He kept up a steady program of construction and reconstruction for 35 years and was his own hands-on general contractor. European ambassadors from Spain and France marveled at his city's grandeur. The centerpiece was the still-standing Registan, a huge plaza surrounded on three sides by dramatic half-domed mosques and *madrasas* towering 150 feet high, covered in intricate blue tiles.

Equally massive and framed by twinned arched gateways, the Bibi Khanym mosque and *madrasa* had been endowed by Timur's favorite wife, a Chinese princess. On the outskirts of town, we also visited the Shah-i-Zinda necropolis, an *allée* of jewel-like tombs tiled in brilliant blue, green, turquoise, white and yellow.

Nearby was the observatory built in 1428 by Ulugh Beg, a historical figure the three of us found much easier to admire than megalomaniacal Timur. In his short reign, this grandson of Timur excelled as a scientist and mathematician. With the aid of a 120-foot-radius sextant, Ulugh determined the positions of 990 stars, and calculated the year's exact duration more precisely than Copernicus 90 years later. His trigonometry calculations were comparably sophisticated. In his spare time, he made notable advances in medicine and pharmacy. Unfortunately, Ulugh lacked similar skill and success in statecraft and was beheaded by his eldest son at the age of 55.

At an artisanal studio, we experienced a geopolitical case study of unintended consequences. Across their Central Asian Republics, the secular Soviets had discouraged the perpetuation of traditional Islamic arts and crafts like carpet-weaving. Now an Afghan refugee family was re-teaching this art to local Uzbek girls. The only reason the teachers were here to undo this Soviet crack-down was that they had been driven out of their own adjacent country by those same Soviets.

A four-hour, early-morning drive took us on to Bukhara. We immediately noticed the contrasts. Historical Samarkand was surviving as a cluster of ancient monuments at the hub of a modern metropolis. The visual effect was of elegant verticality, gleaming in blue-white tiles. Bukhara's historical center was smaller but more intact. Whole neighborhoods were two stories high, predominantly red-brown in bricks and stucco made from local earth.

You could easily get the sense of a Silk Road oasis or caravanserai. Shortly before our arrival, UNESCO had designated Bukhara as a World Cultural Heritage Site, heralding it as the most complete and unspoiled example of a medieval city in Central Asia.

This time our lodgings were in a guesthouse owned and operated by Sasha, a former Russian soccer star now returned to his native Bukhara, and his wife Lena. Their house was constructed in a traditional local form as a hollow square around a vine-covered courtyard, a small garden with fig trees, and open space for sitting outside in the cool of the evening. Sasha's and Lena's cooking was no match for Emma's, but their hospitality was equally warm.

Since they didn't serve lunch, our driver led us to the old-town center for a traditional meal of *shashlik* and trimmings. The plaza where we ate was delightfully atmospheric. Centuries-old mulberry trees surrounded a pond filled with splashing children. On three sides were ancient *madrasas*. On the fourth, a *chai-khana* where old men sat, sipping and gossiping.

After an afternoon's rest, we dined with other guest-house visitors. Sebastiano and Karla were both working in Bukhara under United

Nations auspices. He was an Italian architect specializing in encouraging historically accurate building restorations. Karla was an American advisor helping revitalize local arts and crafts. After dinner, World Cup rugby on television proved irresistible to Sasha, Sebastiano and me.

The next morning, we met Noilla, another moonlighting guide. She reminded us that Bukhara had been an internationally prominent and respected center of learning, first under Buddhist monks, later under Islam. Persian-born Avicenna, the "father of modern medicine", taught here in the early years of the eleventh century. Medieval scholars came from as far as Muslim Spain. For hundreds of years, Bukhara was the largest center of Muslim theology in the world.

Noilla took us to one of the world's oldest standing mosques, Magoki Allori. It dated from the twelfth century but stood on the foundations of another mosque a century older. Below that, archaeologists had identified the foundations of a fifth-century Zoroastrian temple and, still below, an even older Buddhist monastery!

The next day we saw a Muslim mausoleum dating to 900 CE. This was one of my favorite structures in Bukhara, a simple cube faced with glazed bricks in an intricate checkerboard design. It held the tomb of Ismail Samani, founder of the last Persian dynasty to control Central Asia. The Kalan Mosque, a near-twin of Bibi-Khanym in Samarkand, could reputedly accommodate thousands of worshippers. Its signature minaret, splendid and restrained in decorative brick, bore the unfortunate label of the Tower of Death, a legacy of its balcony's past service as an execution launch-pad.

The Ark was the ancient citadel of Bukhara's emirs. Its touristic notoriety depended largely on the pit where two nineteenth-century British spies had been imprisoned and died. The fortress figured prominently in that era's "Great Game" of espionage waged across Asia by imperial Britain and Russia. The emirate collapsed under assault by the Bolsheviks' Red Army in 1920. That siege took a heavy toll on the center's historic buildings. At the time of our visit, the fortress's imposing walls remained in disrepair. But their smooth surfaces and rounded bastions like tapered silos gave an impression of the structure's sophisticated defensive components. By contrast, the last emir's summer palace seemed rather shabby and sad.

More interesting and livable was a nearby nineteenth-century wealthy merchant's house, complete with stables, harem courtyard and an ancient Victrola. Noilla was a good sport to model for us indoor and outdoor costumes of the ladies of that era.

In both Samarkand and Bukhara, we'd noticed that restorations and repairs were proceeding haphazardly but aggressively on the ancient monuments. Just as noticeably, the workmanship and materials of these rushed repairs were inferior to the original artistry. Our hope was that, through UNESCO involvement and the guidance of experts like Sebastiano, shoddy patch-ups could be discouraged, if not halted entirely.

On a happier note, the three of us were repeatedly impressed by the quality of for-sale arts and crafts. Wood-carving, tilework and painting struck us as particularly skillful, much better than kitschy souvenirs. Engineer Leonard acquired a Koran stand carved from a single block of wood into a delicate lattice adjustable to a half-dozen positions. Nancy selected polychromed pen cases and small boxes with reproductions of intricate Persian miniatures. I opted for small watercolors of camels and riders emerging from sandstorms. They are now framed in the entranceway of our California home.

Our return route to Almaty led again through Samarkand and Tashkent. I had to fly back for professional appointments. But Nancy and her father continued overland, first purchasing fifteen pounds of just-picked apricots to share with Almaty friends and neighbors still emerging from winter. When they reached Almaty, they brought glowing reports of steppes dipping down into green, glacier-fed valleys where stocky horses grazed.

For both of us, one of the nicest aspects of our thousand-mile journey was seeing how well Leonard was treated by local folks. They all praised his stamina, intellect and curiosity, refusing to believe he was older than 65. And they unfailingly afforded him the deference that Central Asians give to elders. He'd come half-way around the world to realize a childhood dream and been met with the best of Silk Road hospitality.

*Silk Road tea break. Leonard Swing with guide Valentina, daughter Nancy and anonymous tea critic. Samarkand 1995.*

# Rogues' Gallery

*Dushanbe 1996*

In the Dushanbe Municipal Library adjoining our Project's Legal Information Center, I liked to wander into a cozy alcove cluttered with coffee-table volumes of Central Asian art. The heroic propaganda of Soviet Realism left me cold. But I admired some evocative imaginings of Silk Road legacies.

Word filtered back to my Information Center colleague, Oksana. She shyly informed me that the artist whose work I'd been lingering over was in fact her own father. She kindly invited me to view some originals. I accepted with pleasure and the two of us set off together.

Her father, she explained, had been ailing and was still confined to a hospital. His studio turned out to be a converted garage, 20 feet on a side. It was secluded behind the family's modest home, three steps out the kitchen door and across a shaded courtyard.

The dark space was chock-a-block with clichéd landscapes—posing stags, plunging cataracts, everything but elves. Half-finished on easels or leaning in stacks, the repetitive paintings were little better than railway-station souvenirs. What a comedown for a venerated Hero of the Soviet Union. Obviously the old man needed the money, if only to afford private medical care.

His daughter winced at my evident embarrassment. I tried to appear interested as I tiptoed through canvasses. At last, in a back corner, I uncovered a few of the historical paintings which had established his reputation. One bright carnival scene in front of Timur's Registan at Samarkand was particularly enchanting. I asked Oksana if she'd set it aside for me and backed out of the depressing garage.

When next in Dushanbe, I was ready to retrieve my purchase. Oksana surprised me with the news that her father was out of the hospital and said she was sure he would like to meet me.

Now here we were back in that box of a studio, where the confronted master gave no indication that he shared his daughter's enthusiasm for the intrusion. As if accustomed to his being difficult, Oksana pressed ahead with introductions. I'd asked Saule Nurgaziyeva, accompanying me to Dushanbe from our Almaty Office, to help out with informal interpreting. Picking up on the chill, I apologized for barging in. But the artist would not be appeased.

In his early eighties, A.K. Kaidarov had blotched, fissured skin and dark, sullen eyes. Thick tufts sprouted from pendulous ears. His rasping breaths and stooped posture suggested the old man was losing a compound struggle with emphysema and arthritis. No wonder he felt prickly and put-upon. Humbling enough to be reduced to cranking out sentimental trash without being caught *in flagrante* on his pathetic assembly line.

His wife passed a tray of tea-filled glasses and sugar cubes in through the studio door. Then she retreated across the postage-stamp patio, implicitly declining to add to the awkwardness. Just as well since the rest of us were bumping up against each other and the easels. As we sat and sipped, Oksana tried to ease the tension, softly reciting her father's accolades without provoking his wrath.

The old man fidgeted with irritation, but beneath his dismissive mutters, I sensed embers of wounded pride. As I digested the résumé highlights through Saule's interpretation, I tried to reconcile these honors with Mr. Kaidarov's current isolation. Reaching for common ground, I drew him out on the painting I was purchasing.

"Please tell me about the Samarkand scene, Sir. Is it from life or historical sources?"

"I sketched the acrobats in pencil and chalk. It was 1925. I was just a boy finding my hand. A few years ago, I fished out those notebooks from happier times and retrieved the memories with oils."

"Do you have other sketches?" I mentioned my enthusiasm for artists' working drawings but was also thinking that small studies would be easier to carry on the plane.

His daughter pointed to paper sheets stacked on a tall bookcase. "Show him those, Father."

He visibly bridled. "They are old, Oksana. Leave them be. They are of no interest to an outsider."

Oksana had inherited some of her father's backbone and stood her ground. "I told you, Father. Mr. Sunshine leads a democratic-transition project. You should not assume."

"He wouldn't understand."

Next to me on the threadbare sofa, Saule squirmed at this family squabble. Leaning closer to my ear, she trimmed her interpreting to clipped whispers. I shared her discomfort and confusion. What lay beneath this coded spat?

"Don't be so stubborn," our hostess persisted. "Mr. Sunshine is leaving Dushanbe this afternoon and doesn't know when he can return."

Taking his shrug for acquiescence, Oksana herself climbed onto a rickety chair and eased down the dusty pile. She set them gingerly on the low table in front of our sofa.

I began turning them over, so Saule and I could look at the drawings together. What an odd mixture of materials—cardboard, ruled notepaper, brown butcher's paper, even wrinkled wrapping.

On each sheet was a portrait, in pencil or charcoal. All the subjects were men, gaunt, short-haired or with shaved scalps. The faces varied in age and ethnic type, mostly Slavic but some Central Asian. All were somber, several haunted. Only heads and still faces. No torsos, costumes, or context. No smiles, movement or color.

Within these tight compositional constraints, the studies were brilliant. Subtle shadings of gray, spiked by accents of black, remarkably captured and conveyed a tragic range of human character. Despite no flicker of overt emotion, I was certain that these give-away-nothing countenances concealed resilience, intelligence, sophistication, charisma, rage, disease and despair.

I lost myself in 50 decaying pages and was moved nearly to tears.

"What are you thinking?" the old man asked.

"What I'm thinking, Mr. Kaidarov, is that I like these drawings much the best of all your work that I've seen. Beyond comparison. But what I'm feeling is the despair in your subjects' faces."

"Can you guess what you are looking at?"

"Help me, please."

"Welcome to the Gulag."

Master Kaidarov gazed into the past. "It was just after the Second World War. Mother Russia was gloriously victorious. But Uncle Josef wasn't satisfied. The General Secretary decided to settle a few scores."

Stalin started with the top military brass, the artist explained. Several field commanders had been captured by the Germans on the Eastern Front and repatriated in 1946. To Stalin, they were disgraced. Even those whom later historians would rank among the Red Army's most brilliant strategists and courageous leaders.

"For him, to surrender was to betray. Never mind the tens of thousands of troops spared by those white flags. It was necessary to make an example. Stripped of rank and decorations, the demonized generals were banished to oblivion. Several sites served his purposes. One was Semipalatinsk in northeastern Kazakhstan. Do you know it, Mr. Sunshine?"

"Only by name."

"Consider yourself fortunate. Picture utter flatness, wind-swept, and destructively hot or cold, depending on the season. A perfect choice for isolation and invisibility."

The artist sank back, self-absorbed, as if reliving, not merely recollecting. "Stalin's purge gathered steam. Next in the queue came decadent intellectuals—artists, cinema directors, ballet impresarios, symphony conductors, scholars, professors, philosophers, writers, poets.

"My crime was historical painting. 'Subversive bourgeois nostalgia'. I was picked up in 1947. It took them a while to get down to my tier."

The old man shuddered as if physically chilled. "The camp was so bleak. Leached of all color. Dilapidated dormitories shrouded in fine dust blowing off the steppes. No guard towers or perimeter fencing. Why waste scarce wire? We were warehoused in Limbo. Buried alive."

Saule kept pace, interpreting softly. We were both transported back 50 years.

"As part of our punishment, we were totally deprived of information. No newspapers, books, radio, films or music. The rare family letter was half blacked-out by censors. I drew to preserve my sanity. I didn't want to attract our keepers' attention and risk punishment or confiscation. So I only sketched subjects inside the dormitory. The heads and faces of the damned."

Mr. Kaidarov coughed and leaned forward. With a savage index finger, he jabbed at the top sheet in our stack. "Young Lady, do you recognize this one?"

Saule jerked to attention. Lulled by his monotone, she'd been interpreting on autopilot.

"Field Marshall Ivanov," he barked. "Do you know that name?

"Of course," she stammered, with a twinge of irritation. "We studied Stalingrad in school."

"And him? And him?" The thin sheets scattered under his assault. To me, the names were unknown or only vaguely familiar. However, Saule's shocked face confirmed these were stars from USSR constellations. A fierce patriot and former Young Pioneer, my colleague was being shaken to the core.

I jumped in to relieve her distress. "Mr. Kaidarov, how did you get the paper?"

"Whatever I could scavenge. Wrapping paper from rare packages admitted by the guards, cardboard from boxes. Other scraps. I hoarded pencil stubs and charcoal chips like treasures."

"And the drawings?"

"Stored in a tin box under the floorboards until I could smuggle out a batch, perhaps once a year. Several got through. My wife hid them in a cupboard. They were ugly, but they proved I was still alive. I had no political agenda beyond a stubborn determination to bear witness. I also jotted a secret journal. The notes were cryptic but I knew every line. Most of all, though, I drew. To keep my hand and my eye. My mind and my soul."

The speaker sat up a bit straighter. I sensed he was bringing his salvaged saga to a close.

"We sleepwalked through years. Seven years in hell. I would have died there, but Stalin beat me to it. In 1953. The word flashed through the camp like wildfire. One bunk-mate ran screaming from our front porch. He'd hung on only to spite the hated tyrant. With that spring released, his mind literally snapped. We were trucked out soon afterwards, without identity papers or compensation. Walking skeletons from the Soviet closet."

The artist dropped his bard's cadence and resumed adversarial posturing. "Enough rambling by an old fart. You're not interested in ancient history. Neither am I."

I was deeply affected by his treasures. Equally by his tale. I asked if he'd considered exhibiting the drawings or at least transcribing and publishing the journal.

"Don't patronize me," he spit. "I've been manipulated by the best. First, Khrushchev had me reinstated, when it suited him to distance himself from Stalin. Even pinned a medal on my chest. Then I was dumped again when the pendulum swung back. The bigshots would prefer not to be reminded of an awkward chapter in our again glorious past. Fair enough. I learned from experts how to keep quiet. I'll carry my scribbles to the grave."

I could taste his choking bile but the loss seemed a travesty. "Have you or your daughter tried to make contact with a university or a library? If not within Central Asia, then farther afield?"

"Spare me your bright ideas," he cut me off. "Another enthusiast came here before you. Fussing and fawning, all pledges and promises. Total bullshit. It came to nothing."

"Give me a chance."

Oksana lent her support. "Father, let him try."

The fatigued artist relented and we exchanged strained goodbyes.

I had a specific ally in mind. Back in Almaty, I contacted Adilet, one of our Project's NGO grantees. This determined group was fighting to preserve historical awareness throughout the former Soviet Union. Their mission was to educate the youth, not letting past abuses be denied, papered over or forgotten.

As I'd anticipated, the NGO jumped at the opportunity to help rescue this precious archive. Adilet dispatched two rapporteurs to Dushanbe to tape the old man's recollections, retrieve his drawings and preserve his journal. He was escorted to Almaty to be saluted as guest-of-honor at an exhibition of his drawings and written record. The entire collection was purchased and preserved intact.

The recognition came none too soon. The master was dead within the year.

# Floatin' Thru Kazakhstan

## *Ili River 1996*

Frank gets most of the credit for inspiring our Ili River cruise. The rest of us were more than ready to get out of Almaty, always breathing polluted air and wrestling with national and international bureaucracies. Frank's visit spurred Nancy and me to cast about for something special to share with our visitor from Eastern Kentucky. Travelling by water through the arid steppes of Central Asia seemed about as unusual as we could imagine.

Frank Olson was (and remains) my best buddy. Our friendship stretched back 30 years to our first year of law school together in Berkeley. A kind soul with Quaker roots, he taught high-school kids and counseled prison inmates in Appalachia. Equally appealing to Nancy and me, Frank was a thoughtful houseguest in any country where he visited us—fitting in, pitching in and taking genuine pleasure in things local.

Rounding out our nautical party were Dave and Sue Benedetti and Ben Steinberg, all dear friends and fellow development-assistance professionals based in Almaty. Our ad-libbing tour guide was Ruslan, a former USSR kayak champion now launching an outdoor-adventures business. His younger clients preferred white-water canoeing or glacier treks. But for our mature band, he graciously offered to pull together something less taxing. Ruslan's ad hoc expedition crew included a driver, a cook, and two general helpers, in addition to himself. We'd not be short of support.

We left Almaty on a Friday evening after work, conveyed in a repainted school bus. Arriving two hours later at our first campsite on the Ili River floodplain, we were greeted by a welcoming circle of tired tents and a crackling campfire. We shared inaugural beers as the cook prepared dinner. Two local young men cantered up on the same shaggy, squat ponies that had carried fearsome Mongols to the gates of Vienna. Once they'd satisfied their curiosity and confirmed we were not dispensing complimentary vodka shots, they faded into the darkness.

*First campsite, with raft and bus. Ben, Sue, Dave, Frank, Russell.*
*Ili River 1996.*

Unfortunately, another loud group camping across the river seemed to have brought their own alcoholic provisions. Their carousing, plus the inadequacy of thin Insulite pads under our sleeping bags, kept most of us awake for long hours. Our consolation was dazzling riverside skies. Away from competing metropolitan glare, the Milky Way was breathtakingly close and brilliant. No wonder the heavens had dominated ancient religion and science.

The next morning, after a restorative breakfast of eggs, bread and tea, Nancy and I strolled up to the bluffs overlooking the river. There were no trees, buildings or other intrusions, so it was easy to spot movement in the distance. To our delight, a seemingly unending carpet of camels unrolled across the plain. Finding a defile, they rushed down to the water and began slaking their thirst. These were marvelous, animated beasts, a far cry from lulled curiosities in circuses or Shriners' parades. Bactrian camels, they had one hump and huge shaggy heads. Males and females, adults, adolescents and calves, they ranged in color from almost black to almost white. We admired dark and milk chocolate, caramel, golden beige, pale cream and all shades in between.

The column kept streaming down off the bluff as we drew closer. There were scores, perhaps hundreds, of shapes, a surging mass blurred by the dust. We jogged back to our camp to rouse our friends. When we all returned, two large guardian males interposed themselves and kept us at bay. But we were allowed to approach within 20 feet, plenty near to hear a full concert of snorts, groans, belches and gas, all accompanied by gurgling bellies.

Frank grinned at the team slurp. "Sounds like a gigantic suction pump."

At no time, in this extended encounter did we observe any accompanying herdsmen. They must have been trailing. But to our urban eyes, the self-service consumers were free-ranging.

We looked at our watches and reluctantly withdrew, returning to camp to help pack things up. The crew had cobbled together a wooden-decked raft lashed onto torpedo-shaped pontoons. Ruslan fitted us into stale-smelling life vests for what he assured us was an unnecessary, though prudent, safety precaution. The improvised vessel's permeable deck felt stable enough as we all scrambled aboard to pick our spots. There was ample room to accommodate eight passengers and all our gear. The other three workers moved the bus to keep ahead of our aquatic progress.

The Ili in this stretch and at this time of year was wide and tame. Two hundred yards from bank to bank and four or five feet down to a smooth bed. As a bonus, the water was warm. The river originated in the Tien Shan range of far-western China, in the Xinjiang Uighur Autonomous Region. After passing the Kapshagay hydroelectric power-plant and reservoir near Almaty, it would continue past us to flow into

Lake Balkhash in southeastern Kazakhstan. Balkhash, the third largest freshwater lake on earth, drains a basin the size of California.[12] Fittingly, given most of the terrain the river traversed in its 900-mile journey, "*Ili*", in Turkic languages, meant "bareness."

Frank and I were avid bird-watchers. I was an enthusiastic novice but rarely knew what I was looking at. He'd had the foresight to bring a paperback field guide. The river was a migratory flightpath for dozens of species, so we were thrilled by the abundance and variety. Neon rollers, kingfishers and bee-eaters quickly became routine. But a Himalayan Rubythroat! A gloriously long-tailed Asian Paradise Flycatcher!

Soon our raves drew all but the most resolute dozer into the act. The spotters would shout out colors and markings while Frank thumbed furiously through his pages.

"What was that one?"

"What one? Where?"

A nondescript streak buzzed the raft, perhaps defending a riverbank nest.

"Can't make it out." That was Dave from the bow.

"Give me something to work with, Guys." Frank, looking up from his guide.

"Fas-bird." My wife stirred from her slumber, animated at last by the clamor.

"What'd she say?"

"Can't hear you, Nancy."

"It's a fas'-bird."

It seemed an apt designation for a bland feathered missile. "Fas'-bird" it stayed.

When not rudely rousted, Nancy contentedly catnapped, catching up on lost sleep. Ben, Frank and I periodically jumped into the stream

---

12  Kazakhstan and China remain embroiled in an unresolved conflict stemming from China's plans to dam or even reverse the flow of the Ili River to help support major in-migration into Xinjiang. The Kazakhstan government and environmental experts are concerned the blocked flow could shrink Lake Balkhash to another ecological disaster like the decimated Aral Sea.

to cool off from the bright sunlight. The water was cloudy with silt but free of dangerous debris. In most places, we could stand on the bottom if we got tired of paddling. Ruslan, our steersman, would hover in eddies to let us catch up and climb back aboard.

We pulled up onto an island for a light lunch of soup and bread prepared in advance by the go-ahead gang. Then more swims, more naps and a leisurely afternoon float.

By the time we reached Nightingale Island, with its avian chorus performing on cue, our crew had already set up tents and started stew simmering. They had portaged the gear from the bus on foot and by kayak. The six Americans provided the evening's entertainment with a round of increasingly challenging charades. "Cruising down the River" wasn't much of a stretch. "Be-bop-a-Lula" required more of the guessing team.

After a better night's sleep, already getting used to the hard ground, we were treated to a breakfast of made-from-scratch blinis topped by fresh loganberry syrup. Our foraging cook had picked the berries at dawn while the languishing tourists snored.

We invested a lazy morning in lounging, reading and exploring. I tagged along when Ruslan led the driver upstream for an unsuccessful fishing foray. They had no better luck than our cross-country trek to flush allegedly abundant pheasants. The wily birds, if indeed they existed, were more practical than the humans and stayed out of the mid-day sun.

After lunch, more portaging and repacking, we rode the faithful bus on a now-longer haul back to Almaty. A temporary mechanical breakdown was taken in stride. All charter members of the '60s Generation except younger Ben, we filled the vehicle with our acapella imitations of Pete Seeger, the Mamas & the Papas, and Simon & Garfunkel. Broadway show-tunes provided backup when our pop repertoire thinned. Only Frank kept on key, drawing on his barbershop-quartet experience in the Kentucky hills. But missed notes by the rest of us did nothing to lower the volume or dim our enthusiasm. After decades of postings in remote locations, we were well-accustomed to making it up as we went along.

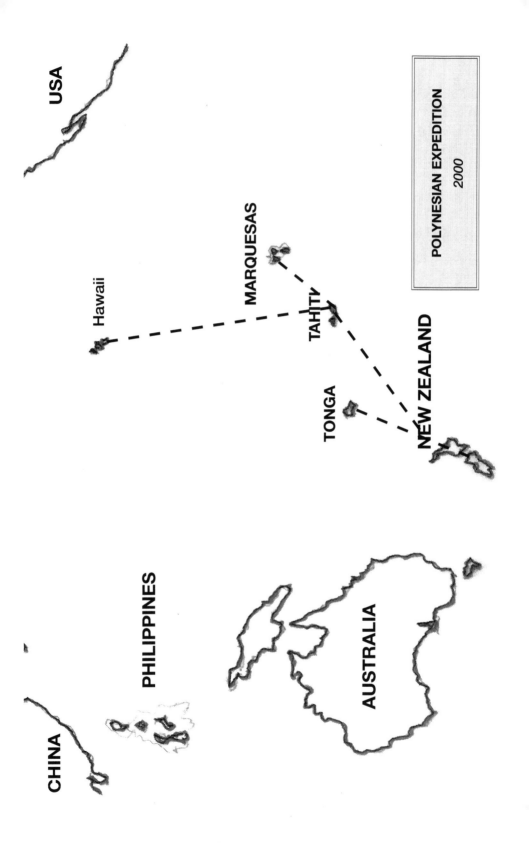

CHAPTER NINE

# POLYNESIA:
# IN THE WAKE OF CANOES

In the autumn of 2000, I was restless between international consulting assignments and making a nuisance of myself around the house. Nancy was immersed in revising a novel and couldn't get away. She suggested I take off on my own for some destination long dreamed of but deferred. Since boyhood, I'd devoured factual and fictional accounts of the Far Pacific—Bougainville, Cook, Stevenson, London, Nordhoff and Hall, Michener, Heyerdahl, and an alphabet of other Oceania visitors and scribes. So when I drew up my travel wish list, Polynesia bobbed to the top.

As the Millennium turned, scientific knowledge of Polynesian migrations was expanding exponentially. Multidisciplinary analysis confirmed that Polynesian ancestors first migrated south from Taiwan and the China coast as early as 3500 BCE. Arriving off New Guinea about 1500 BCE, they exploded into a burst of artistic creativity and navigational bravura. By 1200 BCE, proto-Polynesians had sailed northwest, via Fiji, to Tonga and Samoa. By the beginning of the Christian era, they had reached the Marquesas and Society Islands, then Hawaii and Easter Island around 500 CE. New Zealand, 500 years after that.

Their voyages covered hundreds, even thousands, of miles, across uncharted seas. In sturdy, twin-hulled sailing canoes measuring 50-100 feet from bow to stern, Polynesians were able to cover 100 miles on a good 24-hour run; and to carry provisions sufficient to sustain crew and passengers for three months at sea.

With no knowledge of Pacific geography, no documents to record their routes, no metal, no instruments for measuring time or direction, these courageous pioneers ventured repeatedly into the unknown. They navigated by sun, moon and stars, by winds and currents, watching birds, fish, sea mammals and floating debris for signs of possible landfalls. So dispersed were their potential targets that most of these explorers must have perished at sea. Of those who safely reached new archipelagos, some returned with tales and trophies. Eventually, regular trading routes were established, guided by chanted maps. To put this achievement into historical perspective, while Polynesians were taming the world's largest ocean, European mariners were still hugging the shore.

I wanted to visit this watery trail. I reversed the migration routes in order to do a bit of preliminary research at the University of Hawaii and the Bishop Museum. From Honolulu, my airborne itinerary carried me south to Tahiti and the Society Islands, the Marquesas, New Zealand and Tonga. Leaving home on October 1, I was in the Pacific for two restorative months.

## DAY AND NIGHT

*Nuku Hiva 2000*

A sharp volcanic ridge knifes into the sea surrounding Nuku Hiva, largest island in the Marquesas. On either side of this rain-catching divide, a half-moon bay forms an open fan. The settlements on these twin shores and the two women who dominate them could hardly be less alike. Near-neighbors Yvonne Katupa and Juliette Vaianui occupy, and have largely created, two different worlds.

Nuku Hiva was an exhilarating short hop from Papeete, Tahiti, over luminous turquoise atolls. My pickup-truck taxi bounced for two lulling hours along snaking ridges. Then a roller-coaster plunge through a cleft in 1,500-foot vibrant green cliffs crowned by exposed volcanic pinnacles like giants' drip-castles. Whoosh! Out we popped onto a black-sand shore.

"Hatiheu!" my stoked jockey announced.

After the arid hilltops, the bay-side vegetation was overwhelming. Dense coconut palms, pandanus, mangoes, plumeria, hibiscus, banana, oleander and papaya wove a dense thicket as the slope eased to the water's edge.

My hostess greeted me at her modest *pension* with a welcome glass of mango juice. I guessed Yvonne Katupa to be in her fifties and no more

*Hatiheu Harbor promenade. Nuku Hiva, Marquesas 2000.*

than five feet tall. She radiated hospitable energy and filled an expansive floral-print smock. I'd soon learn that this pint-sized dynamo powered the entire village 18 hours a day.

Locally born and raised, Yvonne had served as Hatiheu's mayor, magistrate, tourism promoter and village elder for nearly two decades. As I observed more than once during my brief stay in her fiefdom, this diminutive matron exercised firm leadership through a deft combination of charisma, cajolery and consensus-building. A tribal chieftain without the headdress, Yvonne held her community together by example and force of will. This, in an era when outward migration and substance abuse were decimating many Polynesian hamlets.

As the only guest in her *pension*, I got to watch her in action at close range. Whether on the front porch, on the telephone or seated under backyard banana trees, Her Honor was on the job. An obviously respected mediator in constant demand, she listened before responding—receiving petitions, bridging differences and contributing requested advice.

Hatiheu was a modest settlement, with only 120 current residents. Yet by tapping French colonial stipends and a network of contacts, Yvonne had attracted to her hamlet a health clinic and a primary school, a library and a community bathhouse, underground electrical wiring, two churches, a volleyball court and a concrete jetty. Without exaggeration, it was a model community.

The docking facility received monthly calls by the posh cruise ship *Aranui*. This pampering vessel carried 90 well-heeled retirees on two-week circuits among the Marquesas for up to $10,000 per person. In Hatiheu, their six-hour shore visit for an archaeological tour, local dance performances and a luncheon feast generated substantial revenues for the community, as well as personal gratuities for villagers drafted as guides, dancers, musicians and waiters. Equally important, as Yvonne quietly explained to me after the one landing I witnessed, this recurring port call gave her an occasion to mobilize the kids and other village residents to sweep paths and lanes, weed flower beds, pick welcoming garlands and generally tidy up the entire settlement.

Early and late, Yvonne found time to chat with me about her values and vision. With no post-secondary education, she'd intuitively developed a pragmatic leadership agenda that balanced vigilant preservation of tradition with encouragement of digestible doses of modernization. Education was her driving passion for village youth. Thirty-two boys and girls attended the local primary school. Adolescents boarded across the island at the Taiohae Academy. The most promising students had a chance to pursue higher technical or university courses in Tahiti. Yvonne worked hard with other elders, sports coaches and two missionary priests to keep local consumption of cannabis and alcohol from spiraling out of control. She was also a driving member of an archipelago-wide coalition to preserve and promote use of Marquesan language.

When not presiding over municipal affairs, Yvonne engaged her passion as a self-taught chef. (Only later did I learn that the leading English-language guidebook to the region had dubbed her the best cook in French Polynesia.) Her cuisine blended Marquesan unpretentiousness

273

with a French twist. Always, fresh local ingredients provided the key.

One evening she served me broiled lobster flambéed in whiskey, butter, garlic, onions and herbs. Breadfruit fritters and roasted taro complemented this entree. A just-plucked mango was my dessert. I chose Tahitian beer as my beverage, although French wine was also on offer.

For a lunch, I enjoyed lightly-sautéed local whitefish with a salad of garden greens. Freshwater shrimp from the stream running outside my bungalow window were deep-fried in tempura batter.

The cruise-ship guests' luncheon menu featured succulent pork baked in the ground on hot stones for five hours, then served with a sauce of chives and coconut milk and a side of marinated baby bananas.

I spent much of my Hatiheu time exploring the sprawling Polynesian ruins. From my reading, I'd discovered that this sleepy hollow had once hosted no fewer than 25,000 inhabitants in the so-called Polynesian "Classical Period" just before contact with Europeans. The same remoteness that had isolated these islands from most humans and other large fauna and flora had also kept micro-organisms away. So the locals were mostly disease-free, a condition that encouraged rapid population growth but tragically also made them easy prey to European infections.[13]

The Hatiheu site of pre-Contact ruins measured nearly a mile on a side, all on the gentle slope descending from cliff bases to the shore. With a local guide, I scrambled over and around walls and terraces, long assembly fields with bleachers, platforms for ceremonies, statues, grave sites and stairways—all carved from lava. Abundant petroglyphs incised into the worked volcanic stone included graceful dolphins, turtles and stick figures. Ferocious effigies explained to me as deities were dwarf-like in stature with bulging eyes.

The entire complex had been excavated by archaeologists from the University of Hawaii. With findings now published and the location still remote, by the time of my arrival the site was fast receding into the jungle. Stairs were buckling, undermined by relentless roots. There

---

13  The other major drivers of population reduction were intertribal warfare in ancient times and economic emigration in the modern era.

*Pre-Contact (17th-century) Polynesian temple platform and guardians. Nuku Hiva 2000.*

were no explanatory signs or protective facilities. I found it incredible that one of the most significant historical locations in the Pacific was so quickly capitulating to neglect. From Hatiheu, the main expeditions colonizing Hawaii had been launched. Nuku Hiva, along with other Marquesas, had been a hugely significant way-station for Polynesian onward migration to Easter Island and New Zealand. Now this heroic hub was crumbling in solitude.

A 90-minute hike up a steep but well-marked footpath led me over the saddle to pristine Anaho Bay. A collapsed caldera more than a mile across, Anaho was more open in vista than Hatiheu, and now inhabited by less than a half-dozen families. The entire bay-front had once belonged to a single landowner. He'd bequeathed equal plots to his four sons, slicing parcels in the Polynesian tradition from summit to shoreline.

The eldest son became a successful contractor, in charge of road-building at the French nuclear-testing site in Tahiti, until that facility was deactivated. He'd put up a family-vacation compound at one end of Anaho Bay but died in a fiery car crash two years prior to my visit. He was survived by his French widow, Juliette, who greeted me now as I made my way through acres of rustling coconut palms.

Juliette Vaianui was long, lean and still. I faced a translucent wraith. Over a chilled glass of wine, this lonely widow shared her immigrant's tale. The Paris-born daughter of a French civil servant and his society wife, Juliette had come out to Tahiti with her parents when her father was assigned a Territorial post. Raised by convent Sisters in mission schools, she had swum as soon as she'd walked, spoken and sung Polynesian as well as her mother tongue. Boarding school back "home" in Europe had been a nightmare for a shy, provincial adolescent lagging years behind metropolitan fads and fashions. She'd returned to the islands as a young adult and soon married a handsome local man on his way up in Territorial business.

Juliette gave birth to no fewer than nine children, six girls and three boys. Two died in infancy, two others before they were ten. One daughter was mentally troubled. The mother hinted at drug-overdose damage. Decades of losses desiccated the marriage.

Juliette never enjoyed the brittle animation of Papeete, the Tahitian capital of French Polynesia. Periodic excursions to France gave her no joy. Increasingly, she found solace in her husband's inherited Anaho retreat. On his death, she withdrew there full-time. When I arrived, the widow had nominally converted the family-vacation property into a *pension*. But I was the only guest. And unlike Hatiheu, the accommodations were shabby in the extreme.

Juliette herself was a curious mélange. At one moment silent and tuned out, she exhibited the eerie calm of an eccentric recluse. Then suddenly she'd erupt into manic chatter, interweaving French and English. Her voice was soft, her laugh thin and reedy. Clearly starved for conversation, she rushed ahead in fits and starts, leaving sentences and topics dangling. Surprising phrases revealed archived residues of wit and vibrancy. Pulses of gaiety raced over a lingering melancholy.

Juliette had pale blue eyes and smooth skin. Wan, almost haunted, she looked every one of her 60 years. Yet under palm shadows, this ethereal figure gave fleeting glimpses of her earlier selves.

Her son Leopold joined us for dinner. He bitterly complained that tourists were staying away, then trotted out a catalogue of reasons why this wasn't his fault. When I suggested an excursion invitation to the *Aranui* management or at least a water taxi linked to Hatiheu, Leopold took 30 minutes to explain why neither would work. Boats and fuel were expensive, spare parts unavailable, pilots unreliable and thieving. Like so many island offspring, he felt constrained by his shoreline and lured by the horizon.

Anaho Bay was serenely lovely at all hours. Bold roosters joined snuffling pigs rooting for shellfish at low tide. Pelicans, terns, gulls and skimmers competed for flight lines paralleling the gentle waves. I swam out through clear water to float above a finned kaleidoscope.

When boastful Leopold failed to produce his promised catch of fish, his seemingly fragile mother hitched up her skirts and waded barefoot on the rocks to spear a formidable octopus. It soon anchored a succulent chowder simmered with coconut milk and lime juice.

In another time, with other players, this gorgeous setting could support a world-class resort. Here and now it was sleeping, a protective shelter for a damaged survivor. I decided not to wish for yet another magnet spa. Unspoiled sanctuaries were already being gobbled up at a terrifying pace.

When I packed my rucksack and took my leave, the pale siren leaned in her doorway, a huge hibiscus blossom intertwined with fragrant frangipani behind her ear.

She laid two glorious seashells in my hand. We both knew I'd never return.

"They come with the full moon" were her parting words.

# SERENDIPITY

## Ha'apai 2000

"Does that inspire confidence, or what? The fucking wing fell off the plane!"

"Freddie, look on the bright side. We're still alive to tell about it."

Sound bites arced across tables. I caught snatches of disbelief, irritation, sarcastic humor and trembling relief. Royal Tongan Airways had just informed its 18 passengers that the single Otter servicing Ha'apai had been declared "un-airworthy" until the errant wing could be re-secured and certified.

The airline's Airport Manager had put chutzpah ahead of customer relations when announcing his take on our near-disaster. "Ladies and Gentlemen, the pilot has assured me that in fact the wing did not completely fall off while still airborne. Total detachment occurred only upon contact with the tarmac when he returned to the runway for his emergency landing."

One or both of these hair-splitters must have gone to law school. But regardless of spin, our take-off had aborted. We'd be stranded over a long weekend while they borrowed a substitute craft from Air Fiji.

The good news was that Royal Tongan had contacted our connecting carriers and informed them of the delay. The airline would also cover our layover lodging and meal expenses. The bad news was that we'd already exhausted Ha'apai's modest tourist attractions. Most passengers were itching to get on with their planned itineraries.

It was no coincidence that all of us had gathered to commiserate in Tony's Café. Tony's was the only commercial eatery in town. Thankfully under the circumstances, it was a pleasant-enough place for nursing grievances. A striped parachute canopy sheltered the courtyard from tropical sun and showers. Bordering pots of flowers and herbs kept the space compact and cozy. Long tables with benches encouraged family-style sharing. Tony, a leathered Aussie, and Tia, his Tongan wife, served up generous portions of tasty burgers and fries, fish, omelets, pizzas and salads. Today their comfort food was much in demand.

The stranded passengers were a typically mixed bag for a South Pacific port. Fit, aging German couples doggedly chasing remnants of a long-gone colonial heritage. Loud, obese Americans. Earnest European university students backpacking between terms. Misery loving company, they exchanged and recycled individual morsels of inconvenience.

Although I wasn't about to broadcast it, I was feeling much less agitated. I had no inflexible onward appointments. There was nothing any of us could do to shorten our delay. Most important, I was silently grateful that, if the damned wing had to fall off, the gods had consented to let it happen on the ground.

As the griping wound down and groups drifted away, I noticed other diners besides my fellow passengers. It was November of 2000 and talk at our table turned to America's election fiasco. No one had mastered the nuances of Florida ballot recounts or hanging chads. Joining this lighter round of chatter was a strikingly handsome, 30-something couple. Both were softly tanned and emitted an aura of welcome serenity. I sensed they were long-term sojourners or perhaps re-provisioning yachties. The man had bright green eyes and a frequent crinkling smile. His partner was as slim and feline as a catwalk model, genuine cover-girl material. The three of us gradually found ourselves alone and exchanged introductions.

Hal and Elena were Toronto-based. Dividing their professional time between television and theater, he designed sets and she costumes for major productions. They intimated, without boasting, that their careers were flourishing. "We both work freelance," Hal explained. "It lets us fly out twice a year."

"So how long have you two kept up your marathon commuting?"

"Eight years for me," Hal responded.

"Four for me," Elena added. "Since we've been a couple."

I was intrigued by their quiet candor and found the pair refreshingly simpatico and self-effacing.

Taking Hal's nod as tacit consent, Elena leaned forward. "Russell, you appear stuck here for the weekend. How'd you like to slip across to *our* island?"

The next morning found me down at Ha'apai's municipal dock at seven sharp, rucksack in hand. Tony and Tia joined me with conspiratorial grins. We clambered into an outboard-powered skiff under the command of our pilot, Star.

Tony confided that Star was something of a local celebrity. Probably well past 60, though admitting only to 50, he retained weathered good looks, a light step and a twinkle of mischief. The Tongan co-owner of Hal and Elena's hideaway, Star was doubly notorious—for his appeal to ladies of diverse ethnicities and eras, as well as an addiction to alcohol that rendered him periodically inert. One smitten Japanese conquest had paid Star's airfare all the way to Tokyo, luckily round-trip. Her banker-husband proved less susceptible to Polynesian magnetism.

Star eased the skiff in and out of Ha'apai harbor's multiple inlets for no apparent reason. I wondered if he might have been hitting the sauce. However, it soon emerged that local decorum demanded that Star not pick up his weekend girlfriend from the same dock on which he'd just taken leave of his wife. Once the new lady had hopped aboard, our now-complete party made the crossing in calm waters.

Hal and Elena had returned to their island the night before. As we rounded the nearest headland, they waded out into the shallows to help pull in Star's skiff and keep satchels dry. The turquoise water, empty white beach and gently curving, palm-studded shoreline were already worth the trip.

The encampment that greeted us was devoid of any frills. The few structures were thatched, faded and sagging. Hal cheerfully demonstrated the modest communal plumbing. A bucket and rope attached to a well did double duty as outside shower and toilet sluice. Hal and Elena occupied one cabin. Star and satellite, the second. Tony and Tia were shown to one hut, I to another. Its amenities were limited to a thin mattress and sheet on a wooden platform, a mosquito net and sighing roof fronds. Everything was within 50 yards of the beach. No extras, but no pretensions.

After a simple lunch catered by Star, we drifted apart for hammock naps and gliding swims. As the mid-day glare subsided, I decided to take advantage of low tide to walk the island's perimeter.

Hal offered two pointers. "The island's deserted. You can't get lost. Just keep the sea on your right. Or your left, depending on your direction!"

Elena was helpfully less pixyish. "Russell, the total circumference is less than 12 miles. No more than four hours walking."

At even a strolling pace, I'd be back before sunset.

The weather was unpredictable. A sweep of the horizon revealed dark rain squalls, clear blue patches, and a full palette of grays in between. I stuck a rain slicker in my rucksack on top of an apple, camera and dark glasses. Thick-soled beach sandals were tucked under the flap in case rocks or coral raised sharp hazards.

From the first step, I eased into a relaxed, rhythmic stride. Like a yogic breathing exercise, repetitive, calming, yet curiously awareness-heightening. My feet soon became sensitized to the sand's varying slope and firmness. Soon I was automatically keeping to the best footing on slightly moist sand.

Beneath mostly overcast skies, the light was subtle and yet wonderfully changeable. At one moment, sun shafts bounced sharply off the tidal surface, forcing me to squint or look away. The next instant, the sky darkened to monochrome charcoal, with horizontal, stinging showers. Then cool, drying breezes, then sudden stillness. The sea colors kept pace. Transparent, brilliant turquoise. Translucent but somber ultramarine. Solid black under patched white foam.

The beach was a medley of comparable surprises. At first seemingly vacant, it began yielding up treasures on closer inspection. Science-fiction crabs bigger than my open palm stood motionless, near-invisible sentries masterfully camouflaged in beige and white. Losing their nerve at my approaching vibrations, they'd sidle away on stilts into gaping burrows. Almost impossibly, in less than six inches of water where the sea met the sand, explosive schools of skittish smelt darted and froze like miniature barracuda.

A hundred seashell varieties had been deposited by last night's high storm tide. Clams a foot in diameter. Lustrous cowries. Fanciful, spiraling augers, horns and tritons. Giant sea-urchin spines buffed to elegant javelins. There was garbage too, mostly plastic debris from fishermen and other sailors. Even this invasive flotsam failed to deflate my buoyancy.

Birds were my only non-marine companions. Squealing waders kept just ten yards ahead of my advance, apparently sensing I presented no threat. Frigate birds soared. Gulls and terns swooped. In my entire ramble, I saw no other human or animal.

It was easy to identify the many tracks of stray dogs and wild pigs. Other larger prints baffled me until Elena later decoded them as free-ranging horses'. Small herds wandered over from the adjacent island along a sand spit exposed only at lowest tides.

Every bend in the coastline brought new vistas. In one stretch, an eight-foot bluff was carpeted in sea grape and grasses, backed by a border of pandanus and coconut palms. On two tidal flats, I came upon ancient Polynesian quarries of exposed volcanic-rock slabs. An assembly line frozen in time, each site contained long rows of three-by-six-foot rectangles in progressive stages of extraction. At one end, guidelines chipped with basalt adzes etched the solid bed. At the other, finished slabs lay ready for floating and transport. Painstakingly crafted components destined for unknown sacred or noble constructions.

I recalled from my readings that similar quarries were scattered throughout the Tongan archipelago. Dating from the thirteenth to the eighteenth century, they were worked under the supervision of a privileged guild of stonemasons. Typical slabs weighed more than a ton. Some were cradled between canoes and moved as much as 60 miles. So much that we know about early Tongan customs comes directly from William Mariner. An English cabin boy shipwrecked in the archipelago in 1806, he spent four isolated years as the adopted son of a local warrior-king before being plucked away by off-course Europeans.

After dozens of straightaways, headlands and conclave bays, I recognized Hal and Elena's beach. Three-plus hours of absorbing walking had left me drained but exhilarated, with gently abraded toes and soles. I was surprised to realize I'd never lifted my camera out of my pack.

Star served up grilled fish, chicken and cooled beers for an evening barbecue. I asked about the tidal slabs.

Hal's eyes twinkled. "I'll show you tomorrow morning. Tony and Tia, you too if you're game. Better wear shoes, long sleeves and hats, if you've brought them." Despite our entreaties, he wouldn't say more.

After breakfast and a wake-up swim, the three of us joined our mischievous scoutmaster, kitted out as instructed. Hal claimed he'd first stumbled upon his surprise when exploring the island years before. But then he'd lost track of it, despite numerous searches.

We suspected our playful host was exaggerating for effect. The low coral island measured only five miles long, one-and-one-half wide. But after just five minutes of slogging through the dense vegetation, our skepticism dissolved. Every stretch of forest looked alike, as did the infrequent clearings. Tall, full-leaved trees screened out much of the light. Draped lianas accentuated confusing shadows and the shoulder-high underbrush was disorienting. Downed trunks and rocks underfoot demanded close attention. We could hear the surf, so getting back out to the perimeter would be no problem. But getting in was another story.

Without Hal as our guide, we'd have had no confident sense of direction or distance.

Tony saw it first. "Jesus wept!"

A giant stone pyramid rose out of the shimmering gloom.

Ten steps before, it had been totally invisible. For long moments, we just stood and stared. Then, like kids, we dashed in separate directions, calling out finds.

I paced off the oblong mound. "Fifty yards long, twenty-five wide. I'd guess eight to the top."

The sides tapered inward, faced in finely-worked, rectangular stone slabs. I stretched my arms across a panel. "Three by six feet, maybe eight inches thick."

Hal stepped up quietly behind me. "Your quarries at the shore."

The slabs were tightly laid in horizontal courses, with no apparent mortar. Most were covered in lush, electric-green moss. A few had been dislodged by persistent banyan roots. Others were missing entirely. These patches exposed a rubble interior.

"Come, look here." Tia found a curbed ramp at one end.

Tony appeared from around the back side. "Its twin's at the other end."

We climbed gingerly to the top, uncertain of our footing. The summit platform was half as large as the base. In its center, we found a complete circle of smaller vertical slabs, almost like tombstones, driven firmly into the surface soil.

We all jabbered at once. Why the mound? Why the ramps? The platform? The circle?

Hal was definitely enjoying our sense of discovery. Tia was a Tongan but said she'd seen nothing like this. I'd done the most reading so I shared what I could remember.

"Pre-Contact Tongans built mounds for different purposes— defense, lookouts, noble burials, even blinds for the chiefly sport of pigeon-snaring."

"This one can't be a fort," Tia objected. "Not with two welcoming ramps."

Tony wasn't so sure. "There could've been wooden palisades. They'd be mulch by now."

From the Bishop Museum, I remembered a sepia photo of a *malae* or ceremonial plaza bounded by vertical limestone slabs. "The anthropologists say those small vertical slabs weren't tombstones but backrests. A cozy club where the chiefs could get high on *kava*, their crushed-root cocktail."

Hal offered up an alternative suggestion. "This pyramid lies directly inland from the main channel through the reefs. The submerged coral would rip canoes apart. Maybe the ring framed a bonfire, strategically placed as a navigation beacon."

Back at camp, he was more talkative about the unexcavated site. "You can appreciate our dilemma. On the one hand, Elena and I are painfully aware that the pyramid's not our private plaything. It lies on our land but belongs to Tonga's national heritage. On the other hand, we can't ignore what happened just one island over."

Elena explained. "As soon as a similar site was reported to the authorities by its owners, ransacking vandals swooped in. They had political connections at the highest level. There was nothing anyone could do about it. Whatever they dug up will never be exhibited for school kids or the general public."

"And just in case you're not sufficiently concerned," Hal wryly concluded, "I haven't even shown you the second pyramid at the other end of our island."

After lunch and a last leisurely swim, Tony, Tia and I packed up our gear and said wistful goodbyes. Our fey hosts saw us off in the shallows.

I'd been having far too much fun to remember that derelict wing.

# FISH STORY

*Turangi 2000*

I'd been moving around New Zealand's North Island visiting Maori Polynesian sites and natural wonders. There were plenty of both on offer. After an up-close look at plunging waterfalls and scalding hot-springs in Tongariro National Park, I was ready for Lake Taupo.

New Zealand's largest lake, with a surface area of 240 square miles and depths down to 600 feet, Taupo filled the caldera of the volcano bearing the same name. When the volcano blew its top in the Oruanui eruption 26,500 years ago, it was the world's largest blast in the past 70,000 years. (A lesser but still cataclysmic sequel by the same volcano in 180 CE turned skies red in China and Rome.)

My guesthouse hosts persuaded me to try my hand at lake fishing. Importation of rainbow trout from California had started in the 1880s, with brown trout from Europe soon to follow. Decades before my arrival, Taupo had become recognized as a world-famous sport-fishing destination. I had barely touched a rod and reel since pier-casting at Newport Beach in childhood. My concern over depleted stocks and the ethics of killing live creatures had kept me away from the sport. But Taupo was supposedly overpopulated and I'd only be keeping what I intended to eat. So I decided to give it a try.

Len, my senior guide, had been fishing for so many years he was nicknamed "the Silver Fox." Locating the big ones was a highly competitive venture. For decades, Len had kept ahead of the pack. Twenty-three-year-old Robby, his protégé, was breaking into the business. Robby had multiple sclerosis and was still grieving for his father felled by a heart attack only months before. But he was warm and talkative in marked contrast to his dour boss.

The pair had pulled their sleek boat up onto the shore. Robby helped me clamber aboard and into a life vest. Then he pushed on the bow and hopped on himself as the craft slid into the shallows. Two trolling rigs had been secured in metal braces bolted to the boat's stern. They would trail artificial lures once we got underway. We'd be using light tackle to increase the odds when playing a fish on the line.

Before we got underway, Len walked me through a clipped tutorial. "Up and down, that's all you need to remember. Raise your rod to slow the fish. Then lower it while you reel in to recover your line. Up and down." The Fox demonstrated the cyclical motion. "Keep it smooth. Never jerk. And don't meddle with the star drag," pointing to the gear on the side of the reel that maintained pressure on outgoing line. "It stays where it's set."

I flashed on Humphrey Bogart barking Katherine Hepburn on the African Queen. I figured my best hope was to practice on minnows before things got serious.

Not another word from Len for the next 30 minutes as he maneuvered our boat into inlets and along the shore. Robby filled the silence with details of water and wind, boats and lures. The pair were looking forward to the coming high season, peaking over Christmas and New Year's, when rich clients flew in from Texas and London. Robby implied that the older man's gruff manner and silence were largely due to his brooding over younger competition.

The line sang out as a fish hit one lure. Both my guides sprang into a practiced routine. Len shifted the inboard-motor's gear to neutral, lifted the curved rod from the brace and handed it to me. Robby reeled in the second line to give me room to play my fish side to side.

"Let him run." The taciturn master was suddenly animated. "Now bring up your rod tip. Steadyyy…"

The fish felt heavy to me. Beginner's luck? I slowly drew it closer as its surges grew briefer. My forearms were aching but the contest was a thrill. The trout surfaced, then bolted again when it got near the boat. I interpreted Robby's grin to mean the glimpsed trout was exceptional.

"Work him, work him," The Fox stood just behind me while Robby readied the net.

"Not too fast. Not too tight. Loosen up." Rattled by the barrage of rapid-fire commands, I tried to comply by lowering my rod tip and pausing in reeling.

"No! Keep up the tension." In that instant, the line went slack.

Len made no effort to conceal his exasperation. "You let him off the hook."

Adrenalin pumping, I found I was just as irritated. "But you told me to loosen up."

"I meant stop your cranking. Not lower your rod."

There was no need getting in a pissing contest. The monster was long gone.

Robby reset the lines while the two of us simmered down. It was a lovely day, with warm sun and a light breeze riffling the water surface. I hooked 11 more trout and landed six, a ratio Robby generously characterized as normal. (The Fox seemed to have lost interest after our blown opportunity for a trophy.) The smaller ones we freed up and tossed back. I gave two fish to my guides and kept the largest one for myself. By California standards, my four-pounder was a leviathan. In Lake Taupo, a trout had to weigh ten pounds or more to cause much of a stir.

Len seemed slightly mollified by the gift but remained taciturn. He told me the hotel I was shifting to later in the day would cook my fish for me. Robby packed it with ice in a heavy-duty sack.

The guides drove me to my guesthouse where I packed up and

checked out. Then on to the Chateau Tongariro where I was splurging for one night. A storied property emulating Canadian icons at Banff and Lake Louise, the Chateau had been built in 1928 and renovated after the Second World War.

At check-in, I self-consciously showed my sack to the front-desk staff. One clerk escorted me to the kitchen. The chef admired my fish and graciously consented to prepare it. I needed only pay a modest charge for the off-menu service and show him my local fishing license. "So the Game Warden doesn't come knocking."

When I took my seat in the handsome dining room that evening, it was already filled with a hundred or so guests. After I'd enjoyed soup and a first glass of wine, the beaming maître d' approached with an expansive silver tray. When she set it down on a stand snapped open by the accompanying waiter, I could only marvel at the presentation. My trout had been posed vertically in a theatrical curve, its body suspended by some concealed support. Skinned but with intact head still ferocious and tail full of thrust. The breaching fish emerged from a lake of multicolored vegetables—bak choy, baby carrots, a full tomato and cauliflower flowerets. On the side, as the server explained, was a sauce blending soy, mustard seed and light honey.

Surrounding diners joined me in spontaneous applause. This was truly a pièce de résistance. It seemed a shame to disturb the mounting, but the proof of the pudding is in the eating. So the maître d' laid the fish down and carved me a generous slice. Some vegetables came across from the tray for good health. The trout's taste and texture were fabulous. As if poached for tenderness but also smoked for robust flavor.

After the initial admiration from surrounding tables, some assertive neighbors lost no time in making their own moves. One demanding gentleman in a checked sport coat tugged at a busboy's sleeve. "Why don't I find that on *my* menu?"

Slightly farther away, a composed, heron-necked matron instructed her waiter, "I'll have what he's having." (*Thank you, Meg Ryan.*)

As I allowed myself to be talked into a smaller second helping, other diners stopped by to float polite questions. Where had I caught my fish? Who'd been my guide? Was I connected to hotel management to warrant such a feast?

I asked the maître d' to please share the better part of the delicacy with her colleagues, if hotel policy permitted. The wait-staff seemed delighted, having observed the preparation and presentation from a distance.

When I told her I was writing my way through Polynesia and would not fail to record this memorable treat, she asked if I'd like to meet the sous chef responsible for my dish. When my benefactor emerged from the kitchen, he didn't conform to my stereotypes. Lance stood six-foot-six, even without his toque. Obviously local talent, his twice-broken nose testified to scars from the scrum.

"Thank you for preparing the best fish dish of my life."

"Glad you enjoyed it, Mr. Sunshine. The head chef looked it up and confirmed today was American Thanksgiving. He thought we should help you to mark the occasion far from home."

I asked this Olympian about his magical sauce. "We normally use it as a salmon glaze. But this trout was so hefty, I hoped it would be a good match."

"Do you still play rugby, Lance?"

"Only on the infrequent weekend. With a growing family and more to learn in the kitchen, it's hard to slip away." He paused. "But I miss the contact."

The head chef had evidently assigned my trout to his understudy as an on-the-job challenge. Everyone at my end of the dining room awarded Lance an honors grade.

◧ ◪ ◨

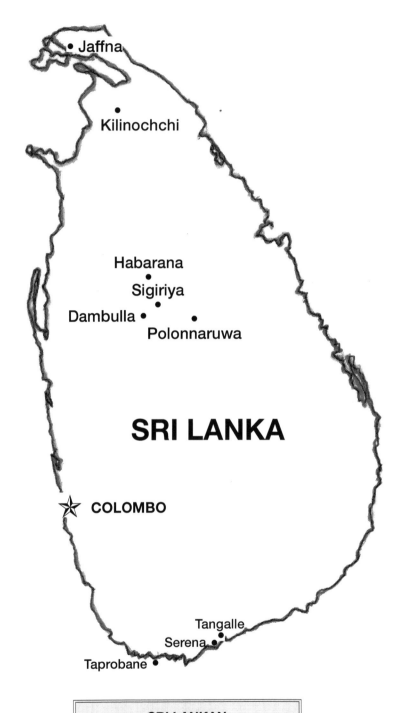

Jaffna

Kilinochchi

Habarana

Sigiriya

Dambulla

Polonnaruwa

SRI LANKA

COLOMBO

Tangalle

Serena

Taprobane

SRI LANKAN
PEACE-BUILDING
*2002–2004*

CHAPTER TEN

# SRI LANKA:
# MOBILIZING BUSINESS FOR PEACE

After two decades of civil war between its Sinhalese Buddhist majority and Tamil Hindu minority, Sri Lanka found itself confronting an unanticipated peace at the end of 2001. A new national government was elected on a platform dedicated to terminating hostilities. The rebel LTTE[14] reciprocated by declaring a pause in its military struggle. By February of 2002, a Norwegian-mediated Cease-Fire Agreement had been signed. Remarkably and unexpectedly, it seemed as if the brutal conflict that had claimed at least 65,000 lives and paralyzed national development might at last be over.

The new right-of-center Prime Minister, Ranil Wickremesinghe, was convinced the key to consolidating this fragile peace was to win the active engagement of the national and international business communities. Heretofore, island corporate leaders had largely remained aloof, "leaving politics to the politicians." The result had been that vested interests on both sides of the conflict who saw

---

14  The Liberation Tigers of Tamil Eelam, the official name of the rebel force. Unofficially, the Tamil Tigers.

benefit in protracted hostilities had not been effectively challenged by Sri Lanka's financial and commercial leadership.

The Prime Minister wrote to the United Nations Secretary–General requesting assistance with mobilizing business for peace. On the basis of my field experience in facilitating national emergence and recovery in China, Laos and the Central Asian Republics, I was invited by UNDP to respond to the request.

I flew out to Colombo to meet and start working for the PM. For his proposed campaign to attract international business, I crafted the theme "Invest in Peace." This brand tacitly delivered two linked messages. Business leaders should proactively commit their resources to peace-building. And Sri Lanka was again a safe environment in which to invest.

I accompanied Prime Minister Wickremesinghe and his delegation to New York City where he launched the Invest-in-Peace campaign in his address to the UN General Assembly. In Manhattan, our UNDP team also introduced him to leading corporate CEOs, investment bankers, journalists and expatriate Sri Lankan entrepreneurs. Many of the latter business leaders were members of the Tamil diaspora supporting the rebels. The UN venue created a neutral forum for this unprecedented bridging dialogue.

The Prime Minister made a hit with New York's world-weary business community. He conceded without spin that he'd have to enact an ambitious menu of law reforms before his country's investment climate could be credible or competitive. Adhering to candor and realism, he stimulated positive publicity and interest.

To sustain momentum, the PM requested UNDP to extend my advisory services. My new assignment was to help implement the Prime Minister's vision. He was determined to harness private-sector energies as the main engine driving Sri Lanka back to peace.

Over the next two years, our UNDP Invest-in-Peace Project assisted the government to make promising strides. We mobilized world-class advisors to help attract new foreign investment and promote sustainable ecotourism. We sparked Japanese investors' interest by organizing Sri Lankan forums in Tokyo, Kyoto and Osaka. We supported a coalition of Sri Lanka's provincial Chambers of Commerce in restoring commercial communications and relationships across conflict lines. And we started resuscitating devastated Tamil communities in the worst-hit North and East by championing training and employment for demobilized youth.

Tragically, national reconciliation then came to a screeching halt. The Opposition party persuaded Sri Lanka's Buddhist majority that total victory was preferable to federated power-sharing with the minority Hindu and Muslim communities. The government changed hands again, civil war resumed and the resulting fatalities were estimated to include at least 40,000 civilians.

At this writing, a deeply wounded nation is progressing towards what hopefully will prove more lasting reconciliation. My former client, Mr. Wickremesinghe, is again occupying the Prime Minister's chair, this time as head of a broad coalition government.

My 2002-04 Sri Lankan residency was my first long-term posting to which Nancy did not accompany me. She opted to remain in our new rural home in Italy, where she found harmony with the local culture and climate. We rendezvoused on holidays in Asia, Europe or half-way between. Emails and phone calls kept us in constant touch. This family decision was the right choice for each of us but a painful separation for both.

# Learn–To–Earn

*Jaffna and Kilinochchi 2003–04*

Touching down in Jaffna was a rude wake-up call. Siva had the window seat next to mine. We looked out at Armored Personnel Carriers flanking the runway.

"I was born here," he whispered. "In Jaffna, 'Pearl of the North'."

Across the aisle, Sonali looked stunned. A year ago she'd been studying law at Harvard. "I can't believe this is my country."

It had been only a short hop from Colombo. Forty airborne minutes but a world away.

In the national capital, it was possible to reduce the civil war to a remote abstraction. Sandbagged checkpoints had been removed from Colombo streets since the 2002 Cease-Fire. Parliamentary squabbling consumed more newspaper ink than the stalled peace negotiations between the government and the rebel LTTE.

Jaffna Airport brought the fragile truce's ground realities back into sharp focus. As we disembarked, the cabin crew remained on board, preparing for an immediate return trip. On the tarmac, rifle-toting troops made certain that we didn't stray or snap unauthorized photos.

Beside the bare terminal building, official vehicles waited inside a barbed-wire cordon to collect their parties. Our UNDP jeep came equipped with a large blue flag, two-way radio, flak jackets and helmets for all passengers. Ram, assigned as our driver, asked us soberly to sign his clipboard roster and then radioed his base to confirm the pick-up.

Although legally still a civil-aviation facility, Jaffna Airport had obviously been expropriated by the military. We rolled through the compound at the posted five miles per hour, past jogging platoons and sentried barracks. Not until we'd cleared the perimeter checkpoint did Ram relax enough to ask our detailed plans for the visit.

I'd been through this transition several times but never quite adjusted to the tension. For my colleagues, it was their first trip to the North since the Cease-Fire. Their uneasiness was apparent. Siva Sivananthan, though a Tamil, was the government's Number Two in charge of Northeast reconstruction. Today he was acutely aware we'd be heading into rebel territory. Sonali Dayaratne, my Sinhalese Project Officer, had always before remained in the South.

Jaffna town retained some of its historic charm and shaded serenity. Until one spotted the scars of machine-gun and mortar rounds pitting facades. The city tolerated a bizarre dual occupation. During daylight hours, it functioned as a government regional center. But at dusk, government troops retreated to their fortified compounds, and kepi-topped LTTE police emerged from the shadows to direct commuting bicycles and maintain law and order.

On through Jaffna and just to the east, our jeep pulled up for border-crossing formalities. Here any remnant of government jurisdiction abruptly terminated. Even a United Nations vehicle could not advance without a rebel visa. An eerie 200-yard buffer zone was stripped of all structures and vegetation. Inside this chute, cheery monitors in International Red Cross armbands looked up from their paperwork to wave us through. Out the other side, we were in Tamil Eelam, sovereign Sri Lanka left behind.

My friends were shocked by the devastation. Every palm tree was a splintered shaft, its crown blasted off by artillery exchanges. Every building was an abandoned shell. At low speed, we rolled through Elephant Pass This strategic isthmus controlling access to the Jaffna peninsula had witnessed some of the fiercest seesaw battles of the civil war. Today it was a lunar wasteland marked only by the occasional rusted tank.

"Why the barbed-wire fences with the skull-and-crossbones?" Sonali asked. "There's nothing left for trespassers to take."

"Uncleared mines," Ram explained. "No pit stops until we reach Kilinochchi."

The rebel capital was another anomaly. Desperately poor after ten years of government embargoes, Kilinochchi's dirt lanes bustled with determined energy. The Tigers had fought to a stand-off an enemy force ten times their size. The hardened guerrilla band was now awkwardly evolving into a civilian administration. The insurgents' authoritarian, spartan instincts were reflected in every block of this severe but clean-swept cityscape.

Despite the grim terrain we'd been traversing, what brought us to Kilinochchi was a happy occasion. We were here to inaugurate Learn-To-Earn. This pilot project was UNDP's first response to an economic-recovery problem that had been vexing the government and LTTE alike.

International donors had pledged $5 billion in peace-building aid, much of it earmarked for re-constructing roads, hospitals and schools in Sri Lanka's hardest-hit Northeast Region. Common sense favored mobilizing the local construction industry to participate in this approaching boom. Yet the industry was debilitated and demoralized, unable to seize the windfall opportunity.

One chronic deficit paralyzing local contractors was qualified construction labor. Local workers existed but lacked skills and certification. Training courses existed but taught mostly theory. Contractors complained that the graduates of these courses could not hammer a nail. Trainees complained there were no jobs to study for.

Our pilot project proposed to break through this impasse by directly linking training to employment. Under Learn-To-Earn, participating contractors would supply unskilled laborers from their workforces as trainees. The contractors would define and control the training syllabuses by selecting priority disciplines—initially, carpentry and masonry—and by specifying required skills within each discipline. They would continue to pay the trainees' wages during on-the-job training sequences, and then guarantee successful graduates a year's employment as apprentices upon their completion of instruction. It was a win/win trade-off. Assured skilled labor for contractors. Assured higher-paying jobs for trainees.

The pilot project's role was to generate take-off velocity for this demonstration initiative. We won support from key stakeholders, including the National Contractors' Association, the government and the LTTE. We helped select training venues, host institutes and trainers. We persuaded the UN-affiliated International Labor Organization to donate Tamil-language training modules. And we procured a seed-money grant from the World Bank to cover trainers' and trainees' expenses.

Pulling through the front gate of the Kilinochchi Technical College where today's launch ceremony would be conducted, we confronted local deprivations close at hand. Here, at the premier vocational-training institution in rebel territory, all the surfaces were rough dirt. The main classroom had open sides, no windows, blackboards or desks, much less electronic teaching equipment. Out in front, the ferocious visage of a Tamil Tiger snarled down from an orange banner on a flimsy flagpole.

A colorful group had assembled for the proceedings. The honorees, Kilinochchi's inaugural class of 29 Learn-To-Earn trainees, stood as scrubbed and alert as first communicants. In keeping with the event's ecumenical spirit, a Hindu priest and his Catholic counterpart chanted complementary blessings. The traditional Sri Lankan oil lamp was lit as a symbol of harmony by four representatives: Siva Sivananthan on behalf of the government, an anonymous Tigers officer in combat fatigues, Mr. Suwarnaraj from the Contractors' Association, and me standing up for UNDP.

Moving inside to fill the classroom, we offered the charter class some inspirational remarks. Siva led off, characterizing this skill-building initiative as a "mini-revolution." For the first time, he explained, Learn-

To-Earn was bridging the gaps that had deprived prior vocational-training efforts of real power to deliver employment. Siva's endorsement carried weight because of his unique résumé, combining Tamil ethnicity and fluency with high government rank. With passion and political risk, he had convinced government skeptics to share this training with "enemy" communities.

Selvin Ireneuss, the CEO of the Joint Government/LTTE Transition Commission, was another individual highly trusted and respected by both parties to the national conflict. The gravely-wounded survivor of a bombing attack, Selvin had persuaded the Tigers leadership that Learn-To-Earn was their vehicle to exploit, not some treacherous Trojan horse. Now he told the local youth that this pilot project offered them a crucial step onto the ladder of entrepreneurial opportunity and professional certification. "Grab that ladder," he urged. "With courage and conviction."

Sharing the rostrum as if government/LTTE joint ventures were a commonplace affair, the rebels' representative encouraged the would-be carpenters and masons to aspire to the same standards of professionalism they associated with medical doctors and accountants. For UNDP, I added that professionalism implied not only specialized technical knowledge but a personal commitment to excellence and integrity.

Homilies concluded, the youngsters stepped forward to receive their Learn-To-Earn materials—crisp overalls, safety helmets and individual tool kits, all decorated with the smart LTE emblem.

As she helped with the hand-over, I noticed Sonali was both beaming and teary-eyed. She knew these customized outfits were no extravagance. In our preliminary planning for the pilot project, we'd quickly encountered a threshold barrier. The caste-ridden Tamil communities from which we needed to draw our training candidates harbored deep prejudice against manual labor. A young man or woman from one of these villages would rather earn a single rupee in a menial white-collar job than ten times that amount in a responsible, but blue-collar, construction position. We were tackling this bias head-on with stylish Learn-To-Earn uniforms and logos. Soon the selected trainees would be receiving recognition from admiring peers, as charter members of an exclusive club.

A group photograph, lukewarm soft drinks, Chinese biscuits and handshakes all around completed our dusty Kilinochchi inauguration. Parallel ceremonies in Jaffna and Vavuniya raised the initial complement to 120 trainees.

From this modest debut, Learn-To-Earn expanded swiftly and smoothly, an idea whose time had come. Shathieskumar, another talented member of our UNDP Invest-in-Peace team, took over day-to-day supervision of the pilot. A Tamil civil engineer, Shathies was the perfect catalyst to facilitate the necessary alliances. He was equally comfortable, and capable, working with public- and private-sector clients, in the North and East as well as in Colombo. More than any other individual, he kept this ball rolling.

The first two classes of trainees completed their instruction, passed certification examinations and returned to their sponsoring contractors, stepping up into skilled-labor positions. The World Bank adapted the Learn-To-Earn prototype for its $70-million Northeast Housing Project. The pilot's menu of construction disciplines broadened to encompass electrical fittings and aluminum fabrication. Additional training hubs added in Trincomalee and Batticaloa spread the program's reach from the North into the East. By Year Three, 400 trainees had passed through our pipeline.

Complementary pilot-project initiatives boosting the local construction industry moved forward in tandem. A leasing plan granted small contractors unprecedented access to heavy equipment. Work-study fellowships attracted young entrepreneurs to the industry. And affordable loans for the first time became available from commercial banks.

Locally adapted spin-offs continued to multiply. But Learn-To-Earn was the pioneer. We figured out a way to help war-zone contractors help themselves, their employees and their communities. One well-driven nail at a time.

# ANCIENT OCCUPATIONS

*Dambulla 2003*

Nancy flew out from Italy to ring in the New Year. One of the highlights of our together-time was a tour of Sri Lanka's Cultural Triangle.[15] We planned to visit three UNESCO World Heritage Sites and sample the island nation's layered ancient history.

For our basecamp we selected the recently opened Kandalama Hotel at Dambulla, the latest major project of Geoffrey Bawa, Sri Lanka's best-known and most-respected architect. Bawa had started out in life as a lawyer, found it boring, and jumped to a fresh start in architecture at the age of 30. Within ten years, he was an Asian icon.[16]

Nancy and I both loved his "tropical modernist" style, featuring natural local materials and ventilation, interior courtyards with water features, and a restrained palette of colors. We'd admired several of Bawa's residential and commercial buildings in Colombo and were looking forward to staying in his striking new hotel. It was tucked into a concave mountainside, in an evident homage to millennia of cliff-face structures dotted throughout the area. The design's elongated horizontal

---

15  The Triangle is Sri Lanka's premier concentration of historical sites, bounded by the two ancient cities of Anuradhapura and Polonnaruwa and the former royal capital of Kandy.

16  Still practicing at 84, Bawa would pass away within four months of our visit.

axis ensured that most rooms, including ours, overlooked a giant ancient reservoir directly below.

Everything about our stay lived up to our expectations. Hotel service was courteous and unobtrusive, the furnishings uncluttered and the food consistently first-rate. We especially enjoyed taking evening meals on the open-air terrace with background melodies by a solo flute. Kandalama's recent international recognition for outstanding energy conservation, not yet common practice in Sri Lanka, was another plus.

The afternoon of our arrival, we made our first site visit, to the nearby Dambulla Cave Temple. This Buddhist sanctuary had seen continuous use from the first century BCE. Its five linked caves stretched in a long row across the cliff face. A wall had been constructed across the fronts of the caves, converting the grottoes to enclosed chambers. The largest chamber measured 160 feet wide and 60 deep. Brightly colored murals totally covered the interior walls and ceilings. The paintings included abstract designs but mostly depicted traditional episodes from the life of the Buddha. An overhanging rock ledge protected the artwork, with a groove carved into the lip to carry off rain.

A prominent position in this Buddhist shrine was reserved for large statues of the Hindu gods Vishnu and Ganesh. The effigies were doused with fragrant oil and garlanded with marigolds, so the deities were obviously still receiving frequent homage. These two religions have contested in South Asia for thousands of years, often with violent results. But here somehow an ecumenical truce was holding.

Our second day's destination was Polonnaruwa, the capital of Sri Lanka's ruling kingdom from the eleventh through the thirteenth centuries CE. The ruins of this remarkable city extended for five miles along a linear grid bordered on one side by a 6,000-acre ancient reservoir "tank." The site encompassed palaces, temples, baths, bell-shaped stupas and free-standing statues of the Buddha. An excellent small museum helped us get our bearings and make sense of this array, using maps, models and a timeline of archaeological discoveries.

Polonnaruwa had played a pivotal role in the competitive ebb and flow of Sri Lanka's religions. From the third to the first centuries BCE, Sri Lanka had offered safe haven to Buddhist monks fleeing Hinduism's resurgence in northern India where Buddhism had been founded. Sri Lanka subsequently "seeded" the spread of Buddhism all across Southeast Asia. But by the late eleventh-century CE, when Polonnaruwa's founder kicked out Indian Hindu occupiers and wanted to re-energize island Buddhism, the religion had been totally decimated. So he had to import monks from Burma who knew the old rites and rituals.

It was exciting to be reminded of this small island's continent-wide influence on religious, educational and artistic developments. The disheartening flip-side, of course, was that Sri Lanka's ethnic and religious conflicts, still inflaming the nation's modern civil war (now thankfully suspended), had roots extending back more than two thousand years.

From the museum, we walked to the Gal Vihara. This massive granite outcropping was carved with four twelfth-century, larger-than-life-size images of Buddha. Three were standing but the most serene figure was a 50-foot-long reclining form. Nearby we visited the Rankot Vihara stupa. Its 180-foot-high, bell-shaped structure was testimony to the ancients' advanced architectural and construction skills.

Nancy and I saved the highlight of our ancient-monuments tour for our third and final day. Sigiriya, a dramatic stone monolith, rose 650 feet straight up from the surrounding plain. Its sheer sides and flat top looked carved by giants.

The history of the site explained its remarkable features. Facts were difficult to unravel from fiction in this saga, but the core narrative was that Sigiriya had been occupied and developed by King Kashyapa between 477 and 495 CE. Having killed his royal father and chased away the rightful heir, Kashyapa the usurper fled to Sigiriya and established an impregnable fortress on the flat top of the mesa.

Expansive gardens created a formal approach to the citadel. Fed by underground pipes and cisterns constructed 1,500 years ago, this park featured small lakes which reputedly once held island pavilions.

*The monolith and its water gardens. Sigiriya 2003.*

The final entrance had once been dominated by a massive lion gate. Now only two 15-foot-high paws remained. But we could imagine the awe caused by passing through the legs of the entire guardian, which must have towered 100 feet up from the ground.

The modern tourist track up the rock face took the form of a zig-zagging, enclosed metal stairway. Nancy has a problem with heights. So, like most visitors on that sweltering day, she halted her ascent after one stage. While she waited in the park for my return, she discovered giant boulders with high niches that apparently once anchored defensive emplacements.

I kept on going, climbing first to a section of the cliff face where the enclosed walkway had been suspended out from the rock surface. This distance protected from tourist hands an ancient gallery of marvelous frescoes. The beautiful subjects of these paintings were 21 voluptuous females, bare- and full-breasted. Wearing elaborate headdresses, most

*Bird's-eye view from on top of the mesa. Sigiriya 2003.*

carried lotus-blossom bouquets. I recalled very similar figures painted in the contemporaneous Ajanta caves in Central India. There, as here, a scholarly controversy still raged over whether these "royal maidens" represented erotic concubines or religious devotees.

Incredibly, nineteenth-century observers reported that the original paintings covered most of the rock's entire west face, an area measuring 500x130 feet. Graffiti references on the immediately adjacent "mirror wall" spoke of 500 figures. That would have been an extravagant spectacle, if not another example of tourist exaggeration.

Beyond the gallery, the mirror wall, named for its shiny surface polished by thousands of fingerprints, was now shielded from further contributions by a clear plastic panel. Archaeologists were restoring and preserving graffiti dating from the eighth century CE.

Right after this stretch, the enclosed stairway gave way to something much more intimidating. Here the trail wrapped around the corner of the mountain up and over an open rock surface, flaking from too much foot traffic. Waist-high metal spikes had been driven into the rock and a rope hand-rail looped between the spikes. But the whole area was exposed to the wind, and the sheer drop was very much in evidence. If that were not distracting enough, pre-teen children who'd been confined in the enclosed stairway were now freed and dashing past more preoccupied adults. If I hadn't been so intent on reaching the citadel, this was one ascent I'd have abandoned with relief.

As it turned out, the summit was well worth the ordeal. A perfectly flat two-and-a-half-acre plateau had once housed a palace and fortress. Apart from scattered foundations, all that remained of this remarkable retreat were the rain-catching cisterns that had enabled its occupation. Views extended for miles in all four directions.

I envisioned Kashyapa's lookouts raising the alarm. After 18 years of refuge in southern India, the deposed heir to the throne had returned to Sri Lanka belatedly demanding revenge. The usurper was defeated in battle on the plain below his hideaway. The bloody saga ended with his suicide.

Sigiriya's palace and fortress were converted to a Buddhist monastery, much later abandoned. Legend has it that not until Major Jonathan Forbes of the 78th Highlanders cantered by in 1813 was the long-forgotten, brush-obscured monolith "re-discovered."

# Taprobane

## *Weligama 2004*

When Kumar and I approached the island along the South Coast road, its profile resembled a giant naval vessel. Anchored in the shallows, prow towards the shore, the entire form was camouflaged in a jungle canopy of lustrous green.

My driver pulled into a parking lot opposite the village of Weligama. King coconuts were stacked in pyramids ready for transport to market. Outrigger fishing canoes were hauled up on the sand. But no signboard, ferry or launch facility acknowledged the island lying directly offshore.

Kumar and I reconfirmed that he'd collect me again in three days' time. Then he hired a local beach-boy to ferry my suitcase. In the swimming trunks and flip-flops I'd put on in advance, I followed the kid across. He hoisted my suitcase overhead, so I did the same with my rucksack. The water was cool but not unpleasant and there was thankfully no surf. We waded in to our waists at low tide and walked single-file for two hundred yards.

As we got closer, I could see that the island was entirely composed of jagged rocks. A metal gangway led up to a small concrete jetty. This landing platform terminated in an imposing white gatehouse framing double wooden doors. I paused at this portal, feeling like I was about to step into a fairy tale. Taprobane had always been one of my Sri Lankan

*The view from the mainland. Taprobane 2004.*

dream destinations. So near and yet so far. Almost touchable offshore. Yet strictly private. Now, for one blissful weekend, I'd have the place to myself.

I clanged the brass ship's bell to the right of the doors. In a few moments, a caretaker swung them open. The boy set down my case and started back towards his village. I turned to the shore and waved to Kumar, now a small figure on the beach. He waved back and set off for Colombo, leaving me on my own.

The caretaker looked in his fifties, Sinhalese but with skin darkened by exposure to sun and wind. He slouched forward slightly as if with arthritis. Still, he insisted on carrying my suitcase. He seemed to have little or no English, so our communications were in mime. He slid a bolt-lock securing the twin doors from the inside and I followed him onto a path.

We walked up a steep, shaded slope on gravel, with a border of matched round stones. The villa on the hill's crown was an architectural delight. Unpretentious in style but rambling in size. A modern homage to Dutch colonial forms. One story, with white stuccoed walls supporting a tile roof in weathered red. Arches protruded over the entryway and large windows. The structure covered the entire hilltop like a custom-tailored hat.

Inside, simple elegance. From the entryway, I could see all the way through to a rear balcony. Everything was white. Walls and terrazzo floors. Filmy curtains draping interior windows and doors.

All open and breezy. An octagonal central chamber with a soaring ceiling over twenty feet high doubled as traffic hub and living room. Off to the right lay a large roofed dining terrace, open to the sea. Both of these common rooms were bordered by tall, slender wooden columns, reaching to larger horizontal beams. The intervals between columns invited relaxed movement through the flowing indoor-outdoor space. Five bedrooms opened off of the hub and the hallway beyond. Everywhere a few pieces of aged teak furniture, relieved by rattan, stood solid and heavy. Some trunks, sideboards and tables looked like Dutch antiques. There were occasional framed photos and maps, one or two vases of flowers, and little else. This was a home for relaxation, not for show.

The caretaker's wife, warmer and slightly more talkative than her husband, greeted me with a fresh-lime-soda and showed me my bedroom. Its high bed sat under furled mosquito netting. A lovely striped throw in gray, coral and aquamarine looked like South Coast handloom.

In a few words we discussed when and what I'd like to eat. After that first delicious lunch, I assured my cook that I would happily consume whatever she felt like preparing. It turned out to be all local and tasty. Fresh grilled fish with rice, vegetable curries, and platters of mangoes, bananas and papayas. In response to my question, she told me that all island supplies, including bottled water, were portaged across from Weligama. She also confided that she and her husband had worked on the island for 24 years, long before my friend's acquisition.

Geoffrey Dobbs had bought and renovated Taprobane for his private use, occasionally renting it out for groups and special events. The island had an exotic history. When the self-promoting French commoner, "Count" Maurice Talvande, purchased it in the 1920s, he changed its name to "Taprobane," the Classical Greeks' designation for Sri Lanka. In the '50s, it was owned and intermittently occupied by the writer Paul Bowles, in between his bohemian stints in North Africa.

Geoffrey was a British-born and -educated entrepreneur. He and I saw eye-to-eye on including colonial structures in Sri Lanka's portfolio of cultural-tourism attractions. From tea-plantation hills to the coastal plains, the island was dotted with legacy properties surviving from the Portuguese, Dutch and British eras. Along with Geoffrey Lipton from the World Tourism Organization and Adrian Zecha, founder of Amanresorts, we were pushing to refurbish these buildings for residential and commercial use, especially as upmarket boutique hotels. But it was an uphill slog. The powers controlling the domestic tourism industry resisted diverting clients from their high-rise resorts. And the national government, sensitive to nationalistic and communal passions, was reluctant to celebrate a colonial heritage.

After crossing swords with the country's tourism establishment, Geoffrey had gone his own way, renovating handsome small properties in Colombo and Galle town and marketing through international media. Well-known and respected in the international travel-and-tourism industry, he had fewer friends on the island.

But I'd become one of them and Geoffrey had kindly offered me his island for a weekend's solitary sanctuary. The virtual isolation was a perfect respite. Geoffrey's invitation had come out of the blue, exactly when I needed it. My recent Project work at Sri Lanka's Board of Investment had been particularly stressful. The island getaway would recharge depleted batteries.

I barely saw the caretaking couple again after the first morning's meet-and-greet conversations. Meals would appear and be cleared. Morning tea was served at my door, lunches and dinners on the terrace. My bed would be made, shutters opened and closed. But the pair were essentially invisible. I inferred that indoors was her domain, outdoors his.

The gardens I strolled through were lush with hundred-year-old hardwoods, bearing banana trees, tropical bushes and brilliant, rampant bougainvillea. Perfumed frangipani blossoms carpeted the paths. In one cul-de-sac, a pair of life-sized bronze cranes dipped long beaks through a stone urn's lily-pad raft.

My favorite haunt was a salt-water swimming pool above the surf on the island's east side. When I lay on the pool deck, I could hear occasional sounds from the mainland. But intervening breezes and currents kept these intrusions to a minimum.

I swam and walked, read and wrote, ate and slept. Never interrupted, never disturbed. It was as if I inhabited a restorative bubble, in the world but not of it. Too soon it was over, but no less precious for its brevity.

You can drive along coastal highways in a dozen countries and spy a rocky formation offshore. What a marvel! Is it better left alone, you wonder? Could it be unobtrusively developed? Could it be occupied without being ruined? Now I knew.

# Country Cousins

*Sri Lanka 2002–04*

Habarana, December, 2002. The delegates hugged the meeting-room corners like shy teenagers at a school social. Too bad we didn't have a dance band to get them moving. Northerners in one corner, Easterners, another, Southern and Central representatives as far from the other two groups as the four walls permitted. We stepped forward as encouraging chaperones.

My colleagues and I were confident that our concept was sound. Sustainable peace-building in Sri Lanka was going to require involvement by the private sector and reconciliation between estranged communities. To help jump-start this process, our UNDP Invest-in-Peace Project had joined forces with International Alert, a British NGO. We'd invited provincial business leaders to a low-key forum in the island's center. Accessible from all points of the compass, but remote from partisan politicians' meddling and media microphones. Habarana Lodge was a perfect venue for this inaugural gathering. Comfortable but not ostentatious, a safe haven for starting to re-knit ties long severed by civil war.

Now the hesitant invitees had been shepherded into a single room. All that remained was to nudge them away from those walls. We ushered the self-protective participants to seats in an informal circle, calling for volunteers to introduce themselves and their provincial Chambers of

Commerce. The first presentations were stiff and hardly audible. But at least people were talking.

A Jaffna Chamber spokesman insisted on speaking in Tamil, through an impromptu interpreter, and then segued into a political harangue praising Prabhakaran, the Tigers' feared generalissimo. We surmised that this threshold diatribe might be the price the speaker had paid to gain the LTTE's authorization to attend.

We asked the Chamber leaders to talk about their local business problems. The responses were hardly surprising—frozen credit, bureaucratic corruption and red tape, blocked supply lines, skilled-labor shortages. Still, the revelation that entrepreneurs at opposite ends of the country and on opposite sides of the post-conflict line were suffering identical constraints made a powerful case for common interests.

One of our core objectives in nurturing this potential network was to engage local business leaders in active peace-building. We'd invited a provocative guest speaker to introduce this theme. Brian Whittaker was a scarred veteran of South Africa's struggle to move beyond apartheid. CEO of that Republic's Business Trust, he briefed the Sri Lankan delegates on why normally conservative business leaders in his country had decided to actively work for political change and racial reconciliation.

"We were corporate heads," he assured them, "not social workers. Bottom-line pragmatists, not ideologues. Our assessment was strictly self-interested. We had something to prove in exercising corporate social responsibility. Something to lose if our country disintegrated into further violence. Something to offer in private-sector leadership, community stature and managerial expertise. Something to gain in social stability, commercial prosperity and personal satisfaction."

"You talk as if we all have common interests," one Northern delegate protested. "I don't believe that. You assume that peace is automatically better than war. I don't believe that either. My community has been shattered by military attacks and occupation, our commerce strangled by the government's embargo. We didn't invite this suffering. But it has made us stronger."

I glanced around. The delegates were squirming a bit. These volatile topics were never discussed among strangers in Sri Lanka. But the impassioned Northerner had their full attention.

"The embargo forced us to rediscover innovation," he continued. "Self-reliance. We dug sand and pressed cane fibers for construction materials. We grew local foods and listened to our grandparents about traditional herbal medicines. We even converted vehicle engines to run on kerosene. Now the Cease-Fire has been declared and the only peace dividend I can see is a floodtide of Southern traders, goods and services pouring through our reopened gates. These invaders and their underpriced products are submerging local entrepreneurs. Southern banks are opening Northern branches to take our deposits but offer no loans. We learned survival behind the blockade. Its rushed removal is worsening our lives and our businesses. Not bettering them."

One Southern business leader responded. "My father told my brothers and me of Jaffna. He remembered your spicy prawns. And your friendliness. I never had the same chance. War has kept us apart, within the same small island, for two decades. I want to come and see for myself. And if you wish, I can pledge the support of my Chamber to help yours get back on its feet."

That first self-conscious conversation had resumed every two months for the next two years. Nine participating local Chambers swelled to 21, eventually covering every province and ethnic community in Sri Lanka. Rotating the venue allowed each Chamber to host a session, brief their guests on the local economic climate and meet potential customers and suppliers.

The delegates pressed UNDP and International Alert for training. Soon they were strengthening their presentation and advocacy skills. Another workshop offered principles and techniques for community-level conflict resolution. Steadily, the informal roundtable developed capacities and connections. It adopted the name "Business-for-Peace Alliance" to celebrate the partnership's twinned commitments.

BPA's forward progress was not all smooth sailing. One of two contesting national Chambers of Commerce, both based in Colombo, perceived the swelling provincial consortium as a direct threat to its hegemony (and not incidentally to its preferential access to development-assistance grants.) The well-connected big fish nearly succeeded in depriving the new Alliance of crucial United Nations support.

Nor was communal violence possible to ignore. One Sunday afternoon a respected economics professor addressed the visiting Alliance delegates in Batticaloa, voicing his dream for Eastern Province regeneration. Within 24 hours, this visionary had been gunned down on his doorstep by a terrorist masquerading as a student.

Despite resistance and setbacks, however, over time the Alliance evolved from a talking shop into an effective sponsor of pilot projects. In the process, almost entirely without publicity, BPA matured into a potent national player.

*Colombo, December 2004.* With my Sri Lankan posting now winding down, I was detecting parallel arcs between my individual assignment and broader national developments. Probably hubris. For sure, the initial burst of economic and political optimism I had shared and promoted had recently been largely deflated.

The venue for today's meeting of the Business-for-Peace Alliance was a sad case in point. Two short years ago, developers had unveiled glossy plans for restoring Colombo's venerable Grand Oriental Hotel to anchor an ambitious harbor renaissance. In its heyday, the Victorian relic had hosted Kipling and Coward, divas and diplomats. The boosters touted the property's unparalleled view of the capital's booming container port, the nation's commercial gateway. Now the giant cranes that had pivoted and hoisted round-the-clock were immobilized by bankers' and traders' loss of confidence. And the flaking walls of the hotel's dining-room walls had never received their promised renovation.

Thank God some initiatives were resisting this depressing trend. Our BPA was one stubborn, shining example. The energy, unity and confidence of Alliance members buzzed around a single table. What a distance we had travelled together from the fellowship's prickly launch.

Here were those same pioneers. But Habarana's shy, polarized envoys were unrecognizable. Each animated face summoned memories.

Sinhalese Suresh, who had designed and led cross-country Peace Visits for local entrepreneurs and their families to get reacquainted with peers on the other side of the post-conflict line.

Christian Dudley from central Kandy, championing the Alliance as a catalyst for small-business credit, bridging the communication and credibility gap between local branch banks and would-be borrowers.

Tamil Jeyasekaran, President of the Jaffna Chamber, who'd invited Buddhists, Muslims and Christians to his Hindu wedding reception. He teased that the matrimonial conclave had been "the prototype Business-for-Peace Alliance."

*Nationwide Chamber of Commerce leaders assemble to bless an "ecumenical wedding." Colombo 2003.*

Daya Gamage from Ampara in the South, standing up in a packed Ministry of Commerce auditorium to challenge condescending national-government bureaucrats. "You say you understand ground conditions in my community?" his voice boomed from the floor to the rostrum. "Well, I've been local Chamber President for the past four years and I've never met you before today. I'm pleased to make your acquaintance."

Nanthakumaran, convincing fastidious Japanese importers at the Osaka Small Enterprise Forum to place bulk orders for organic food products from his Vavuniya farm. "You like pickles?" Reaching into his briefcase like a magician, "I've got your pickles. How many containers would you like to order for starters?"

Pooranachandran, another respected Tamil leader, leading the Alliance team to the government's Peace Secretariat to lobby successfully for the re-opening of an additional fishing channel in Jaffna Harbor and for 24-hour traffic on the principal North/South arterial highway.

Azmi from the far South, making the case for a provincial Chambers consortium independent of capital-city domination. "The Colombo Chambers invite me to their meetings. There's even a chair reserved at the back of the room. But I'll be walking with a cane before they ask my opinion. And long deceased before they hand me a gavel."

Wickram, deftly keeping vital communication channels open between business communities and the LTTE leadership.

Ram, the once tongue-tied provincial contractor, delivering a major presentation to South Africa's business leadership in Pretoria and receiving a standing ovation.

VJ from Matara, chief organizer of Peace Bridge, the Alliance-sponsored provincial-trade-and-investment fair that would be the first of its kind in Sri Lanka.

Back in the present, Dahanayaka, the group's eldest member, was raising his glass in a toast.

"I'm from Galle, as most of you know. Sri Lanka's southernmost and loveliest city. If you'd asked me three years ago to name what Jaffna meant to me, to my shame but in all frankness, I'd have said 'the enemy'."

"And now, Father Daya, now what do you say?" a younger voice rang out.

"Now I say Jaffna is Pooranachandran." Dahanayaka placed a wrinkled arm around his Tamil seatmate's shoulders. "My good friend and new Northern business partner."

It was the last time we'd meet. I looked around at these grassroots champions who had reaffirmed that living and working in the provinces, far from Colombo's elite, did not make them second-rate. I saw brave leaders who had rediscovered they could stand together for peace. An extended family had re-knit its connections. That's why I had come. And why I felt I could now move on.

# Eyewitnesses

## *Tangalle 2004*

It was the end of my three-year UNDP mission to Sri Lanka. Nancy flew in from Italy to help me pack out. We wanted to squeeze in one final beach weekend before returning to Europe. Even though it was the Christmas holiday, I'd been able to book my favorite South Coast resort for our getaway, the Serena Hotel near Tangalle.

When Kumar pulled into the hotel driveway, Nancy spoke up in surprise. "We're heading up?"

"Yes, the hotel's on the hilltop."

"Not right on the beach?"

"You'll see. Serena has a fab beach. But that's only part of what makes it so special."

I could hear my wife was disappointed not to be staying directly by the water. But she seemed to be cheered by Serena' gorgeous tropical gardens sloping down around the hotel's secluded cottages. The resident proprietors had devoted 17 years to landscaping five lush acres. And the half-moon bay at the bottom of our hill was perfect for strolling on sand and rocks.

We spent two lovely days lolling by the swimming pool, walking on the beach, consuming delicious fresh seafood and resting up from our relocation labors.

*Serena's half-moon bay. Tangalle 2004.*

December 26 dawned bright and clear. We had the breakfast terrace to ourselves. The other guests must have been sleeping off Christmas cheer. The privacy suited us fine. We were eager to get down to the sand for a last wet-footed walk. Kumar was due just after lunch to collect us for the drive back to Colombo.

The gravel path serpentined under a canopy of shade trees. Dense clumps of hibiscus provided riotous color. Plumerias added seductive fragrance. Chatting as we rounded a bend, we almost stepped on a monitor lizard, lounging smack in the middle of our right-of-way.

"Nancy, take his pic! He must be three-feet-long! Look at his belly, like a giant toad that swallowed a tire."

Our family photographer hesitated. I knew we had a surplus of lizard portraits in our family scrapbooks. But this one seemed symbolic. "We need a memento of our last day."

Before Nancy could get her camera out of her beach bag, the ungracious reptile lumbered into motion. At an impressive clip, it waddled into a bamboo thicket, my sporting wife in hot pursuit.

"He went in to your left," I kibitzed.

"He's gone down into a drain," she called. "I grabbed a shot. But there probably wasn't enough light."

We resumed our stroll. The hotel gardens ended above a sheer drop. A retaining wall ran the width of the cliff, breached by an eroded concrete stairway down to the beach. From our elevation, the view was fabulous. An arc of deserted, rock-studded sand framed the symmetrical cove. Even the bamboo kiosk that doubled as bar and dispenser of beach supplies was locked up tight. Normally, it would be a bustling depot. The bay stretched nearly a mile across, on this sunny morning as still as a lake.

Three figures sprinted out of the shore-front brush and along the water's edge. They were locals, weathered adults barefoot in shorts and T-shirts. Charging up the steps two at a time, the men pushed past us at the top. "*Muddha! Muddha!*" they shouted, jabbing fingers out to sea.

I climbed up onto the seawall to get a better look. Across the flat surface came a dark line. A wave, I wondered? From the clifftop, it looked unimpressive. Then I realized it was approaching faster than a ski-boat. And it was very, very high.

"*Whomp!*" The wave slammed first into the mangrove thicket curving out to our right. Just behind the grove, the surge flooded the neighboring farmer's field, plucking out concrete fence posts like matchsticks. To our left, the water swamped the bamboo bar. Farther along, it climbed halfway up the trunks of soaring king-coconut palms.

The spray broke over the top of my head, 30 vertical feet above the beach.

"Get back!" Nancy yelled. I jumped down and stood next to her.

The penny dropped. We'd lived in Hawaii some years before and had visited the site of Hilo's 1960 destruction. Now her eyes were wide. "A tsunami." We got the word out at the same time.

As we watched, the whole process reversed. Unbelievably, the entire volume of water was sucked out of the bay, draining the seabed to strand flopping fish. In the middle distance, offshore rocks had been scattered humps above the ocean surface. Now they stood revealed as a single contiguous ridge.

Back down the stairs streaked the three locals. Out across the empty bathtub they scrambled and slid, grabbing for the largest suffocating fish to feed their families.

"No! Come back!" we both screamed. Thanks to Hilo, Nancy and I knew that what went out would return with a vengeance.

Our English-language warnings made no impression on the ecstatic trio. But the hotel owner came running across the garden and his coastal dialect had more effect. The three men turned, figured out what our host was yelling, and sprinted back towards the stairs as the returning water picked up speed. This time the wave came loaded with uprooted tree trunks and those lethal fence posts.

Would the men make it? The first two cleared the top step. But the third guy had a limp. He clambered up one leap ahead of the onslaught. While we stood and stared, the force demolished the stairway, ripping out cliff-bolted stanchions.

The three men, fish forgotten, danced and hugged with adrenalin joy.

In and out, the surge sequence repeated a half-dozen times, each less severe than the original. A small crowd of hotel guests gathered above the wall, gawking at the natural spectacle. Somehow we all still thought the phenomenon was only local in scope. And, thank God, no one had been hurt in our secluded bay.

As mid-day approached, the harsher reality began to intrude. Electricity lines were down, and with them, television and radio service. Mobile phones were on the blink. From neighboring beaches and tourist facilities, silent figures staggered onto our hillside grounds. Their stories were increasingly traumatic.

One Scandinavian family struggled in—towering father, dazed wife, two children, all holding hands. They'd been swimming off a nearby beach when the first wave lifted them onto the front porch of their rented cottage. The man had the presence of mind to lead his family up the interior stairs to the second floor. From there he punched a hole in the thatch and pushed the others through onto the roof. The four clung in terror to the roof frame as the currents swirled by, thick with corpses.

Other survivors told of a French woman and her three-year-old daughter. The child had been ripped from her arms and swept out to sea.

Our hosts released the hotel staff to rush home to village relatives. Some got through. Most were blocked. The returnees whispered of death and destruction. Sri Lanka's entire South Coast had been smashed—Galle, Matara, Tangalle and Hambantota. Maybe the East Coast as well. No one knew. That was LTTE territory, outside government control.

Over the course of a long afternoon, as cellphone connections flared in and out, Nancy and I received two calls. Kumar managed to report that he was blocked 30 miles south of Colombo. The entire Southwest Highway had been closed by the police after two buses, countless cars and even a packed train were swept away. I encouraged him to circle around, up into the hills, then down through Ratnapura.

The UN Country Director got through to me after hours of trying. He was relieved to learn Nancy and I were safe but concerned that another vacationing expert was still incommunicado.

Just before our phone battery failed, Nancy reached her best friend in Los Angeles. Bettina kindly offered to contact our families across the United States, assuring them we were unharmed.

That evening, our hotel proprietors switched on the television, drawing power from their on-site generator. Scattered news bulletins began to add up. Colombo and its environs had escaped largely unscathed, around the corner of the island from the brunt of the waves. Sri Lanka's Southern and Eastern strips were devastated, as were exposed coastlines in Thailand. Indonesia, the epicenter of the massive earthquake that had launched the devastating wave, was hit hardest of all.

Our host wandered among his huddled guests, murmuring over and over "Never in 40 years. These things don't happen here." TV commentators extended that time-line back even further. No prior tidal wave had reached Sri Lanka in the 140 years that reliable records had been kept.

Kumar finally appeared after ten p.m. He was badly frightened, more by what he'd heard than what he'd seen. On the car radio and along his route, rumors were rife that another wave was about to strike. He urged us to leave Tangalle instantly, but we knew an all-night drive made no sense in his condition. Nancy led him down through the gardens to the cliff's edge. Only when our driver had viewed the calm sea and then realized on the hike back up the hill how far we were staying above the water, could he be persuaded that we were all safe. We'd arranged quarters and dinner for him before he'd arrived. Now he wolfed down a meal and collapsed in exhaustion.

The next morning Kumar drove us eastward to Tangalle town, then inland through the mountains and back to Colombo. A working port, Tangalle had taken the full fury of the assault. After flash floods had poured down from the hills the year before, the municipal authorities had constructed a concrete flood canal straight through the town center, from the slopes to the sea. The tsunami exploited this conduit in the opposite direction, like a besieging army. It shot projectiles up the vulnerable channel at speeds scientists later estimated at 90 miles per hour.

Volkswagen vans lay upside down in living rooms where front walls had been ripped away. Seaweed streamers were pasted to facades like grotesque festival decorations. A hulking commercial trawler rode high-and-dry on rocks in front of the windowless Tangalle Hotel. Residents stood hollow-eyed on curbs, rocking back and forth in obvious shock. Bruised, bloodied and bandaged, many were holding hands.

Official tallies put Sri Lanka's death toll at 30,000. In fact, those numbers were no better than rough guesses. Most of the victims were fisher-folk camped by their outriggers, unregistered on any legal rolls.

Relief efforts mobilized quickly. Back in Colombo, Nancy and I did our small part, sending clothes, rice, beans and cooking oil to a Southern emergency center. We tucked in a bag of sweets for the children, so they'd have an ounce of reassurance in a world turned upside-down. The Business-for-Peace Alliance performed a major role, coordinating and tracking aid shipments to ensure accountability. Two of my former

Project Officers headed up reconstruction efforts on the hardest-hit East Coast.

My Alliance colleagues hoped that the disaster would give government and LTTE leaders a historic opportunity to collaborate on relief. But we were all disappointed. Twenty years of military hostilities had generated too much mistrust to permit impromptu cooperation, even to cope with a natural disaster. Meanwhile, politically connected opportunists seized and fenced off choice ocean-front properties now abandoned by the fishermen.

One friend spoke for the rest of us. "Just like all crises, this one brought out the best and worst in men."

Nancy and I had witnessed the sea's awesome power and lived to tell about it. Except for that pause for a garden snapshot, we'd have been down on the beach. To think we owed our lives to a camera-shy lizard.

ITALY

Venice

Florence

Perugia • • Assisi
*UMBRIA*
• Amelia

ROME
✩

SARDINIA

SICILY

UMBRIA:
GREEN HEART OF ITALY
*1995-2012*

## Chapter Eleven

# ITALY: LIVING
# THE MEDITERRANEAN DREAM

## Meant To Be

*Amelia, Italy 1995*

First, we lost our house. Notification came out of the blue in an envelope dropped in my mail slot at UNDP's Country Office in Vientiane, Laos. The enclosed letter bore the seal of Stafford County, Virginia where we owned our home. In a curious blend of upbeat public-relations prose and lawyers' jargon, the text got right to the point. To anticipate the projected expansion of metropolitan Washington, DC, our satellite county was planning ambitious infrastructure upgrades. In our valley (which not coincidentally had the lowest density of registered voters in the county), the contemplated improvement took the form of a massive reservoir. Our house and a dozen others were to be legally condemned by right of eminent domain and our lots submerged by the artificial lake. We had no choice in the matter, since this condemnation was for a public purpose. But we would be paid fair market value for our property.

Although a total surprise, this governmental decision upset Nancy and me far less than it did several irate neighbors. They considered bringing a class-action lawsuit to try and block the confiscation. For our part, we didn't love our house, didn't fancy futile litigation, and thought we'd be better-off to take the money and run. So we accepted the authorities' offered price. But we asked for quick payment to help us afford new quarters when my UN/Laos contract expired in 18 months. By the time the county bureaucracy had cut a check, we'd moved on to a new development-assistance project in Kazakhstan. Check deposited, we had no house and an inflated bank account.

Next, in Kazakhstan, Nancy and I became eligible for "R&R" (Rest and Recreation). This recuperation policy of my client, the United States Agency for International Development, awarded two weeks of paid family vacation to its employees and contractors working and living for two or more years in what USAID designated as a hardship post. Central Asia qualified in spades. But to keep its beneficiaries from going hog-wild, the U.S. government had selected R&R destinations in advance. From Almaty, ours was Rome. Now we had no house, money in the bank and a paid vacation in Italy.

That R&R selection suited us to a T. We'd been smitten by Italy ever since first passing through on undergraduate travels. Our enthusiasm had only ratcheted up when working as guest instructors at Rome's International Development Law Institute (IDLI). There was almost nothing about the country that didn't appeal—history, culture, landscapes, art and architecture, music, cuisine, climate. Most of all, the ebullient Italians. We'd even dreamed of retiring there. Now we could do some advance reconnaissance.

The final inducement, as if we needed additional encouragement, occurred when touring in Bukhara. Over breakfast at our guesthouse, Sebastiano, a UNESCO architectural historian and Italian to his fingertips, expropriated the topic of our upcoming R&R excursion. He grabbed a felt-tipped pen and a paper napkin. "I will tell you what you must do. Here is Rome," he began with a black dot. "Here is Umbria, the green heart of Italy," tracing a semicircle above the dot, with brio. "You must stay within 90-minutes' drive of Rome, so you can use Fiumicino Airport to reach your international consulting assignments. The area within this arch," crosshatching boldly, "allows you to do just that. By good fortune, this same semicircle contains paradise. Drive around. See for yourselves. Find your new home. You are favored by the gods."

Our Italian connection was definitely meant to be. At the least, we'd enjoy a cross-country romp. As a bonus, we might find a reason for not postponing relocation until retirement. No American house, money in the bank, two airplane tickets and a treasure map. How could we resist the Fates' compelling invitation?

Once we got to Rome, our friend and IDLI's Chief Financial Officer, Pasquale Ferraro, added a practical suggestion for organizing our R&R itinerary. Tecnocasa, a new real-estate chain similar to the Century 21 franchises we were familiar with in USA, had just opened in Italy. Pasquale proposed keying our Umbrian stops to the hill towns in which Tecnocasa had outlets. As we passed through, we could ask the local agents if they had any properties to show us that met our criteria.

In truth, those criteria were a bit vague. We fancied a smallish country house, mostly restored but with some work still to be done. Precise specifications probably wouldn't have made any difference. Whether by inexperience or training, the scattered Tecnocasa agents politely listened to our priorities and then blithely ignored them. With Latin self-confidence, they enthusiastically showed us whatever they had on offer, from drafty farm houses to elegant villas. The resulting site visits were mostly a waste of time. But we treated the whole excursion as a lark and saw some enchanting vistas in the process.

My favorite property was a sloping agricultural estate overlooking the walled medieval town of Bolsena and the volcanic lake of the same name. The owner, whom I immediately labeled *"la contessa"*, took my arm and not so subtly ignored Nancy. The lady walked us past orchards and vineyards, not neglecting Etruscan ruins. Her lilting monologue wove in her landed-gentry heritage. "During the World War, when I was a small child as you can understand, we had to run from the great house to the wine-storage cave when the bombers flew overhead." (She tactfully omitted the detail of those planes being American.)

By the time Her Ladyship got around to showing us the actual decrepit house that was for sale, I realized its only two noteworthy features were the skeleton of a grand staircase and a retrofitted third-story water-closet suspended over an exterior wall. As for the fire pit burned in the living room floor, "It was a terrible error in judgment for my brother to use immigrant labor to harvest the grapes. Absolute barbarians."

"When she finishes peeling you figs," my wife whispered, "her Asking Price is six times our budget."

Nancy was charmed by our first glance of a meandering monastery perched above Aquasparta, with a view to die for. The main chamber retained fragments of thirteenth-century biblical frescoes. An elevated parapet might do wonders as a writing studio. Unfortunately, our walk through the interior traversed six inches of compacted droppings from a full menagerie of farm animals. I had a hard time hearing the agent's ebullient pitch. In a hairpin turn immediately above the property, tractor-trailers were shifting gears to make the grade.

On our last morning before turning in our rental car, Nancy shared a brainstorm over a final cappuccino. "I think we've been going about this the wrong way."

"Honey, don't tell me that now," I protested. "Tomorrow we're boarding our plane."

"Instead of *searching for* our dream house," she continued, "we should be *making* our dream house. Instead of looking for the perfect place, we should choose something imperfect, but with potential, and then steadily improve it."

I wasn't immediately persuaded but could appreciate the practicality of my wife's revised approach. Applying these fresh criteria, we selected one of the first properties we'd visited, an unromantic square farmhouse near the hamlet of Montecampano outside Amelia. We rushed back to Amelia's Tecnocasa office and requested a return tour.

An engineer's daughter, Nancy had always been better at visualizing improvements. She walked me around, inside and out, asking that I imagine what could be, in place of what was. Scalped terrain somehow symbolized her approach. Scraggly roses stubbornly survived from what must once have been a garden. Why not again? To the south lay a bleak concrete slab for drying livestock manure. This could be a patio next to a glassed sunroom to catch winter light. The former stable and manger had already been upgraded. We could finish the job and end up with an expansive living room. The *a la moda* pink and turquoise bathrooms could be redone in natural earth tones. The kitchen would have to be totally outfitted, but this could be to our taste. More important were the modern plumbing, wiring and heating already installed by the owner. We had no desire to slog through a complete A-to-Z reconstruction. Energized by our now-shared vision, we asked Maria, the Tecnocasa agent, to telephone Signor Bruno, the Rome seller.

Even filtered by her diplomatic translating, his rebuff came through loud and clear. We were 50 percent too low. I explained that we weren't trying to be sly. What we were offering was what we'd received from the Virginia authorities. The next day, we had to fly back to Kazakhstan. I had Maria give him bilingual Pasquale's name and Rome phone number, so we could be contacted if the seller changed his mind.

She relayed verbatim his parting shot: "I will never make that call!"

Back in Almaty, our Italian adventure quickly faded in memory as local obligations reasserted their demands. In no way bitter about having failed to purchase a retirement nest, Nancy and I both felt we'd had a rollicking vacation. As a bonus, we'd learned much of value for future prospecting.

Three weeks later, the phone jangled in the middle of the night. Fumbling for the receiver, I heard Pasquale Ferraro's amused voice from the far side of the world.

"Russell, *caro*, I hope you are sitting down."

"I'm lying down, Pasquale. It's three o'clock in the morning."

"Well, sitting or lying, you're now the proud owner of an Italian farmhouse. Signor Bruno accepted your offer."

Our lark had become our life.

*Before: bare bones with potential. Montecampano 1995.*

*After: the results of a decade of TLC. 2005.*

# Zack Attack

*Montecampano 1997*

It was an abrupt turnaround, even for our nomadic family. One hour after Nancy and I had landed at Rome's Fiumicino Airport to begin our Italian residency, I kissed her goodbye and jumped on another plane to Bangkok. Our plan had been to proceed overland together to our just-purchased farm house in Umbria. But a last-minute invitation to lead a field team of consultants in Laos was too good to pass up. So Nancy would have to start homesteading for three months by herself, in the middle of an Italian winter.

She was a country girl from West Virginia, thoroughly comfortable living alone in the woods. But we'd already agreed on our acquiring a dog for companionship and to alert us when visitors approached our large rural property. Nancy set about making inquiries. We'd always had Labs, much taken by their loyalty and gentle dispositions. However, none were on offer in our area, so the Amelia vet suggested an alternative.

A local family that ran an agricultural-equipment business had an adolescent German Shepherd and wanted to give him away. Imagining an aggressive guard dog, Nancy had strong reservations. But she arranged to meet him. It was love at first sight, on her part and it seemed also on his.

His owners had named him "Zaccaria" but that was soon shortened to "Zack." Nancy sensed the dog may have been harshly raised and neglected. He cowered if she passed by with a broom or a stick. And he bowled her over when she served his chow. But she had long experience training dogs. Within days, Zack got the message that she would never use force for discipline, and that no one would compete for his food.

When I came back, there was a brief awkward transition as the four-legged male reassessed his rank in the household hierarchy. Then we promptly and warmly bonded.

Zack was splendiferous. Black and tan with classic German Shepherd features. Eighty pounds of pure muscle, he was keenly intelligent and a quick study. His phenomenal hearing and sense of smell never ceased to amaze.

In the prime of health, Zack needed lots of exercise. Nancy and I split the twice-daily dog-walking chores. We would traipse along the dirt tracks that divided the planted fields surrounding our property. For millennia, Umbrian farmers had prudently preserved natural woodlots between their plowed parcels. These linked greenbelts did triple duty as sources of wild game, timber and erosion-control. Here too we would roam, with Zack joyfully flushing the occasional giant hare or feral cat.

High on the hill directly behind our house, Zack snuffled into an ancient stone ruin and was soon loudly barking. He backed out whimpering, with a snout full of porcupine quills. Fortunately, with Nancy's steady hand, we were able to extract the fish-hooked spines with only a few drops of blood.

One afternoon, Zack and I were returning home along a shady lane at the base of that same hill. A young man from the nearby hamlet of Montecampano rounded the bend, overtaken by his yapping dog. I spotted the fellow's cradled shotgun and recognized the loud-mouthed miniature as the terrier/hound mix that local hunters preferred when going after small game.

Even this early in our stay, I was already no fan of the hunting clan. At dawn they'd be blasting away in the surrounding fields and woods, decimating the declining wildlife. That said, I knew hunting had deep roots in Umbrian culture, combining provisioning with sport for millennia.

I vaguely recognized this teenager and we exchanged greetings. Zack calmly sat down and waited for the humans to stop talking. With no advance warning, the hunter's agitated mutt launched himself through the air and landed biting and scratching on Zack's undefended face.

Zack rose to four legs and tried to shake off the nuisance. This only caused the determined attacker to dig in his claws and hang on. At last aroused, Zack slammed his assailant to the ground, tossed the smaller dog somersaulting into the air, and then burrowed into his exposed belly when he landed on his back.

"No, Zack!" I shouted, at last recovering enough to intervene. But he was now too excited to obey. I lunged at my dog's collar, anxious to pull him off before he did serious harm. Concentrating on avoiding flashing teeth, I sensed movement out of the corner of my eye.

The young man was raising his weapon and cocking both barrels. His whole body was trembling beneath panicked eyes.

"Stop! No!" I yelled, leaping into the line of fire. Not a smart move under any circumstances. But I couldn't believe this freaking bozo was going to spray Zack with birdshot at point-blank range. My Shepherd would be blinded at best and might even be killed. In the process, of course, the guy's own attached dog would be wounded or destroyed.

I pivoted to slam the barrel down and spun back to separate Zack from his prey. Clumsily, I snapped Zack's leash to his collar and yanked him off the small dog. Ready to go one more round, the flyweight feinted another assault. But I shouted him off and both animals were suddenly subdued. In the bizarre silence, the young man was still shaking.

As my own adrenalin subsided, I was furious at the near-tragedy. Especially since the macho miniature had started it all. I dragged Zack away without another word and stomped home to tell Nancy about my close encounter with a violent native.

Two days later, the same young man drove up our driveway. Nancy and I were gardening, with Zack nearby. I looked quickly to make sure the car didn't contain the testosterone tyke. I assumed the chagrined teenager had come to apologize so I stepped forward to shake his hand.

Instead, without any greeting, he handed over an envelope. I opened it to find a veterinarian's bill, not from Amelia but from Terni, the county seat ten miles away. A quick mental calculation converted lira to $500.

"What is this?" I managed in my rudimentary Italian.

"Compensation for my hunting dog's injuries. His internal organs required emergency surgery."

"Bullshit!" I laughingly responded, trusting the obscenity required no translation.

"You must pay," he insisted.

"So, sue me!" I snapped. The young man jumped back into his car, turned around and drove away.

At Nancy's suggestion, I sought cross-cultural advice from Umbro Rosati, our one English-speaking local friend. Over espressos at Bar Leonardi, Umbro gave this American lawyer a candid briefing on local realities.

"Yes, of course, Russell, I understand. Your neighbor's dog attacked Zack, not the other way around. Yes, of course, both dogs were unleashed, not just yours. But you must understand that, in Umbria, where the hunters' lobby is so strong, only hunting dogs are authorized to run loose, not watchdogs or pets."

"I hear you, Umbro. Legally, there was wrong on both sides. But the vet's bill is a joke. He must be a cousin, or on the take!"

"This is a negotiation, my friend. The bill is only their opening gambit."

My tutor walked me through an Amelia perspective on our dispute. The demand for reparations was all about face. The young man had undoubtedly been mocked by his older brothers for letting an unarmed foreign newcomer make a fool of him. And injure his dog to boot. Since the foreigner was presumably well-heeled, the best way to restore family pride was to soak him for an inflated medical bill. Fortunately, the Terni vet, who depended on business from the large local hunting fraternity, would be pleased to do his inventive part.

Umbro leaned across the café table to summarize my options. "You can resist this shakedown, Russell, by hiring a bilingual lawyer. That would have to be from Rome. And would cost you a fortune. Equally important, after years of delays, you will still lose."

My friend paused for a sip of water to let each point sink in. "In the meantime, you'll have poisoned your family's relationship with the Montecampano community."

"So what should I do?"

Umbro delivered his advice with a shrug and a grin. "Counter-offer $100."

That's what I did. In the end, we settled on $200. Umbro enjoyed his mediator's honorarium of fine *prosecco*. Zack reluctantly adapted to a retractable leash.

After years of reciprocal avoidance, the no-longer-so-young man and I began to exchange waves from our passing cars. He may have learned the risks of barks worse than bites. I definitely had learned the value of respecting local norms.

Only proud Zack was unrelenting. Ever protective of his beloved owners, amazingly tolerant of ear-pulling infants, to his dying day he remained disdainful of yapping mutts.

He is sorely missed.

*Zack guarding the tulips. 1997.*

# The March of Millennia

## *Amelia 2000*

Nancy and I were honored to be invited to march in the *Corteo*. The costumed, torch-lit procession was the centerpiece of Amelia's medieval mid-August pageant. Strictly speaking, participants were supposed to be residents of the historical center within the walls. But the sponsors were always casting broader nets and we'd been adopted as rural "cousins" of a respected *Amerini*[17] family.

Now here we were, in the cramped servants' quarters of a borrowed palace, getting suited up like a high-school sports team. We were *Crux Burgi*, the Merchants' Cross, so we'd march beneath a magenta-and-navy banner. Pageant competition was fierce among the five *contrade* or medieval neighborhoods. Judged on costumes and drumming, the winning neighborhood would display a handsome trophy for the entire year.

The summer pageant was an all-volunteer production. Conducted by and for local residents, not for tourists. *Contrade* raised funds with street barbecues and bake sales. Nimble fingers stitched and mended costumes months in advance. The five drum troupes trained new talent, repaired snares and basses and practiced signature rhythms allegedly

---

17  Amelia's name in Classical Roman times had been *Amerina*. Proudly identifying with that heritage, the town's modern residents called themselves "Amerini."

handed down for centuries. Neither jazzy nor martial, these syncopated beats had magical power when bouncing off medieval walls.

Luciana, normally a droll dairy-shop proprietor but tonight our *Crux Burgi* Warden, was making the rounds of the dressing rooms. "You know the rules, Ladies. No make-up or wedding bands. Get rid of your spectacles, Signor Sunshine. Benjamin Franklin won't be inventing for another 400 years!"

Male and female participants had separate costuming spaces. But there was much earthy banter along the hallway. And no serious attempts to conceal half-draped bodies. Amelia's hairdressers had been working since morning, fashioning elaborate head-dresses incorporating braids, woven ribbons and veils.

Some *Amerini* marched for years. Others dropped out after a year or two, freeing slots for fresh recruits. In our snug locker-room, I recognized townsmen and neighbors from eight to 80.

"Get your shoes on and move outside." Luciana was cracking the whip. "If you can't resist one last cigarette, Marco, smoke it on the pavement."

In our compact outdoor assembly area, our drill-sergeant chivied the marchers into our designated order. Teenagers joked and jostled nervously before getting into character. My hooded robe and leather-bound tome marked me as a judge. The heavy wool garment itched, but I was glad to have the insulation in the cool night air. Friends said that, in other years, they'd sweltered in summer heat waves. Nancy was dressed as a nursemaid, doing her best to keep three "noble" children from bolting.

The first trumpet fanfare tumbled over the rooftops. High above us at the summit, the *Corteo*'s lead party of Town Council dignitaries must be setting out from the Cathedral steps, basking in the Bishop's blessing.

Soon we could spot the flicker of approaching torchlight, pulsing along the facades lining the curved street above us. The jingle of burnished trappings of a mounted knight. (It took me a moment to recognize the solemn visage as Robby, our gas-station attendant.) The lead banner with Amelia's coat-of-arms. The current City Council members were decked

*Contrada musicians marching to a medieval drumbeat.*
*Amelia Corteo 2000.*

out as their medieval forebears, resplendent in velvet and fur. Two rows of liveried musicians followed with long brass horns.

Our *Crux Burgi* contingent awaited its cue to feed into the procession. "Off you go!" Luciana pulled at an uneven hem. "Keep up but don't bunch up. No sleep-walking!"

*My one night in the judiciary. Amelia Corteo 2000.*

Down we wound along the cobblestoned lane, settling into a measured pace. No more banter now. Not a smile, wave or wink. All were silent and serious. Even the spectators, crouched on shop thresholds or leaning over balconies, were respectful and reserved.

Maintaining solemnity was no problem for me. Without my eyeglasses, I had only six inches of vision. My judicious concentration remained squarely on the heels in front of me. They belonged to Marco Mucca, our plumber. In his silk tunic and cap, he and his aquiline nose could have passed as the Duke of Urbino. So many of our marching neighbors stepped out of medieval altarpieces and Renaissance portraits.

As we processed, I was struck again by Amelia's ancient wealth. With never more than 10,000 inhabitants within the walls, the historic center had contained no fewer than 15 *palazzi* of noble families. Presenting mostly nondescript fronts to the street (reputedly to reduce property-tax assessments), these huge mansions concealed stately inner courtyards, salons, beamed ceilings and elaborate frescoes.

I loved the second-floor plaque commemorating the one-time residence of Christopher Columbus's principal champion, Antonio Geraldini. This courtier had extracted final approval and funding for the "Indian" expedition from Isabella and Ferdinand. His reward was appointment in Santo Domingo as the first Governor General of the Hispanic New World. Directly across the street stood the local branch of our bank, Monte dei Paschi di Siena, the world's oldest continuously operating bank, chartered in 1472.

At the bottom of the hill, we entered the old town's chief thoroughfare, the *Via Romana*, complete with 2000-year-old paving and sewer channels six feet under the modern surface. Then the marchers poured out through Amelia's main gates and took up positions around the city *piazza*. Behind the last *contrada*, the giant wooden portals slammed shut, announcing with a thud the climax of the pageant.

A spokesman for the ancient town spoke loudly to another character, costumed as a Papal Envoy up from Rome. In 1346, as tradition had it, the Vatican had tried to reassert periodic hegemony by collecting local tribute. The local official boomed out Amelia's revered response:

"Your Excellency, we are not Papal vassals. We are *Amerini*, independent and democratic. Here is our Charter. We pay no tribute to outside authorities, secular or ecclesiastical. Our gates are closed to you. You, Sir, are not welcome here!"

The marchers shouted on cue. "A-P-C-A!" (The acronym for the elders and citizens of Amelia).

Cynics would later inform Nancy and me that the Vatican had not taken "No!" for an answer. Mercenary troops returned in force, occupying Amelia and imposing Papal taxes for the ensuing centuries. But for one bright and shining moment, apocryphal or historical, the little guys stood up to tyrants. And since Italy's history from the fall of Rome through World War II had been a series of occupations by foreign invaders, this small ceremony resonated with broader significance. Compromising my judicial composure, I beamed with adopted pride.

The rest of the week-long festival was always a treat. It featured jousting, crossbow contests, neighborhood taverns run by residents, and Amelia's renowned *Sbandieratori*.

*Il Gruppo Sbandieratori* was a troupe of 20 local men and boys coached and led by Federico, our electrician. In splendid livery, they twirled and tossed six-foot-square heraldic flags attached to weighted staves. Alone, in pairs and foursomes, they hurled the spinning banners into the air, catching them with a flourish. The color and movement were fantastic, whether in sunlight or spotlight. This antique sport was reviving across Europe. But we were confident our guys were the best. And in fact they'd won trophies in Prague, Zurich and Lyon.

Amelia was reputedly one of Italy's most ancient settlements, long predating the Roman Empire. The walls encircling the historic town-center survived from either the eleventh or seventh century BCE, depending on which authority you credited. This inspiring perimeter contained stones as big as automobiles, expertly fitted together, without mortar, like notched pieces of a giants' jigsaw puzzle. They'd been erected

*Amelia: our neighboring Umbrian hilltown. 1999.*

by the Umbrii, Italic tribesmen separated by the Tiber River from Etruscans to the west.

Strategically sited above a sheer gorge, Amelia evolved into a major intersection of east/west and north/south overland routes. Tolls were collected, the hub prospered and, by Classical Roman times, Amelia even presided over a Tiber port 10 miles away.

Nancy and I gradually became familiar with the concentric series of interior town walls pierced by fortified gates, ascending to Amelia's scenic summit. It was evident these rings had served as a sequence of defensive ramparts during protracted sieges. Within each stone band, terraced gardens and water wells had kept besieged citizens alive.

Amelia's cathedral at the top of the hill was relatively unimpressive by Italian standards. Rebuilt in the 1890s after a catastrophic fire, its main claim to fame were cannonball-pierced standards from the Battle of Lepanto in 1751, when an Italian-led fleet had repulsed an Ottoman assault. More imposing was the 12-sided watchtower standing just next door. It survived from the eleventh century CE.

For us, Amelia's treasures from Imperial Roman occupation were much more exciting. One was a giant cistern from the second century CE. It continued to serve as central Amelia's principal water supply until the mid-twentieth century! Rain-fed, through rooftop pipes and plaza drains, this series of nine subterranean chambers was ingeniously engineered by staggering the connecting outlet channels so that no direct stream of water could build up speed to put pressure on the reservoir's down-hill walls. Now empty and occasionally open for viewing, this marvelous structure had been Amelia's insurance policy.

Another favorite local relic was a larger-than-life-sized bronze statue of Germanicus—son, father and brother of Roman emperors. Dating from the first century CE, this magnificent symbol of imperial power had been unceremoniously unearthed just outside Amelia's main gates during excavations for a mundane apartment house. In typical Italian fashion, the statue was withheld from public viewing for 20 years while bureaucrats in Rome, Perugia and Amelia arm-wrestled over the trophy. In the end, a tenacious and popular Amelia mayor withstood provincial and national pressures and made Germanicus the anchor of a new municipal historical museum.

This stubborn pride in local legacies was not driven by hubris or avarice. For our *Amerini* neighbors, heritage was who they were. Community meant continuity.

# Might Have Beens

*Montecampano 2006*

I was up a ladder pruning table grapes on the trellis above the cistern. Zack's ears perked up. Then I heard car tires on the gravel lane outside our front gates. I climbed up the hill and saw a young man standing outside the bars.

"Signor Sunshine, you probably don't recognize me."

"I am sorry. Please help me remember."

"I am Lorenzo, the son of Bruno, who sold you this house. We met in Rome at the notary's offices. I was much younger then."

I clicked the remote device in my pocket and the heavy gates swung open.

"It's a pleasure to see you again, Lorenzo. Please drive in and park in front of the house."

When Lorenzo climbed out a second time by our front door, a young woman stepped cautiously from the passenger seat.

"Don't worry about Zack," I reassured her. "He's curious but gentle."

"This is Monica, my fiancée," Lorenzo introduced her. And then hesitantly, "We were in the area. And I had always promised to show her the house."

I guided them to the shaded patio table and fetched *prosecco* and glasses.

They admired the flower gardens tumbling down the hill. I gave Nancy due credit and apologized for her being away. She'd been called to the bedside of her ailing aunt in South Carolina.

Lorenzo swept his arm. "This was *my* house. Not really, not yet. But I was the first-born son. It would have come to me one day."

"I'm so sorry for you," I said, "that things did not work out."

"It wasn't greed," he pressed on. "To look forward to it, I mean. I had worked on the restoration weekends and summers for five years, helping my father and his crew. We put on a new roof," he gestured with pride to his partner. And reaching for her hand, "Monica has heard all this before. She says it's all I talk about whenever we drive north from Rome."

"Then she must see inside. You too, of course, Lorenzo. It will look very different with our furniture. But you will recognize your handiwork in the fixtures and ceilings. Please wander around. Upstairs and down."

I let them in the front door and led Zack back to the patio. Ten-year-old memories surfaced like the bubbles in my glass.

When Nancy and I had returned to Italy from Kazakhstan in late 1996 to sign legal documents transferring title to the house, we'd quizzed Maria, Tecnocasa's Amelia agent, on what had changed the seller's mind. Signor Bruno had been so adamant when first rejecting our offer. As Maria's recapitulation made clear, it was a very Italian story.

The seller was a housing contractor based in Rome, she explained. He'd bought the Montecampano house when it was an abandoned hulk and labored on it for years whenever he could spare time from his business. From the beginning, he'd planned to restore it for his own use. First, for family vacations while the children were still young. Next, as a retirement retreat. Finally, as a bequest to his son. He'd spared no pains or expense—top-of-the-line plumbing and wiring, solid oak doors. This was his dream house.

On the day he swiped the last brushstroke of paint, his wife served him with divorce papers. "You are no longer married to me," she had cursed. "You're married to that god-damned house!"

With that rupture, Bruno's dream had become a nightmare. To relieve the pain, he put on the market the property he had planned to hold forever. But seething with anger, he was determined to justify his emotional and financial investments. So he inflated his Asking Price. And in doing so, he prevented the closure he needed and craved.

By the time we came along, the house had been for sale for 18 months. After we decamped back to Kazakhstan, Maria had confronted her client. She told him she'd be willing to show his house for as long as it took. But the Americans were cash buyers and were offering a fair price. With due respect for his bitterness, she recommended that he consider dislodging the millstone from around his neck and getting on with his life. After weeks of fuming, Bruno reluctantly concurred. Maria gladly made the delayed phone call to Pasquale Ferraro, and the rest was history.

When Lorenzo and Monica found me on the patio, there were tears in their eyes.

"He misses here very much." She spoke for the first time.

"This house is yours, not mine," Lorenzo underlined. "But I like your beautiful things."

"Thank you. We've lived in so many countries that we transport memories with us like nomads. We're grateful to your father for using natural materials in his restoration. They are faithful to the house's origins. A *casale*, not a villa. And, for us, the subdued tones and surfaces give daily pleasure."

We walked around to the north terrace. The flowerbeds below the railings were bright with color.

"My father had no time for gardens," Lorenzo pointed. "He preferred lasting materials."

"What happened to him?" I inquired. "After the house. I hope he is well."

"Successful, but never the same. He bought another country house. Bigger and more expensive than this one. South of Rome this time, near

Anzio on the coast. But his heart wasn't in it. He never completed the reconstruction."

"Can you finish it and live there?"

Lorenzo was silent for a moment. "I don't like the heat. I'm more comfortable in the hills." He gazed at Amelia's cathedral capping the town profile on the horizon. In the foreground, a sea of sunflowers bordered our olive grove.

As I walked them to their car, I handed Lorenzo a card with our phone number. "Please assure your father that we have treated his property with respect. By all means, convey our invitation to come see for himself. Whenever it suits him. He can just phone in advance, to make sure we'll be here to welcome him."

"I will tell him, I promise."

But the father never came.

# Tightly Knit

*Amelia and Montecampano 1997–2012*

It was the Italians, most of all, who made our extended sojourn in Italy such a joy. More than the landscapes or the light, the history or the architecture, the music or cuisine (although all these attractions were a daily gift). From shopkeepers and casual acquaintances to helpful neighbors and intimate friends, our fellow Umbrians were delightful companions and persuasive life-teachers.

The timing of our arrival, in the mid-1990s, was highly auspicious. Southern Umbria had not yet been discovered by foreign tourists, much less overrun and occupied like Tuscany to the north. We counted only a handful of foreign residents within a ten-mile radius of Amelia. This scarcity had positive consequences for our reception. We were not feared or resented as part of an influx driving up property values. The *Amerini* could define relationships with us on their own terms. It also helped that, having lived in a dozen foreign cultures, Nancy and I knew to tread lightly. After our enthusiasm and respectfulness had been assessed as genuine, we were not merely accepted but warmly welcomed.

Right from the outset, when I was working in Laos and Nancy was settling in, she began to experience acts of exceptional kindness. Town contacts invited her home for dinner to meet their families. Neighboring farmers brought fresh eggs and homemade wine. The artisans who knew

Nancy was "camping out" in mid-winter without a kitchen or central heating labored evenings and weekends, without overtime, to get our household systems up and running.

On March 8, International Women's Day, Bruno, Amelia's hardware-store proprietor, stepped out of his shop to greet Nancy on the pavement.

"Signora Nancy," he saluted her, "all of us know your husband is away on overseas business. But no lady should go unappreciated on this special day!" From behind his back, the gentleman produced a bouquet of fresh mimosa, the traditional Italian blossoms for this occasion.

When I did return, another concerned merchant asked my wife if I were unwell.

"Kind of you to ask. He's home safe and sound." Then giving it more thought, "Could I ask why you were worried?"

"I am so relieved. My wife couldn't help noticing that Signor Russell rushed into the supermarket yesterday and then drove out of town again after just buying milk."

Amerini never failed to make time to meet and greet. The speculation on the street was that I must be seriously ailing.

The way locals responded to our first attempts to speak Italian gave more evidence of the pervasive sociability. Since almost no *Amerini* spoke or understood English when we arrived, if Nancy or I needed a bank or a bathroom, we had no choice but to start employing our new vocabularies. We began with some trepidation. In France, we'd both had unpleasant experiences with locals sneering at foreigners' pronunciation and grammar. To our relief and delight, our Amelia neighbors were polar opposites. In place of "I cannot understand you, Monsieur. What is it you are trying to say?", we heard "Si, si, you are doing so much better!"

Nancy had an easier time of it, with her ear for languages and jump-in-the-deep-end enthusiasm. I was more shy and stilted, but soon found myself giving it a go. It eased my learning curve, of course, that half of Italian is spoken with the hands.

Also encountered and appreciated daily was the relaxed bonding of generations. In our experience, this wasn't always the case in Western industrialized countries, with preoccupied two-income couples, game-mesmerized kids and segregated elders. Here grandparents of 80 were lovingly saluted, even by self-absorbed teens. The elders helped tend infants and toddlers, not only relieving the kids' parents for a few precious moments but also making both the seniors and the youngsters feel loved, noticed and important. When grandparents developed inevitable infirmities, most were cared for at home by their families.

Nancy and I were invited to a low-key, extended-family gathering with Reno and Fosca, the parents of Umbro, who'd resolved my Zack crisis. Even though it was a weekday evening, their home was swarming with siblings, in-laws and grandchildren.

Responding to my staring at the cordial chaos, Umbro asked with a wink, "So what are you seeing, my Montecampano friend?"

I thought by now I knew him well enough to reply in kind. "It's what I'm not seeing that's on my mind. No stolen glances at cellphones or wristwatches. Even though all your relatives are working folks and the kids have loads of homework, everyone seems to be enjoying the family time without holding back."

Umbro's comment was only half in jest. "Russell, please don't be offended. We have a little joke. Americans live to work, but Italians work to live."

Pervasive courtesy and consideration also snuck up on us in unaccustomed ways. We began to pay attention to *la bella figura*. This Italian expression did not refer to a woman's sensuous profile but to the social duty everyone owed (to him- or herself, family and community) to make a good appearance. This had nothing to do with wealth or flamboyance, although, to be sure, some celebrities carried it to excess. Instead, it simply meant doing the best you can with what you've got. .

For us, Olga was the epitome of *la bella figura*. A mature woman, she was by no stretch a conventional beauty. Yet she consistently turned herself out well. And not just neat-and-tidy, but with panache. Olga had a deft eye for fabrics, garments, colors and jewelry that suited her. She knew how to combine components into a distinctive personal style. She helped us appreciate that, for Italians, taking care with one's appearance and comportment was considered not vanity but good sportsmanship.

We also learned that while *Amerini* were focused on their own province, mostly wedded to traditional agriculture and living a universe away from sophisticated metropolises, they were often receptive to outside ideas. The first year Nancy and I donned Halloween costumes and went knocking on doors in the historical center, our new friends didn't know quite what to make of us, this being a holiday that had not yet invaded Umbria. The next year, Giuseppina and Alberto, Valeria and Mauro, and their kids of all sizes greeted our knocks wearing brown paper sacks with cutout eyes over their heads. "Treek or treat!" they beat us to the punch. An annual custom had been launched that continued until tots were young adults.

This reminiscence is mostly about our Italian friends. But our lives in Amelia were also enriched by fellow foreign residents. Nancy and I came to perceive these expatriate neighbors as having arrived in three waves.

The first wave came to Italy in the late 1950s and early '60s. Most were British and female. They came as students, fell in love with Italians, mastered the language, married and stayed on to raise bicultural children. In our circle, this group included our dear friends April, Deirdre and Ruth, plus Andrew as a male counterpart. Marie-France, a Provençal variation on this theme, was the proprietress and master chef at Amelia's first boutique hotel. First-wave marriages, like all marriages, didn't always endure. Or the women outlived the men. But the immigrants stayed on in Amelia, in part because it had become their adopted home, in part to be near now-adult children and grandchildren.

The second wave, in which we counted ourselves, arrived decades later. This mixture of nationalities came already married, whether to someone from their own country or another foreigner. They'd become enchanted with Italy, often when visiting earlier, and found ways of returning as residents.

Our second-wave friends included Claudia and Michael who lived directly across the valley from our property and would literally look out for us when down from Vienna. They too had originally planned to restore a *casale*. But their purchase proved too far-gone to support renovation. So they commissioned and built an inventive modern house with a dramatic interior wall of local stone and sweeping views up and down the valley. They deliberately sited their structure down the slope so that it was virtually invisible from cars passing on the Amelia-Orté road just above. Michael explained that they did this not only to preserve their own privacy but also to respect the sensibilities of *Amerini* who might prefer traditional architecture.

This same low profile was sustained by Claudia and Michael's fellow Viennese, their next-door neighbor Anna Maria. In years of interactions with the townsfolk, Anna Maria never disclosed, much less boasted, that she was in constant demand from Europe's leading impresarios and opera houses as one of the Continent's premier costume designers.

On our side of the valley, Ozlem and Jacques were our best second-wave friends. Ozlem was a former Turkish university professor, Jacques a still-practicing Dutch hydraulic engineer. When he wasn't supervising his firm's harbor-dredging projects on the Italian mainland or in Sardinia, the couple would hitch their small sailboat to their SUV and cruise in and out of Eastern Mediterranean coves.

Both these waves of our foreign friends shared our zest for things Italian and respect for Amelia's special integrity. We would gather in small groups, speak English when alone, and share distant adventures. This circle's diversity added a nuanced layer of enjoyment to our Umbrian sojourn.

Unfortunately, the foreigners we categorized as third-wave were much less attractive arrivals. Investment bankers and other millionaires from London and farther afield, they discovered Umbria in the 1990s and began acquiring or constructing villas as second-home trophies. They would fly in with an entourage for long weekends, sit outside

Amelia's Bar Leonardi and loudly mock the perceived foibles of local tradesmen and neighbors. The Great Recession curbed this offensive inflow. But abandoned third-wave construction projects put a dent in the local economy.

Nancy and I were fortunate not only in our town friends but also in the *Amerini* who came out to work with us on our rural property.

Marco, our plumber, was a multi-talented jewel. Far beyond tightening kitchen faucets or closing stubborn toilet-bowl valves, Marco was equally competent repairing hundreds of yards of underground pipes that descended the hillside to link our property to the municipal water mains. If a problem involved water, he could handle it. A gifted raconteur and mimic, Marco would regale us with hilarious jokes after work was completed. Jumping around his car, switching between characters and voices or gesturing in lucid mime, he spared no pains to ensure we could keep up with his comic routines, despite our limited Italian fluency and utter ignorance of local dialect. And if his small daughter were sitting in his truck, he'd bend to the windows and play to that gallery as well.

In more serious moments, Marco would quiz me intently about my views of Sunni/Shia conflict in Iraq or the historical origins of America's Electoral College. Insatiably curious and well informed, he didn't need a university diploma to care about the world.

The one thing Marco was not good at was accepting payment. He never failed to come running night or day when we called with a plumbing emergency, even though he lived in town and we were miles out in the countryside. But he was never comfortable taking our money when a job was finished. "Next time," he would protest. "You can pay me next time." I had to slip euro notes into his pocket while Nancy distracted him.

Marco's generosity was typical of all the artisans who came to help at our property. They literally traced their values and lineage to ancient guilds of traditional craftsmen. Gianni, our gifted mason, put this heritage in context for me after making a highly unusual error. Gianni was constructing a brick stairway down from our patio to the terraced gardens below. Nancy was outside the country but had left him a design sketch to follow.

One morning I stepped outside the house and was alarmed to see that Gianni and his crew had started routing the stairway to the left instead of the right. Worse, the work had advanced quite far along. We consulted Nancy's sketch and Gianni's error was immediately apparent.

"What are we going to do?" I asked.

"You do nothing. I rip out the work and begin again."

"But what's it going to cost for the extra labor and materials?"

"It costs you nothing. Did *you* read the paper upside down?

"Gianni, please let me pay a fair share. I should have been supervising more closely."

As our conversation continued over coffee on the patio, Gianni laid out his artisan's perspective.

"Signor Russell, you and your wife are well-known and respected in Amelia. But, if I may be frank, you have been here only five years. My family has been here for generations. We will always be here. If I cheat you—on prices, on quantities or quality—even if you don't know it, I will know it. I will have betrayed not just you but myself. And not just myself but my family and my profession.

"Please go back inside your house and let me correct my embarrassing error. By mid-day, it never happened. Who's to say? Perhaps you and I only imagined it."

And turning to our ever-attentive German Shepherd, "*Zaccaria, silenzio!*"

Nancy and I were especially fond of Graziano, our handyman. Five-feet-five, with forearms thicker than my biceps, Graziano was a compact fireplug. Five years older than me, he could lift twice as much. More important, he could do any outdoor chore proficiently, with a consistent economy of labor and materials. Whether transplanting trees, tuning a lawnmower or wielding a chainsaw, Graziano had confidence grounded

*Multi-talented Graziano preparing the excavation for our new bombola (propane tank). Montecampano 2003.*

in experience. He took the lead when we replaced rotted posts and stretched six-foot fencing along the perimeter, to keep Zack in and wild boars out. More fun was building a quartet of thigh-high beds from volcanic *tufa* blocks, so Nancy and I could plant and weed vegetables without bending to the ground on creaky knees.

Graziano's childhood had been incredibly hard. The occupying German forces had confiscated all foodstuffs in Umbria, leaving local families struggling to escape starvation. He and his siblings scavenged the hillsides for nuts, berries and mushrooms. On the worst days, they brought home only bunches of grass for their mother to boil a broth. Like others in his generation, his growth was consequently stunted. But he more than made up for diminished stature by exploiting leverage and know-how.

I used to marvel at how this gruff yeoman farmer paid attention to detail. He'd trim downed limbs into uniform fireplace-fitting logs. With an ax, he'd halve and then quarter fat stumps as if discerning invisible guidelines. The antithesis of delicate, Graziano would sweep every leaf, pluck every weed, not for our sake but for his own. At first, like many of his peers, he disdained Nancy's efforts to build flower gardens around our house. Only edible fruits and vegetables warranted care and cultivation. Over time, however, and without any explicit softening of his position, he subtly took co-ownership of beds and blossoms.

"Let me show you our iris," he would take me by the arm when I returned from an overseas assignment. "Look how much they have spread since last year."

Graziano taught me to lean long wooden ladders into the olive foliage during the harvest, trusting the branches to absorb my weight without fearing a 20-foot plunge. How to strip every stem of ripe fruit. How to spread the nets underneath the trees on the hillside slope. How to turn, without bruising, the harvested olives drying on our northern portico.

For the entire two-month harvesting season, the local mill would operate round-the-clock. Driving up when our appointment came around, Graziano and I would schlep 100-pound sacks onto the weighing platform and then tip them into the hopper. The assembly line separated the olives from leaves and stems, washed the fruit, pressed out the liquid and discarded the pulp, centrifuged the liquid to separate water from oil and finally decanted the glorious jade-green nectar from taps at the other end. Fatigued but elated, we'd position our 12-gallon aluminum containers to capture the flowing oil. The huge interior was misty with olive-oil perfume.

Dear Graziano ultimately succumbed to abdominal cancer. We stood with his family at his bedside during the last hours, holding his gnarled hands and saying goodbye. We called him brother, and he was. Every year on the anniversary of his passing, we carried flowers from "his" garden to the cemetery.

Passing too is the entire way of life we observed and shared in Montecampano and Amelia. The younger generation is no longer content with small-town constraints and traditional occupations.

Our friend Elisabetta runs a children's clothing store in Amelia. Her daughter, Valentina, whom Nancy tutored in English conversation, is building a career as a forensic pathologist practicing in Perugia and Siena.

Alberto and Giuseppina own a local furniture store and gift shop. Daughter Deborah, another of Nancy's protégés, is getting her degree in International Finance at Milan's prestigious Bocconi University. Debi aspires to a banking career in New York or London.

Even local youngsters who don't leave the area are not necessarily following in parental footsteps. Our next-door neighbors Paolo and Ornella come from a long line of farmers. Both labor 15 hours a day tending livestock and crops. Their son Guisue is apprenticed to an uncle's bakery. His sister Ionis, after training for the tourism industry, has settled for early marriage and clerking in an Amelia supermarket. These siblings are turning their backs on wine grapes and olive oil. Paolo and Ornella and hundreds like them may have to close down family-farming operations when they can no longer manage heavy lifting. However Italy weathers the Great Recession's stubborn aftermath, traditional Umbrian culture, firmly grounded in small-scale agriculture, is undeniably in contraction.

When Ozlem drove us out through our Montecampano gates for the last time, I sat beside her and tried to look ahead to our new life in California. In the back seat, Nancy was sobbing uncontrollably. In our dozen relocations around the world, she had never done that before.

*Amerini at play on our terrace. Beloved friends never to be forgotten. 2005.*

# EPILOGUE:
## AT HOME ABROAD

Nancy and I could happily have stayed in Italy. But she began suffering from a reaction to sunlight that caused debilitating and frequent migraines. Her doctors reported that the only promising therapies had serious side effects. They recommended she move to a cloudy, foggy climate.

After multiple reconnaissance missions, we've landed up on California's Central Coast. Our town is cozy, offering the cloud cover Nancy needs, plus friendly neighbors, varied restaurants, and otters and redwoods short minutes from our door.

I continue to be energized by international travel. (Domestic too, but that's another story.) If these tales have done their intended job, they've conveyed a hopefully contagious passion for the far and away.

Certainly, one source of my enthusiasm is the need to see things for myself. I do appreciate photos, diagrams and text descriptions. But more as an invitation—not the real thing. Yesterday, friends Khing and Yvonne posted images from their current tour of Machu Picchu. Their color shots of Inca terraces were dramatic. And it was inspiring to see fellow senior citizens smiling at high altitude. Yet I wasn't in the place myself. I couldn't climb the steps or inhale the thin air. This magical retreat's powerful history did not come alive for me from a distance.

If going to a foreign destination is indispensable, staying on a while can be even more worthwhile. I love diving into an unfamiliar environment, figuring out how it works for its inhabitants and how I can begin to fit in. Of course, coping with what's new and different on the road can be wearing. But I've learned that keeping my advance expectations few and flexible does wonders to reduce disappointments. As Nancy's late father counselled his teenage daughter when she was departing for India, "Don't look for hamburgers in somebody else's country." Besides, experiencing the new and different is the whole point of going in the first place. Open eyes and an open mind can convert disorientation to discovery.

One of my all-time-favorite overseas experiences was living alone for three months in a Japanese neighborhood while conducting a seminar at Nagoya University. Two Teaching Assistants picked me up at the airport and deposited me late at night at my small apartment. Since they were junior academics in a hierarchical system and I, an "international expert", they didn't presume to give me any cues or clues. So I stepped out my door the next morning into an alien world. I could not speak or read one word of Japanese. Only numbers and universal symbols were comprehensible. The English-medium graduate school where I'd be working was miles across town. None of my residential or commercial neighbors spoke English. For my entire sojourn, I communicated by mime. Buying groceries or a café meal, watching TV, riding subway trains or busses—everything was a puzzle. And an adventure. My isolation became a problem-solving game. Keeping alert but not anxious, navigating without language. It helped, to be sure, that my Nagoya neighbors were unfailingly kind and attentive to my evident limitations.

No matter how enthralling a foreign place, interactions with foreign people can be even more rewarding. What makes foreigners so distinctly stimulating is that they are similar and different all at the same time. Their similarities in interests and experience give me a starting point for communication and cooperation. Their differences—whether in language, education, politics, history or religion—offer me fresh perspectives that challenge my assumptions and possible prejudices. And when both parties invest in a cross-cultural relationship, the breakthrough to shared respect and understanding can be electric.

As a bonus, friendships forged with fellow Americans overseas, who like me are coping with the unfamiliar, can have a special intensity and resilience.

Decades after venturing forth, I remain in caring contact with most of the foreign and American friends mentioned in these tales. Craig, Jane and Mr. Moon. Liu Pei Long. Sipraseuth, Michael and Monique, Charlie and Ameerah. Roza, Saule, Ivan and Oksana, Valodya, Frank, Ben, two Davids and Sue. Sonali, Shathies and Suresh. Fellow Amerini one and all.

Next month I'll be off for a visit to Yucatan. A fascinating and exotic corner of Mexico. With fabulous Mayan history and monuments. Best of all, I'll be staying and catching up with dear friends Foster and Kathy, thoughtful Americans who have crafted a nurturing bicultural life.

For me, few activities can compare with international travel for learning, touching and stretching. I've still got a list of beckoning destinations that I hope to see for myself before globalization makes synonyms of "here" and "there." Near the top are the San Juan Straits and Norwegian fiords. And don't count out Belmopan, Port Louis, and Thimphu. If we meet on the trail, I'll be the one with the white beard.

That same beard has been a lucky talisman on the international road. Not only did it boost my consulting fees as it matured from brown to white. Sometimes it also served as a bridge across cultures and generations.

One late December morning in an Amelia elevator, a wide-eyed four-year-old gazed up at my beard and tugged at his father's sleeve. "Papa, Papa! Babbo Natale!" [Santa Claus!]

I knew my line, even in Italian. "And have you been a good boy this year?"

"Si, certo, Babbo Natale!" The impassioned affirmation came without a heartbeat's hesitation. "Certo!"

That kid's going places.